Unconditi
Unionist

# Unconditional Unionist

The Hazardous Life
of Lucian Anderson, Kentucky Congressman

BERRY CRAIG *and*
DIETER C. ULLRICH

McFarland & Company, Inc., Publishers
*Jefferson, North Carolina*

Library of Congress Cataloguing-in-Publication Data

Names: Craig, Berry, author. | Ullrich, Dieter C., 1964– author.
Title: Unconditional Unionist : the hazardous life of Lucian Anderson,
  Kentucky congressman / Berry Craig and Dieter C. Ullrich.
Description: Jefferson, North Carolina : McFarland & Company, Inc.,
  Publishers, 2016. | Includes bibliographical references and index.
Identifiers: LCCN 2016038332 | ISBN 9781476663692 (softcover : acid
  free paper) ∞
Subjects: LCSH: Anderson, Lucian, 1824–1898. | Legislators—United
  States—Biography. | Unionists (United States Civil War)—
  Kentucky—Biography. | Kentucky—History—Civil War, 1861–
  1865—Biography. | United States—History—Civil War, 1861–1865—
  Biography. | United States. Congress. House—Biography. | Mayfield
  (Ky.)—Biography.
Classification: LCC F455.A53 C74 2016 | DDC 976.9/03092 [B] —dc23
LC record available at https://lccn.loc.gov/2016038332

British Library Cataloguing data are available

ISBN (print) 978-1-4766-6369-2
ISBN (ebook) 978-1-4766-2664-2

Front cover: Lucian Anderson (National Archives and Records
Administration)

Printed in the United States of America

*McFarland & Company, Inc., Publishers*
  *Box 611, Jefferson, North Carolina 28640*
  *www.mcfarlandpub.com*

To the late Martha Nell Anderson,
Lucian Anderson's great-grandniece
and the last Anderson to live
in "Lush's" 1850s vintage home,
Mayfield's oldest building
when it was razed in 2016

# Table of Contents

# Preface

Kentucky Congressman George H. Yeaman of Owensboro, played by actor Michael Stuhlbarg, got his fifteen minutes of fame in *Lincoln*, the 2012 Academy Award–winning movie. Yeaman gambled, and lost, his seat when he voted for the Thirteenth Amendment to the Constitution, which abolished slavery. But Lucian Anderson, another Bluegrass State lawmaker, risked more than his political career when he, too, voted "aye" on January 31, 1865. He put his life on the line.

Anderson, a Union man from Mayfield, Kentucky, one of the Bluegrass State's most rabidly rebel towns during the Civil War, had already endured death threats. Guerrillas murdered his close friend and Unionist neighbor. Confederate raiders swooped into town and kidnapped Anderson. Though his father was revered as the town founder, Anderson was the town pariah.

Anderson's story, even more than Yeaman's, is the stuff of Hollywood. We are historians, not moviemakers. So we present this first biography of Anderson, who is all but forgotten in Mayfield and throughout his native state. Except for his tombstone, there are no monuments to Anderson in Mayfield, the Graves County seat, where a Confederate memorial stands in front of the courthouse.

Besides Yeaman and Anderson, two other Kentucky congressmen, William H. Randall of London and Green Clay Smith of Covington, voted for the Thirteenth Amendment. They were from Unionist districts and won reelection. Yeaman was defeated. Knowing he could not win, Anderson did not seek another term.

Regrettably, our research turned up nothing definitive to explain why Anderson went against his community and stood for the Union and against slavery. He came from a prosperous, slaveholding family. He owned slaves, possibly even when he voted for the Thirteenth Amendment. If Anderson kept a diary, it does not survive. Nor does a collection of personal papers. In an 1871 newspaper article, Anderson, an attorney, mentioned that his

1

**William H. Randall (National Archives and Records Administration).**

records were destroyed during the war. Most likely, guerrillas who burned the Mayfield courthouse in 1864 also burned his law office on the court square.

Our book is based largely on primary sources, notably newspaper articles, letters, government publications and other contemporary documents.

We hope it will paint for the reader an accurate portrait of Anderson as a significant historical figure in his native state.

After *Lincoln* was released, Owensboro, the Daviess County seat, rediscovered and celebrated Yeaman. Organizers arranged a special showing of the movie on January 31, 2015. Afterwards, Yeaman's portrait was unveiled at the courthouse.

The film also spun off some publicity for Anderson, Randall and Smith. Anderson was featured in stories in the *Mayfield Messenger* and in other Purchase publications. The *Louisville Courier-Journal*, the state's largest newspaper, published an op-ed column that likened the four congressmen to the eight senators John F. Kennedy wrote about in *Profiles in Courage*.

Yet no commemoration of Lucian Anderson was held in Mayfield on or after the centennial of his equally crucial vote that helped put slavery on the road to extinction. He was back in the local news in early 2016, when his home, built in 1851 or 1852, was razed. When it was torn down, the wood-frame house was Mayfield's only surviving pre–Civil War structure.

Probably few citizens knew the significance of the dwelling and the man who lived in it during America's most lethal conflict. Indeed, the now empty lot at 321 North Sixth Street is yet another reflection of Anderson's virtual anonymity in Mayfield, where he was born, reared and lived most of his life. We hope this book will help bring him some long overdue recognition for his important, if largely overlooked, role in helping rid his country of slavery.

# 1

# An Unlikely
# Anti-Slavery Man

*Profiles in Courage*, John F. Kennedy's Pulitzer Prize–winning book, is about eight United States senators who exemplified Ernest Hemingway's notion of "grace under pressure." They endured "the risks to their careers, the unpopularity of their courses, the defamation of their characters, and sometimes, but sadly only sometimes, the vindication of their reputations and their principles."[1]

If someone were to write a second volume of *Profiles*, Congressman Lucian Anderson of Mayfield, Kentucky, ought to be considered for inclusion, though he is not in most history books. On January 31, 1865, he and three other House members from slave state Kentucky elevated principle above politics, courted defeat at the next election, and voted for the Thirteenth Amendment to the Constitution, which declared that "Neither slavery nor involuntary servitude, except as a punishment for crime whereof the party shall have been duly convicted, shall exist within the United States, or any place subject to their jurisdiction."[2]

Southern sympathizers in his hometown threatened to murder him and burn down his house. Three months after he was elected, Confederate raiders kidnapped him. He evidently did not believe discretion was the better part of valor because he tried to convert his captors to the Union cause.[3]

Anderson was one of the most hated men in the history of Mayfield, which was decidedly secessionist during the Civil War. A local historian suggested that Anderson's enemies—many of them former longtime friends and political allies—hesitated to kill him only because his father, John, was credited with founding Mayfield in 1823.[4]

The community is almost squarely in the middle of the rural, tobacco-rich Jackson Purchase, the Bluegrass State's only Confederate-majority region. Also the state's westernmost territory, the Purchase was dubbed "the South Carolina of Kentucky" for its secessionist sentiment.[5]

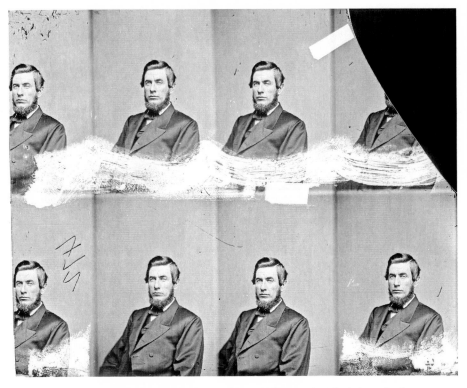

Lucian Anderson (National Archives and Records Administration).

Anderson's roots went about as deep as roots go in Mayfield, the seat of Graves County. He was born in 1824 in the family cabin close to the court square. Going on two centuries later, it seems few townsfolk know who Anderson was. Virtual anonymity is not his only unhappy fate. During his day, his name was routinely misspelled "Lucien" in newspaper stories and even in official documents. He is "Lucien Anderson" in the *Biographical Directory of the United States Congress*. Perhaps that is why he often went by "Lush"—pronounced "Loosh"—and sometimes "Lu."[6]

It seems unclear why he embraced the anti-slavery cause and ultimately joined the Republicans. He may have owned slaves when he voted for the Thirteenth Amendment. Though he sided with abolitionists, Anderson dodged the "abolitionist" label. "This charge of being an abolitionist ... cannot deter or drive me from a full discharge of my duty," he declared in the House of Representatives in March, 1864. "I was born and reared in the State of Kentucky; have been identified with slavery all of my life; own slaves to-day." Nonetheless, Anderson pledged that "my slaves, nor all the slaves in Kentucky, cannot make me disloyal or traitorous to my country. If slavery is being destroyed it is the result of this wicked Rebellion; and my judgment is that when the Rebellion is destroyed this institution will go with it." Yet in June, 1864, he was a Kentucky delegate to the National Union Convention in Baltimore that re-nominated President Abraham Lincoln on a platform that endorsed a constitutional amendment to "terminate and forever prohibit the existence of Slavery within the limits of the jurisdiction of the United States."[7]

Nearly every white Kentuckian despised the party of "Lincoln and Liberty" because it opposed slavery. Nothing—neither letters, nor a diary or personal papers—evidently survives to explain why Anderson voted to end the South's peculiar institution. When his slaves became free is apparently not known. One wonders if he emancipated them before January 31, 1865, or immediately after. Or did they remain his chattels until three-fourths of the states—Kentucky not among them—ratified the Thirteenth Amendment in December, 1865?

Anderson was a late convert to the anti-slavery cause. But like two of Kentucky's best-known foes of human bondage, James G. Birney and Cassius Marcellus Clay, Lush was a lawyer-politician who came from a well-to-do slaveholding family. Birney was born in Danville in 1792; a Madison County native, Clay was fourteen years older than Anderson. Birney, who briefly served in the Kentucky House of Representatives, first endorsed colonization, or buying blacks out of bondage and resettling them in Africa. The idea was obviously racist and based on the assumption that African Americans and whites could not live in the same country. He

James G. Birney (Library of Congress).

switched to abolitionism and published *The Philanthropist*, an anti-slavery newspaper. Eventually, he left Kentucky for Cincinnati and New York, became secretary of the American Anti-Slavery Society and ran for president on the Liberty Party ticket in 1840 and 1844. Clay was a student at Yale College when, in 1832, he heard a speech by the outspoken Boston abolitionist William Lloyd Garrison that won him over to the anti-slavery side. A cousin of Henry Clay and dubbed "The Lion of White Hall" for his mansion, "Cash" Clay was elected to the state House of Representatives as a Whig but as his anti-slavery views waxed, his political career waned. In 1843, he survived an assassination attempt and seriously wounded his assailant with a Bowie knife. Despite the attack and death threats, he founded *The True American*, an anti-slavery newspaper, in Lexington in 1845, a year after he freed his slaves. He printed the sheet in a stout brick building whose defenses included pair of little brass cannons, lances and muskets. Ultimately, a mob shut down his press but he resumed publishing his paper in Cincinnati.[8]

**Cassius Marcellus Clay (Library of Congress).**

On the other hand, Anderson was avowedly pro-slavery even on the eve of the nation's most lethal conflict. When the Civil War began in 1861, he, like most Kentuckians, favored the Union and slavery. At least until August, 1863, when he was elected to Congress on the conservative Union Democratic ticket, he viewed the war as a fight to preserve the Union, not to abolish slavery. The Union Democrats, Kentucky's majority party, were pro-war, pro–Union and pro-slavery. They denounced abolitionism and secession with equal fervor. In other words, their Unionism was qualified. But Lush joined the Unconditional Unionists, a minority of Kentuckians who pledged to stand by the Union even if slavery were abolished, and he allied himself with the Republicans in Congress. Anderson and the Unconditional Unionists became the nucleus of Kentucky's fledgling Republican Party.[9]

Yet Anderson was staunchly anti–Republican in 1860, when Americans voted in the most crucial presidential election in their history. Southern pro-slavery extremists dubbed "Fire Eaters" threatened to secede from the Union if the anti-slavery Lincoln won. As the campaign began, it was obvious that Mayfield and Graves County leaned toward John C. Breckinridge of Lexington, Kentucky, the pro-slavery Southern Democrat. Lush's man was Northern Democrat Stephen A. Douglas of Illinois. Not surprisingly, Breckinridge won the county in a landslide. Though he carried Kentucky, Constitutional Unionist John Bell of Tennessee finished second in the county. Douglas came in third; Lincoln, universally loathed by county whites, did not collect a single vote. His statewide total was a mere 1,364.[10]

Stephen A. Douglas (Library of Congress).

If Lush had some kind of "Road to Damascus" experience that turned him against slavery and toward the Republicans, there is apparently no record of it. His detractors claimed he was a rank opportunist, a politician who simply went with the winning side—the North by the time he was elected. The war's two big pivotal battles were fought in July 1863: Gettysburg and Vicksburg. Both were signal Union victories. On the fourth, General Robert E. Lee retreated south with his battered Army of Northern Virginia, never again to invade the North. On the same day, General Ulysses S. Grant accepted the surrender of Vicksburg, the last major Confederate strongpoint on the Mississippi River.

Yet in 1863, the Union Democrats ruled Kentucky politics. If opportunism were Anderson's main motivation, he surely would have stayed with them. Or, when the war began, he would have thrown in with Mayfield's secessionist majority. Instead, he became a Union Democrat and the secessionists scorned him. When he became an Unconditional Unionist, secessionists and Union Democrats alike declaimed him. Reflecting majority white opinion statewide, five other Kentucky congressmen—all Union Democrats— voted against the amendment. The Union Democratic-majority Kentucky legislature refused to ratify it. Of the four Kentucky congressmen who cast "aye" votes for the amendment, Lush had the most to lose—a prosperous law practice, status and, most of all, his life—in standing for the Union and against slavery. Two of the others came from pro–Union sections of the state: Green Clay Smith of Covington—a nephew of Cassius Clay—and William H. Randall of London, in mountainous southeastern Kentucky. While pro-slavery and pro–Confederate sentiment was strongest in the Purchase, it was weakest in the Kentucky highlands.

To be sure, Smith and Randall also exemplified what Kennedy called "profiles in courage." But they were on firmer ground with their constituents than were Anderson and the other "aye" voter, George H. Yeaman of Owensboro. Covington is the seat of Kenton County, London of Laurel County. Both counties furnished many more men to the Union forces than to the Confederate army. Owensboro is the seat of Daviess County, which sent troops to both sides in close to equal numbers. Graves County furnished the Confederate army close to one thousand men. Union military records credited Graves with 156 white and eighty-nine African American enlistments. Put another way, rebel soldiers outnumbered Yankees by more than four to one. All told, around five thousand Purchase men volunteered for the Confederate army and approximately six hundred whites and 250 African Americans donned Union blue. Kentucky-wide, between ninety and one-hundred thousand whites and blacks fought on the Union side, and between twenty-five and forty-thousand put on Confederate gray.[11]

The Purchase's intense Southernism was also evident in May, 1861, after Kentucky declared itself neutral. Neutrality was popular in every region of the state except the Purchase, which demanded nothing short of secession. A movement grew to forge a military alliance between the Purchase, if not the First Congressional District, and Tennessee. Such action would have been akin to secession. The idea was seriously discussed at a late May convention of the district Southern Rights, or secessionist, party in Mayfield. Ultimately, the delegates agreed to stick with Kentucky for fear that throwing in with Tennessee would harm—even destroy—the secession movement elsewhere in the state. Still, the Mayfield Convention was evidently unique; apparently no other section of a loyal border state contemplated disunion on its own.[12]

In the end, the convention re-nominated Democratic congressman Henry C. Burnett of Cadiz on the Southern Rights ticket. In a June, 1861, special congressional election, Burnett was the only secessionist who won; Unionists swept to lopsided victories in Kentucky's nine other districts. In November, 1861, Burnett and several others at the Mayfield Convention helped die-hard secessionists create a bogus Confederate government for Kentucky behind rebel lines at Russellville. Burnett presided over the conclave which, dubious as it was, got Kentucky admitted to the Confederacy as its thirteenth "state." Burnett became one of the state's Confederate senators.[13]

Congress expelled Burnett as a traitor in December, 1861. Unionist Samuel L. Casey of Caseyville succeeded him in a January special election. Lush followed Casey, capturing his seat in the regular 1863 statewide elections. Casey and Anderson won because Kentucky authorities, backed by Yankee soldiers, disfranchised Southern sympathizers and Confederate soldiers as traitors and allowed only Unionists to vote.[14]

There seems to be nothing in Anderson's background to suggest he would turn against slavery and become a "Black Republican." Lush's slaveholding father was a native South Carolinian, and his mother was Virginia-born. John died in 1842; Nancy, in 1864. It is evidently unknown whether she was pro–Union like Lush or was pro–Confederate like his big brother, Ervin, the county and circuit court clerk when the war started.[15]

Even so, Lush's youth perhaps hinted at where he might end up. He exhibited a stubbornly independent streak, at least for Mayfield. While Ervin was a devout Democrat, like most Graves Countians, Lush joined the Whigs, the party of Henry Clay, Kentucky's greatest statesman and most popular politician ever. Clay died in 1852, and when his beloved Whig Party collapsed two years later, twenty-seven-year-old Lush Anderson joined his brother as a Democrat. Local voters rewarded Lush's conversion by electing him to the state House of Representatives in 1855.[16]

Anderson served just one term but continued to practice law, apparently with success. Lush's politics evolved again soon after the presidential election. By January, 1861, most Bell and Douglas men in Kentucky merged as the Union Party. On the other hand, the majority of Bell and Douglas voters in the Purchase joined the Breckinridge backers in the Southern Rights party. Lush and precious few others carried the Union banner in deepest western Kentucky.

Indeed, the Unionists were outcasts in the Purchase. Yet their steadfast support for the Stars and Stripes in Kentucky's "South Carolina" made them heroes to leading Unionists throughout the state. Anderson's admirers included a trio of powerful newspaper men: George D. Prentice, editor of the *Louisville Journal*; editor John H. Harney of the *Louisville Democrat*; and Albert Gallatin Hodges, who published the *Frankfort Commonwealth*. Hodges stuck with Anderson to the end. Prentice and Harney condemned him when he became a Republican ally and Unconditional Unionist.[17]

Anderson almost failed to make it to Washington. Before he left home, rebel cavalry galloped into Mayfield and shot up the town, then unguarded by Union troops. Part of the band ambushed, derailed and robbed a passenger train from Paducah. The marauders also killed one, possibly two, Unionists and abducted Lush. Evidently, they thought he was more valuable alive than dead and ultimately swapped him for a Confederate congressman the Yankees had behind bars up north.[18]

Most of the raiders were from the Purchase; some were likely Graves County men. Even "Lush" had rebel relations, besides his big brother. Their sister, Mary Elizabeth, was married to Confederate Colonel Albert P. Thompson of Paducah. He was killed in the battle of Paducah on March 25, 1864.[19]

It is not known if Mary Elizabeth shared her husband's sympathies. But her brother's turn against slavery evidently began with his switch from Union Democrat to Unconditional Unionist. When he was sworn in as a congressman in January, 1864, he joined the Republican caucus and helped elect Schuyler Colfax speaker. Colfax was an Indiana abolitionist Republican. In addition, Anderson agreed to the enlistment of African American soldiers into the armed forces and proposed legislation to pay loyal Kentuckians for the loss of their chattels should the state abolish slavery. Nonetheless, Lush did not claim to be an abolitionist nor, technically, was he a Republican. Unabashed Republican abolitionists like Colfax and Representative Thaddeus Stevens of Pennsylvania, demanded that the federal government end slavery with no compensation for slaveholders.[20]

Back home in Graves County, Anderson's support, small as it was to begin with, was all but gone by early 1864. Most of his Unionist friends turned against him. Enmity against Anderson increased when he backed Lincoln for another term. Too, secessionists and Union Democrats alike bitterly assailed him for supporting Brigadier General E.A. Paine's July appointment as commander in the Purchase. Paine cracked down hard on the still rebellious region where smuggling was widespread and where Confederate guerrillas roamed almost at will, sheltered, armed and supplied by a largely friendly populace. Purchase whites, secessionists and Union Democrats, vilified Paine, considering him the worst sort of Yankee. He was an abolitionist, a Republican and a friend of Lincoln who refused to denigrate African Americans. Accused of multiple crimes, including bribery, extortion and murder, Paine was removed in September. Anderson was charged with being in cahoots with the general; the duo allegedly lined their pockets with illgotten gains. In 1865, a court martial exonerated Paine on all but a minor charge. The House cleared Anderson. Evidence is strong that Paine and

Anderson's "crimes" were their anti-slavery and pro–Union and pro–Lincoln opinions.[21]

Lucian Anderson's story is the stuff of movie lore. Hollywood ignored him in the 2012 Oscar-winning film "Lincoln," which starred Daniel Day Lewis as the sixteenth president. Only Yeaman made it into the final cut, and just briefly; Michael Stuhlbarg, who closely resembled the Kentuckian, played Yeaman. Nobody played Anderson, Randall or Smith.

Nonetheless, Anderson and Lincoln became friends. He visited the president at the White House. Lincoln reportedly was fond of the Andersons and gave Lush's wife, Ann, an ornate bejeweled necklace that was clearly visible in a portrait of her. The whereabouts of the jewelry is evidently unknown.[22]

Ann's spouse worked hard for Lincoln's re-election in Kentucky, but to no avail. General George B. McClellan, the pro-war Democrat who ran on an anti-war platform, lost the election but won Kentucky. Lincoln polled about 30 percent of the vote—his worst showing in any state. McClellan carried Graves County.[23]

Anderson must have concluded that his support for Lincoln and the Thirteenth Amendment all but doomed his chances for a second term in the August, 1865, elections. The fate of the amendment was the main issue in Kentucky, where almost all whites opposed ratification. The war's end in the spring sealed Lush's political fate. It was obvious that the Democrats would become even stronger with the return of the Confederate soldiers. The party called itself the Conservative Democrats, or simply Conservatives. Anderson knew he had no chance to win against a Conservative so he chose not to run. Lawrence Trimble, the anti-war Democrat he beat in 1863, won on the Conservative ticket. (Trimble ran as a Unionist in 1861 and lost to Burnett.) Also, a Conservative unseated Yeaman. Though Randall and Smith were reelected, they were widely denounced in Kentucky beyond their districts.[24]

Anderson, Randall, Smith and Yeaman fare better among twenty-first century historians. James C. Klotter, the state historian of Kentucky, agreed that the four congressmen understood that their votes for the Thirteenth Amendment might be career-enders. "Yet they knew it was the fair thing to do and the right thing," said Klotter, a Georgetown College history professor and author.[25]

Anderson, Randall, Smith and Yeaman also found themselves at odds with Kentucky senators Garrett Davis and Lazarus W. Powell; the two Union Democrats voted "nay" when the upper chamber of Congress approved the amendment on April 8, 1864. The General Assembly's refusal to endorse it completed Kentucky's rejection of the Thirteenth Amendment.[26]

The votes of Anderson, Randall, Smith and Yeaman should prove even to the most cynical voters that a "principled politician" is not necessarily an oxymoron. Despite his cameo appearance in *Lincoln*, Yeaman is still largely unknown in Kentucky, too. Anderson, Randall and Smith have virtually disappeared into the deeper mists of Bluegrass State history as well. Yeaman tarried as a Union Democrat, but ran for relection as a Republican. Yet Anderson, Randall and Smith helped lay "the foundation for a permanent Republican party in the state." The three congressmen

> unlike most Kentuckians ... were able to see and accept a new United States rising out of the ravages of the Civil War, a new federation of states with slavery gone. They foresaw what was to come and pointed the way to a new future that need not be feared nor despised by those living in the border commonwealth.[27]

The quartet's descent into near anonymity likely was hastened by Kentucky's intense postwar Southern sympathy. "The conservative racial, social, political, and gender values inherent in Confederate symbols and the Lost Cause appealed to many Kentuckians, who despite their devotion to the Union had never entered the war to free slaves," Anne E. Marshall wrote in *Creating a Confederate Kentucky: The Lost Cause and Civil War Memory in a Border State*.

> In a postwar world where racial boundaries were in flux, the Lost Cause and the conservative politics that went with it seemed not only a comforting reminder of a past free of late nineteenth-century insecurities but also a way to reinforce contemporary efforts to maintain white supremacy.

The Kentucky legislature, whose white supremacist Democratic majority included a number of former Confederate soldiers, officials and secession supporters, also voted down the 14th Amendment, which made African Americans citizens, and rejected the 15th Amendment, which gave black men the vote.[28]

Lush Anderson surely headed home to Mayfield with some trepidation. He, too, must have been surprised that he was able to resume his role as a leading citizen, apparently with ease. He restarted his law practice and evidently did not lack for clients. It was said that Anderson was such a good lawyer that even the most ardent of ex-rebels were willing to overlook his politics, which shifted one more time before his death. Lush eventually abandoned the GOP for the Prohibition Party. His vocation changed some, too. He founded a bank in Mayfield and became part of a Florida land company. When he died in 1898 at age 74, the Democratic *Mayfield Monitor* remembered the old foe of slavery as one of the town's "most noted citizens." In *Story of Mayfield Through a Century 1823–1923*, D. Trabue Davis praised Anderson as "a man with a community spirit that goes down on the pages of history with great honor." Davis got the rest of his tribute wrong, claiming Anderson "was for a number of years in congress" and "has the distinction of being the only man south of the Mason-Dixon line that voted for the 14th Amendment to the federal constitution." Yet J.H. Battle, W.H. Perrin and G.C. Kniffen's *History of Kentucky* correctly credited him with voting "for the Thirteenth Amendment, abolishing slavery throughout the United States."[29]

Except for his tombstone, there are no monuments in Mayfield to Anderson, though a stone memorial to Graves County's Confederate soldiers stands in front of the courthouse and an iron Confederate memorial gate parts to let visitors into Maplewood Cemetery.

Lucian and Ann Anderson's tombstone (Berry Craig).

Lush is mentioned on a state historical marker next to the First Presbyterian Church, which his father helped start. Yet Anderson is cited only as one of three congressmen who attended the house of worship; the plaque is silent about his vote for the 13th Amendment. Built in 1851 or 1852, his single-story, wood-frame at 321 North Sixth Street was Mayfield's last surviving antebellum structure. Razed in early 2016, the house had been moved twice from its original location near the court square. There was nothing to denote that the house belonged to Anderson; it was occupied by Martha Nell Anderson, his great-grandniece, until her death in 2014 at age eighty-seven. She is buried in Maplewood Cemetery though her great-grandfather Ervin, the congressman, his parents, siblings and other family members are buried in the Anderson Cemetery a short distance from where Lush's house stood. Hidden by a low brick wall and partially obscured by houses and businesses, the burial ground is not widely known in Mayfield.[30]

Klotter added,

**Lucian and Ann's home (Berry Craig).**

The memories of the postwar society that rejected their stands and their votes relegated [Anderson, Randall, Smith and Yeaman] … to obscurity. But the good thing about history is that it rescues the obscure, honors the worthy, and remembers the past. History now praises them, while their society condemned their courage. Their example remains important for present-day politicians—indeed, for all of us.[31]

# 2

# Stepping to
# a Different Drummer

Mayfield did not amount to much when Nancy Davenport Anderson gave birth to Lucian, her sixth child, in the family's new dwelling. The Anderson home place was anything but cozy. The "crude log structure," was supposedly the first house in Mayfield, but nothing marks the site of the founder's dwelling. Lucian came into the world on June 23, 1824. His brother, Ervin, who arrived in 1820 or 1821, was said to be the first white child born in the county. Early Mayfield was little more than a huddle of rude cabins and log-walled stores on two streets. Most of the buildings faced a tiny log courthouse on the public square, which crowned a low hill with gently sloping sides. Mayfield was well situated for commerce, communication and growth; the town sprouted almost exactly in the middle of the Jackson Purchase, the Bluegrass State's last frontier.[1]

Kentucky's westernmost region, the Purchase belonged to the Chickasaw Indians until 1818 when President James Monroe commissioned future president Andrew Jackson of Tennessee and former Kentucky governor Isaac Shelby to buy the land on behalf of the United States. For reasons not clear, the deal, which took the form of a treaty, bore only Jackson's name. The Chickasaws knew Jackson and Shelby by reputation; both were famous—likely infamous from the seller's perspective—for fighting Native Americans, most recently in the War of 1812. Reputedly, the Chickasaws especially disdained Shelby and "were loth to treat with him" while they "had learned both to fear and respect" Old Hickory. Also, it was said that Shelby fell ill during the negotiations, leaving Jackson to do most of the parleying. Or the agreement was called the Jackson Purchase Treaty because the "Hero of New Orleans" and his Tennessee land speculator friends "were the driving force behind the effort to break the 1805 treaty with the Chickasaw that had assured them that the United States would never again ask them for land 'as long as the sun shines and the grass grows.'"[2]

When the Native Amer-
icans signed the pact on October 19, 1818, they ceded their
territory for $300,000, payable
in $20,000 annual installments
over fifteen years. The approximately 8,100 square mile
region took in Chickasaw
country between the Tennessee
and Mississippi rivers, north
to the Ohio River and south
to the Tennessee-Mississippi
border. In 1819, the United
States Senate approved the
treaty and Monroe signed it.[3]
Kentucky and Tennessee
agreed to split the Jackson
Purchase at thirty-six degrees,
thirty-minutes latitude, which
was believed to be the boundary between the two states.
Kentucky entered the union

Andrew Jackson (Library of Congress).

in 1792, Tennessee five years later. However, when surveyors were divvying
up the Purchase, they discovered that the state line east of the Tennessee
River was about ten miles north of true thirty-six-thirty. Despite the error
that favored Tennessee, the old border stayed the same. Ultimately the two
states agreed to rive the Purchase at true thirty-six thirty. Tennessee got the
lion's share of the territory; Kentucky's cut was about 2,100 square miles. As
time passed, "Purchase" and "Jackson Purchase" came to refer to only to Kentucky's section of the territory. The Volunteer State's portion became "West
Tennessee."[4]

Like all pioneers, Purchase newcomers toiled to build farms, homes and
communities. But they did not have to blister their hands or strain their backs
hewing their version of civilization from forests primeval. While other parts
of the Bluegrass State, notably the Appalachian Mountains, were thickly tim-
bered, almost all of Graves County was a prairie that Native Americans created to attract game. "The greater part of the county was almost entirely
devoid of timber" and covered "with a tall grass in which but few shrubs of
any kind were to be seen, except along the streams." Whites called the grass-
lands "barrens," though the soil was rich and fertile. The prairie provided
more than ample grazing for buffalo, elk and deer, creatures Native Americans
hunted for food, fur and hides. The Indians preserved the barrens by burning

the grass every spring for many years. Woodlands, mostly oak and hickory, grew back with white settlement. But for a long time, big trees were rare in many places. Early Purchase dwellers swore that along the road connecting Mayfield and Murray, the seat of Calloway County, there was scarcely enough timber to cut a switch.[5]

Like many pioneer towns, the Graves County seat sprang up haphazardly "without any definite plans with regard to the regularity of the streets, and the boundary lines of the city." Mayfield grew slowly at first "but eventually as the settlement increased in its general scope the people began to realize the importance and necessity of laying off the town and properly recording it." In 1821, the Kentucky General Assembly named the whole Purchase Hickman County after Captain Paschall Hickman of Franklin County, who was killed in the Battle of the River Raisin during the War of 1812. As the Purchase population swelled, the legislature subdivided Hickman into smaller counties, starting with Calloway in 1822. The region's second county was named in 1822, though spelled differently, for Colonel Richard Callaway, the famous Kentucky pioneer. Graves came next, in 1823. Graves is the namesake of Major Benjamin Graves of Fayette County who also perished at the River Raisin.[6]

Graves is an almost perfect rectangle because the Purchase was the only part of Kentucky surveyed and platted based on the innovative Land Ordinance of 1785, which was designed to pave the way for the orderly settlement of the old Northwest Territory which was ultimately divided into the states of Ohio, Indiana, Illinois, Michigan and Wisconsin. The measure created a township and range system, which was supposed to prevent land ownership disputes caused by more inexact surveying systems. Early Kentucky courts kept busy with lawsuits stemming from vague or overlapping claims. A township contained thirty-six sections, each one-mile-square, or 640 acres. Settlers or land speculators who bought sections could subdivide and resell them.[7]

History is silent about why the Andersons moved to Graves County. But cheap, available land lured hundreds of families and individuals. A land office opened at Wadesboro, a tiny community that survives astride what is now the Calloway-Marshall County line. At first, land sold for one dollar an acre, with most settlers buying a 160-acre quarter section. Later, the price of a section fell to eighty dollars—or fifty cents per acre—and finally to forty dollars, or twenty-five cents an acre.[8]

While Mayfield is the virtual hub of the Purchase—the "Pearl of the Purchase" to proud locals—the community is also just about dead-center in Graves County. How Mayfield got its name is unclear. There is a Mayfield, England, where, according to legend, Dunstan, the patron saint of blacksmiths, was working at his forge one day when he espied Satan. Dunstan snatched his fire tongs and grabbed Old Scratch by the nose. Alas, the Prince of Darkness escaped to continue his evil-doing. It is unlikely the Graves

County seat is named for the English village. Just as improbable is the suggestion that some of the first settlers, perhaps including the Andersons, named Mayfield for the beautiful fields of wild May flowers they admired. Almost certainly, somebody named Mayfield for nearby Mayfield Creek. Allegedly, the shallow, meandering waterway is the namesake of George Mayfield who died at the Alamo with his good friend and hunting companion, Davy Crockett. Yet there is no that proof Mayfield ever traipsed western Kentucky. The most likely—but still unverified—source of the creek's name was a murdered Mississippian named Mayfield. A rich man, he enjoyed betting on the horses at a racetrack at or near the site of Hickman, the Fulton County seat. Kidnappers allegedly carried him to the future site of Mayfield, where they apparently held him for ransom. After carving his name on a tree, he tried to flee, but was shot dead, his body tumbling into the creek, or so the story goes. Poor Mayfield's corpse was never found, and the tree, long since gone, served as his only tombstone.[9]

John Anderson purportedly put Mayfield on the map on August 15, 1823, when he landed his town a post office. On March 27, 1824, Mayfield's first board of trustees recorded the community's original plot, "an area of 160 acres lying in Section 10, Township 3 north, Range 1 east." The five-man panel included John Anderson and his older brother, Crawford. The tract encompassed thirty-five blocks, seventy-two lots and a public square. It also included "9 streets crossing each other at right angles, 5 running east and west and 4 running north and south." The main street was Broadway and each street was to be an impressive sixty-six feet wide.[10]

Lucian Anderson came to support the enlistment of African Americans like Samuel Crawford whose grave is in Mayfield (Berry Craig).

John and Crawford Anderson's ancestors evidently migrated to America from Scotland before the Revolutionary War. Lucian's father was born on December 11, 1794, in Greenville District, South Carolina. His mother's birthday was October 7, 1795, though where is not certain. Her hometown may have been Halifax, Virginia. John and Nancy wed on August 23, 1816, either in the Palmetto State or in Christian County, Kentucky. The Anderson family, including young John, had left South Carolina for Kentucky, apparently in 1798. They walked 350 miles, trudging through the Appalachian Mountains to Nashville, Tennessee's capital, where they bought rafts and floated down the Cumberland River to Eddyville, Kentucky. They migrated another fifteen miles or so inland before homesteading near Princeton.[11]

The Andersons were among thousands of easterners who headed over the mountains after the Revolution and the War of 1812. The West—the vast territory between the Appalachians and the Mississippi River—was the land of opportunity, or so pilgrims like the Andersons thought. Kentucky, the gateway to the West, was the perceived Garden of Eden without forbidden fruit and minus Beelzebub posing as a serpent. Perhaps the Anderson family believed the tall tales of explorers who claimed Kentucky "teemed with game waiting to be killed." Here, too, "the clear streams were filled with delectable fish eager to be caught," and the meadows and woodlands contained a bounty of turkeys and other fowl eager to wind up on a pioneer family's table. A future governor claimed the land was so fertile that when he poked his walking stick in a corn patch, it sprouted a nubbin. John and Nancy had eleven children, perhaps lending some credence to a boast by another proud pioneer Kentuckian who swore that in his part of the country Kentucky, "female Animals of every sort are very prolifick, it [']s frequent for ewes to bear 3 lambs at a time, & women and cows to have Twins at a time." Evidently, all of the Anderson offspring came singly.[12]

Princeton, now the seat of Caldwell County, was a small but fairly prosperous community. Yet the prospect of starting fresh in the Jackson Purchase obviously appealed to young John and Crawford. The latter and his family apparently beat John and Nancy to the newly opened land beyond the Tennessee. Crawford reportedly arrived as early as 1818 and started a farm near Viola in north Graves County. Supposedly, he had a horse named Duncan that drowned in a nearby creek, which was named in commemoration of the deceased steed. In 1838 John recorded in a little leather bound book that he brought his family to a spot "on Mayfield Creek in the woods two & half miles north of the town of Mayfield (or where the town now stands for it was then in the woods)." Anderson penned that they were "three days on the route encamping in the woods of night and threading our way through the thickets by day." They arrived "at the place of our future residence" on October 27, 1819, "my family then consisting of myself & wife one Negro girl named Felicia and my three sons that are now dead towit Vincent Wadsworth Anderson and John Davenport Anderson and Rollin Lee Anderson." John Anderson built cabins and stayed on his farm until December, 1824, when the family moved to Mayfield to be closer to the courthouse. Governor John Adair named Anderson the county's first county clerk and circuit court clerk. Evidently it was common in early Kentucky for one man to hold both posts.[13]

The Andersons were typical of county pioneers in that they came as families. Sometimes, an individual family member, or part of a family, arrived first, bought the land and made other necessary arrangements for settlement. Then, they would summon the others. Such may have been the case with Crawford and his family.[14]

John Anderson must have been one of Mayfield's busier citizens. He kept office hours at the courthouse, which was completed in November, 1824, at a cost of $139. H also ran a tavern at his house under a license the state granted him in 1825. By 1830, Mayfield, population forty-four, boasted three taverns and two, perhaps three, retail stores, one of which Anderson owned. He ran his enterprise with his sons, Vincent and Davenport. The proprietor

Graves County courthouse and courtsquare today (Berry Craig).

purportedly brought the first stock of goods to Mayfield and Anderson and his offspring "soon established a fair trade in this sparsely settled country." In addition, Anderson farmed and owned several slaves. Evidently, holding fellow human beings in bondage did not disturb John's Christian sensibilities because about 1832, he helped start the town's Cumberland Presbyterian church. Mayfield's first religious organization, it became the First Presbyterian Church in 1909. Until a permanent house of worship was built, the little congregation gathered on Sundays in homes, presumably Anderson's among them. Sometimes, they met at the courthouse, which doubled as a community center for several years.[15]

At the courthouse, Anderson attended to secular matters. His clerical duties perhaps included keeping records for court proceedings, such as trying offenders charged with mischief like shooting "off a gun or pistol" or running or galloping "a horse creature" through town. Parties found guilty were subject to a fine of "not less than two or more than four dollars."[16]

However, prosperity—at least for the time and place—and community leader status did not shield the town founder from tragedy. John and Nancy lost six of their children to various diseases. Most or all of their offspring are buried in the Anderson family cemetery between North Sixth and Seventh streets in town. Rollin Lee succumbed to "typhus fever" in 1838 at age nineteen. In his journal, John Anderson scrupulously detailed the teen's horrible death. His account documents standard nineteenth century medical treatments for typhus that modern doctors would dismiss as fatal quackery.[17]

Davenport and Vincent died in 1837. Vincent had left Mayfield for Clinton, the Hickman County seat, to work in the clerk's office. But he fell ill and on his deathbed, the recently married Vincent, persuaded his bachelor brother to take his job and provide for his widow. "Alas!" John Anderson lamented, "cruel relentless death was there aiming a deadly shaft at [Rollin's] vitals." On June 3, 1838, he began suffering violent headaches. He called for a local doctor; typhus was the feared diagnosis. The physician prescribed "pills" and "copious bleeding," after which Rollin rallied. John rushed to his son, expecting to witness his recovery, yet he relapsed. Rollin's fever spiked; he drifted into delirium and shocked his father with outbursts of "vulgar or profane language." Desperate to save his patient, the doctor "blistered him severely ... right upon the region of the lung, and in the course of the next 24 hours he cut all his hair from his head and caused it to be rubbed profusely with tincture of Canthardy which reduced his whole head to a solid blister."[18]

Anderson poured out his anguish:

> I never shall forget his agonies he begged most piteously for a knife to put an end to his sufferings Oh! God am I destined to see all my children die in the order of nature to be reversed in my case and instead of my sons being spared to comfort me in my old age

and commit my body to the tomb am I to witness the destruction of my whole race? Save me Oh! God from this melancholy fate.[19]

Rollin succumbed on June 12. John paid the doctor, bought a coffin and arranged for a wagon and driver to bring Rollin's corpse home. He also "dispatched a messenger to Mayfield to advise my family of the melancholy event...." Rollin was buried just before sundown on June 13. "My family cemetery is situated about 400 yards north of the courthouse ... on a narrow ledge of land on the right side and overlooking the western road to Paducah," he described the burial plot around which the town grew. "Here now I have six children buried & have only 5 left and here I intend to be buried myself." When Anderson watched the burial of his son, he "was forcibly struck with the great truth that 'there is nothing firm and enduring but heaven.'"[20]

The historical record reveals next to nothing about Lush's childhood. One source held that after he left school, he clerked for his father at the courthouse until the town founder died. "My education has been limited to a good English one never having had the benefit of what is now termed a classical education," he explained in a letter he dictated after he was elected to Congress. Meanwhile, Ervin became county and circuit court clerk upon his father's death and evidently held both posts until 1851. Lucian worked for his elder sibling until 1844 when he quit to study law under the tutelage of his brother-in law, Richard L. Mayes, who wed Lush's sister, Elizabeth, in 1839. A Fayette County native, Mayes lived in Cadiz, the Trigg County seat, before moving to Mayfield. Twenty-one-year-old Lucian earned admission to the bar at Hopkinsville, the Christian County seat, on October 30, 1845, but he ultimately moved back to Mayfield and became Mayes' law partner. They advertised their firm as "Anderson & Mayes, Attorneys at Law and Collecting Agents." Like Lush, Mayes supported the Union cause during the Civil War.[21]

By the mid–1840s, Mayfield and Graves County had grown considerably in wealth and population. In 1846, the year Lucian married fifteen-year-old Ann Rebecca Lochridge, the county's taxable property was assessed at $1,136,400. Graves encompassed 339,194 acres valued, on average, at $1.90 per acre. The 1840 census enumerated 7,465 residents county-wide. Besides a courthouse, Mayfield boasted five lawyers, four doctors, four stores, a number of mechanics' shops and approximately 100 people. In 1832, John Anderson was part of a four-man committee charged with drafting a plan for a new courthouse "more in keeping with the dignity of the growing county, which they did." Their plan was rejected in 1833 but a new committee named "the same year, drew up satisfactory plans and specifications," for a $5,400 structure. The new two-story brick courthouse, forty-feet square, was built in 1834. The facility included "a large court room, two jury rooms and one grand jury room." Lawyer Lucian doubtless became a familiar sight in the county temple of justice.[22]

Mayes may have helped whet Anderson's appetite for elective office. Graves County voters sent Lucian's tutor to the 1849 convention that drafted Kentucky's third constitution. Kentucky entered the Union as a slave state, and the new charter preserved slavery. Mayes was apparently a pro-slavery Democrat like most local voters in the First Congressional District, which was dubbed Kentucky's "Democratic Gibraltar." Nonetheless, Lush became a Whig, the party of Clay.[23]

Born in Virginia in 1777, Clay moved to Lexington in 1797. He steadily climbed the political ladder from speaker of the Kentucky House of Representatives to U.S. House speaker. Clay also was secretary of state and a U.S. senator. Nicknamed "the Great Pacificator," he is best known for helping broker three compromises to preserve the Union.

Like Clay, the Whigs were nationalistic and looked to the federal government to help boost business and industry. Clay proposed the American System, which featured a protective tariff to benefit America's fledgling manufacturers, a Bank of the United States and federal funding for internal improvements, or upgrades in the nation's transportation network. The Whigs were strongest in the northeast and in the new states emerging from the Northwest Territory. The Democrats, led by Andrew Jackson, were generally suspicious of large businesses and banks. They also opposed the American System, calling it special interest legislation. At the same time, they believed the federal government should stay out of the economy, and they favored universal white suffrage. Almost all Democrats were pro-slavery or at least acquiesced in slavery and the South was the party's stronghold. The Democrats often called themselves "states' rights men," meaning they supported the right of states to sanction slavery. There were, of course, exceptions to general characterizations of the two parties. Whigs tended to be wealthier than Democrats, but there were poor Whigs and rich Democrats. While most northern Whigs came to oppose slavery—Lincoln among them—almost every southern Whig was as pro-slavery as any Democrat. Jackson proved himself as nationalistic as any Whig by asserting the supremacy of the federal government over South Carolina during the nullification crisis, which was settled by Clay's second compromise.[24]

Clay ran for president the first time in 1824, when the first settlers were building cabins and starting farms and communities in the Purchase. His opponents were Jackson, William Crawford of Georgia and John Quincy Adams of Massachusetts, the ultimate winner. Only Clay and Jackson were on the ballot in Kentucky. Clay collected nearly seventy-three percent of the vote in his home state.[25]

Clay won every Kentucky region except the Purchase, whose hero was

Old Hickory. The region supplied Jackson nearly seventy-two percent of its vote. Jackson beat Adams in the 1828 presidential election and even carried Kentucky. Statewide, Jackson got 55.5 percent of the vote. The territory that bore his name led every other part of the state in supporting him. Eighty-seven percent of Purchase men who went for the polls voted for Jackson.[26]

The legal age for voting was twenty-one, so Lush could not have voted until 1845, the year after Whig William Owsley was elected governor. The Whigs controlled state politics from the 1830s to the 1850s. Between 1836 and 1851, Kentucky elected seven straight Whig governors. After Jackson, a Democrat did not carry Kentucky in a presidential race until James Buchanan won the state in 1856. On the other hand, the Purchase, except for Paducah and McCracken County, a Whig enclave, remained loyal to the Democrats. In presidential elections from 1832 to 1856, the region's vote was more than two-thirds Democratic.[27]

Even so, Lush became Graves County attorney in 1851, though it is not certain if he was elected or appointed. Either way, he was one of the few Whigs who ever held office in the county, though he soon resigned, for reasons apparently unknown. He also ran for the state House of Representatives on the Whig ticket in 1851, finishing a creditable second in a three-man race. Democrat A.H. Willingham turned back Anderson, 524–459 with Democrat W.M. Cargill finishing third with 428 votes. Lush's strong showing might have been a big reason why in 1852, the state party chose him as a Whig presidential elector for General Winfield Scott. Dubbed "Old Fuss and Feathers," Scott was one of American's top commanders in the Mexican-American War of 1846–1848. His Democratic opponent was Franklin Pierce, who was one of Scott's brigadier generals in the conflict, which the United States won.[28]

Anderson stood up for his party at the McCracken County courthouse in Paducah on October 6. The citizenry gathered "to hear a discussion of the principles and questions at issue between the two parties in the present canvass," according a correspondent for the then Whiggish *Louisville Courier*. The crowd, "quite respectable" in size, was about evenly divided between Whigs and Democrats, and Anderson started the program with a ninety-minute speech "in which he showed up some of the most striking inconsistencies of the Democratic party." His "burning words and scathing sentences" exposed "the glaring untruths of which" the Democrats were guilty.

> He proved most conclusively, that notwithstanding they arrogate to themselves as a distinctive and peculiar trait of Locofoco policy, "that the will of the majority should govern," they did openly and beyond contradiction, "palsy the will of their constituents" by the nomination of Frank Pierce.[29]

Lush lambasted the Democrats; his thrusts at the party "and their *blood stained war-worn Gen. Pierce* ... pierced their victims to the very heart." His

**Winfield Scott (Library of Congress).**

praise for "our noble chieftain, Winfield Scott, was characterized by an eloquence and point rarely heard in any community"; thus "the house rang with cheers and deafening applause." Anderson urged the men of his party to "be of good cheer" because Scott was a "Hero of a hundred battlefields" while Pierce "was a man unknown, and *not to be trusted.*" The Democrat's military career, according to Lush, "was marked by nothing else than fainting fits and well executed feats of the gymnasium." (During the battle of Contreras, Pierce's horse stumbled and fell, pinning the general and injuring his knee. Tied to his saddle, he led his brigade in the subsequent battle of Churubusco, but passed out from the pain. Whigs charged that he fainted from fright.)[30]

The *Courier* scribe claimed that Lush wrapped up "amidst three overwhelming cheers for" the nominee and his running mate, William A. Graham of New Jersey while "the Democrats writhed" from Lush's "sarcasm and the thrusts of the 'trenchant blade' of his eloquence." The correspondent added, "To show how they take it, one of them remarked to me the next morning, to this effect: that his speech was the bray of an ass, and his audience a set of *ignoramuses.*" On the other hand, "the Whigs pronounce it the best speech of the campaign, and his audience the most intelligent that has assembled here during the canvass." Lush "is yet a young man," the correspondent mused, "and if he continues to improve, he will be one of the shining lights, and one of the best speakers in this District."[31]

Naturally, the *Courier* man was unimpressed with the rejoinder from Lush's fellow Mayfield lawyer, William R. Bradley, the district Democratic elector. "A more 'lame and impotent' speech was never heard," the correspondent hooted, claiming, "A candid Pierce Democrat admitted to me afterwards, that he was a fool to attempt to measure arms with Anderson." Lush had stumped nearly the whole district and had won over several Democrats in

**Franklin Pierce (Library of Congress).**

McCracken County, the correspondent said. "Our honorable representative, and almost every 'striker' in the district, are endeavoring to bolster up a weak cause, and are making speeches daily fearful lest this stronghold be successfully attacked by the enemy, and yield in some measure to the valiant charges of our little army." The correspondent concluded, "'Our fires burn brightly,' and if the Whig party be not crowned with success on the second day of November there is no truth in the present indication and signs of the times."[32]

The signs proved wrong. Scott won Kentucky, though barely, while Pierce captured the White House and swept every First District county but Livingston. Pierce trounced Scott in Graves, 971–446. The margin was closer in McCracken, that Whig island in a Democratic sea; the vote was 416 for Pierce and 385 for Scott.[33]

Two years later, the Whig Party shattered over the controversial Kansas-Nebraska Act. Democratic Senator Stephen A. Douglas of Illinois sponsored the measure, hoping it would smooth the way for the construction of a transcontinental railroad from Chicago, his hometown, to California. To win Southern support for the line, he proposed creating Kansas and Nebraska territories, through which the railroad would run, and permit the citizenry to vote slavery in or out. Douglas called it "popular sovereignty," a term he and Senator Lewis Cass used to describe their middle position between the pro and anti-slavery sides. The North reacted with fury because the legislation would, in effect, repeal the Missouri Compromise of 1820, under which Maine came into the Union as a free state and Missouri as a slave state. The agreement, Clay's first compromise, also stipulated that after Missouri statehood, slavery would be prohibited north of thirty-six degrees, thirty-minutes latitude—the Show Me State's southern border—in the rest of the Louisiana Purchase. Slavery would be legal below the line. Kansas and Nebraska were north of thirty-six, thirty. Southern Whigs joined with the Democrats in passing the act, which Pierce supported.

The measure split and ultimately destroyed the Whig party. The act also triggered civil war in Kansas territory between pro and anti-slavery settlers, the former group aided by armed pro-slavery Missourians known as "border ruffians." Virtual outlaws whose ranks included Frank and Jesse James, they crossed into Kansas and terrorized opponents of slavery, killing them and destroying their homes and farms. Dubbed "bleeding Kansas," the conflict was a presage to the Civil War, America's most lethal conflict.

Most northern Whigs, including Abraham Lincoln of Illinois, joined the new Republican party, founded in 1854 on anti-slavery principles. Lincoln, like most Republicans, favored a gradual end to slavery by stopping its spread into territories. A vocal minority of Republicans were abolitionists. They favored the immediate destruction of slavery, arguing that human bondage was un–Christian and mocked the democratic principles upon which the country was supposed to be founded.

Without a party, what was Lush to do? Many, if not most, southern Whigs became Democrats, however reluctantly. But others, especially in Kentucky, embraced the nativist, anti–Catholic and anti-foreign American or Know-Nothing party. The party was semi-secret. If an outsider asked about the party, a member was supposed to reply, "I know nothing." Some Kentucky Whigs, including Anderson, became Democrats, which cheered party members and party papers nationwide. The Democratic Raleigh, North Carolina, *Semi-Weekly Standard* lauded the converts in Tennessee and in the Bluegrass State. "In Kentucky the fight waxes hot, and we are assured that *the order* is reeling under the heavy blows which it receives from Whigs and Democrats," the capital city paper editorialized. "The son of the late lamented Clay is out in open opposition to the order, and six of the twelve Scott electors are ranged in a similar position of antagonism." The paper listed Lush among the half-dozen anti–Know Nothings.[34]

On August 6, 1855, the state elected Know-Nothing Charles S. Morehead governor over Democrat Beverly L. Clark by a close margin of 69,816 to 65,413. The Know-Nothings also won a majority in both houses of the legislature and took six of the state's ten seats in Congress. Yet not all Know-Nothings were nativist bigots. Some liked the party because it downplayed the slavery issue, which many Kentuckians feared might destroy the Union. Even so, on Election Day, Know-Nothing mobs rampaged through Irish and German neighborhoods in Louisville to keep the "undesirables" away from the polls. At least twenty-two people were killed; many more were injured, and several immigrant-owned homes and businesses were burned or looted.

The death and destruction would have been greater had Mayor John Barbee, a Know-Nothing, and other influential citizens not intervened to protect people and property.[35]

The Know-Nothing tide that swept Kentucky was barely a trickle in Graves County, which voted for Clark over Morehead, 1,230 to 539. Every other Democrat on the county ballot, including Lush, won by margins of at least two-to-one. In his second bid for the state house, Anderson easily outdistanced Know-Nothing S.M. Leeman, 1,210 to 529.[36]

On September 27, representative-elect Anderson showed up at a Paducah meeting of the First District Democrats "and Anti-Know Nothings." The gathering was large, according to the *Louisville Courier* but not as big as anticipated "on account of sickness in the country and other causes." Anderson and other former Whigs spoke. Ex-Whig Archibald Dixon of Henderson was invited to speak but was unable to attend. Somebody read a letter from Dixon, a former lieutenant governor and senator, confirming that he intended "to co-operate in future with the Democratic party." It was his opinion that

> the Democratic party, although weakened in the free States, is still national, and still co-operates with the Southern Democracy, in opposition to the Abolitionists and Freesoilers of the North, who, to destroy the institution of slavery, would rend the Union asunder, and bury beneath the ruins of the Constitution the liberties of the country.[37]

Dixon and Anderson were invited to a Lexington Democratic meeting in October. Dixon agreed to attend, but Anderson told the men hosting the gathering that he could not come.

> I write you not for the purpose of descanting upon the propositions and organizations of our opponents, but for the purpose of assuring you, that I am with you in your efforts to 'save the Union from the attacks of abolitionism on the one side and sectional and religious bigotry on the other."

Lush explained.

> You are aware that I have always been a devoted Whig, but when that party became disorganized, and a great majority of those who once composed that party merged into a know-nothing party, I could no longer act with them, but I took my position beneath the Democratic flag, believing that beneath its ample folds the country must look for protection and safety.

Anderson pledged to remain a Democrat "until know-nothingism is crushed, and the Union placed upon a tranquil and solid basis." He assured the Lexington Democrats that "nothing would afford me more pleasure than to be present with you on the occasion referred to." After the "Bloody Monday" election-day riots in Louisville, the American party faded away. The Known-Nothings simply called themselves the "Opposition."[38]

Though Anderson served only one term in the legislature, he stayed active in Democratic politics. His law practice evidently flourished, which may be why he opted against a second term. Besides, Frankfort was a grueling 260 miles away over mostly bad roads and his family was growing. Henry Clay—"Harry"—and Nancy Augusta Anderson were small; Robert Lochridge was a baby. Though he had multiple mouths to feed, he felt he had enough money to invest in the Paducah and Tennessee Railroad Company, which the state legislature incorporated in 1854. The firm aimed to run tracks from the McCracken County seat through Mayfield and on to the Tennessee state line.[39]

Meanwhile, Anderson's investment must have paid off. By the end of 1854, workers had laid tracks all the way Mayfield; the trip to Paducah took a mere two hours. By 1860, the rails stretched another twenty-three miles to the Kentucky-Tennessee state line. The station, just inside Kentucky, was named Fulton for Fulton County, which surrounded it. Ultimately, the Paducah and Tennessee became part of the New Orleans and Ohio line that connected the McCracken County seat with the Crescent City, 570 miles southward.

Henry Clay (Library of Congress).

(Columbus, about thirty miles west of Mayfield, became the northern terminus of the Mobile and Ohio line.) Between Paducah and Fulton, the rails bisected Graves County, leading John C. Noble's *Tri-Weekly Paducah Herald* newspaper to claim that the line afforded the county "an unparalleled increase in wealth and energy almost impossible to realize." The railroad turned Mayfield from "a dull, sluggish, uninteresting little village that only lacked a pair of tombstones to announce her decease" into "an active, prosperous, commercial town," according to the editor. Anderson might have objected to Noble's less-than-kind characterization of pre-railroad Mayfield. He and Noble became sworn enemies in 1861 when the editor made the *Herald* one of the most rabidly secessionist papers in the state.[40]

On January 8, 1856, Lush attended the state Democratic convention in Frankfort, a contentious gathering at which the president of the state Know Nothing executive committee was espied in the gallery, triggering "a loud uproar" and a cry of "interloper" toward the unwelcome visitor, according to the *Louisville Courier*'s correspondent. But the Democrats mainly went after each other when the committee on resolutions declined to recommend the endorsement of former House Speaker Linn Boyd of Paducah for president. Undaunted, Boyd's backers pushed a proposal to give the strongest Democratic counties the most votes on the floor. The speaker's "friends reside in the Jackson's Purchase and in the Mountains, where the Democrats are almost unanimous," the *Courier* reporter explained. Before the pro–Boyd resolution was voted on "or rather choked down," it provoked "a terrible outburst of indignant eloquence." A score of delegates, Lush among them, spoke simultaneously "and if they could not get the attention of the Chair, would address the meeting at random." Lush "pulled off his coat, and said that he must be heard—that there must be an expression of the Convention's sentiments." It is not clear from the story if Anderson was pro or anti–Boyd. But other delegates "doffed their coats and cravats" and delegates climbed on tables and chairs. "Tammany Hall in its palmiest days never presented such a Democratic pandemonium," the correspondent mocked. Congressman John C. Breckinridge of Lexington and other party bigwigs managed to restore order, but Boyd's endorsement was doomed by "the overzealousness and intemperate haste of his friends."[41]

In September, Lush was asked to a Democratic mass meeting on the Tennessee side of Boydsville, a tiny community that straddled the state line between Graves County and Weakley County in the Volunteer State. The festivities were to begin with a torchlight parade on the night of the twenty-sixth followed the next day and by "a

**Linn Boyd (Library of Congress).**

dinner ... prepared for five thousand persons." Boyd, Anderson and Graves County Judge A.R. Boone represented the Bluegrass State. The Tennessee delegation was more impressive. The dignitaries included Governor Andrew Johnson, former governor Aaron V. Brown, state Representative Buck Travis and Daniel S. Donelson. In 1864, Johnson was Lincoln's running mate. Donelson's older brother, Andrew Jackson Donelson, ran for vice president in 1856 on the Know-Nothing ticket topped by ex-president Millard Fillmore. The younger Donelson would become the Confederate general for whom the rebels named strategic Fort Donelson, which Ulysses S. Grant captured in 1862.[42]

Meanwhile, the Democrats ran James Buchanan of Pennsylvania for president and Breckinridge for vice president. On Election Day, "Buck and Breck" easily outpaced Republican John C. Fremont and Fillmore, who became president upon the death of Zachary Taylor in 1850. Fremont was not on the ballot in Kentucky, which went for Breckinridge over Fillmore, 74,642–67,416. Graves County returned its usual lopsided Democratic majority, furnishing Breck 1,380 votes to 475 for Fillmore.[43]

**James Buchanan (Library of Congress).**

In 1857, the notorious Supreme Court decision in *Dred Scott v. Sanford* further inflamed tensions between slave and free states. The court's pro-slavery majority ruled that Congress had no power to exclude slavery from the territories and that African Americans, slave or free, were not citizens. At the same time, the bloodshed continued in Kansas. While pro and anti-slavery Kansans slew each other, each side organized its own territorial government—the free state supporters at Topeka and the pro-slavery forces at Lecompton. In Washington, Buchanan went along with most congressional Democrats who demanded that Kansas be a slave state. Anti-slavery Republicans were equally determined to keep slavery out of Kansas, which became a free state in 1861.

When Kansas joined the Union, slavery was thriving in Lush's part of Kentucky, and he was one of the stoutest defenders of the institution. More than any other factor, an expanding slave-based economy made the Purchase "the South Carolina of Kentucky" during the Civil War, according to historian Patricia Ann Hoskins. She likened the region to parts of the South that underwent similar simultaneous and significant growth in their economies and enslaved populations. There, slave owners were vocal secessionists and non-slaveholders favored secession to uphold white supremacy. Thus, secession reflected white solidarity. Hoskins concluded that "flush with material progress and long overlooked by the rest of the state, the Purchase during the secession crisis revealed itself as never before to be different from the Commonwealth."[44]

Like Lush, nearly every white Kentuckian was pro-slavery, though Kentucky was not a large slaveholding state compared to the cotton states. Because none of Anderson's personal papers evidently survive, it is impossible to know if he had any ethical or religious qualms about human bondage. But he spoke publicly in favor of slavery.

Kentucky, in the early nineteenth century, began developing an agricultural system mainly based on tobacco and diversified farming that did not require the large numbers of laborers needed on southern cotton, sugar and rice plantations. As a result, a significant slave trade began in the state about 1830 when large numbers of blacks unneeded in Kentucky were sold "down the river." "My Old Kentucky Home," the Bluegrass State's official song, is a slave's lament at the prospect of being sent to a southern plantation. It is not known if Lush rues the breakup of slave families, one of the cruelest aspects of the institution.[45]

Though Anderson, like his father, owned slaves, a large majority of Kentucky whites never did, but not because opposition to slavery was widespread in the state. Simply put, most whites could not afford to buy slaves. At the same time, they understood that slaves kept them off the very bottom rung of society. Slaveholders skillfully played the race card, ever telling poor whites that their skin color alone made them better than all African Americans and that all whites, regardless of their wealth and social standing, were naturally united by their whiteness.[46]

Doubtless lawyer Anderson was familiar with Kentucky's slave code, laws that defined slaves as chattel, or moveable property. They had no legal rights. The slave system was based on punishment—including torture and death. The most common punishment was whipping. But government authorities also beat slaves for public crimes, and county seats and other communities had whipping posts. Slaves were lashed, tortured or executed in the presence of other slaves. Slaveholders knew the certainty of punishment was as effective as the punishment itself. "Masters had few restraints upon the punishments they inflicted, and a number of slaves were killed or permanently crippled."[47]

It is not known how many slaves Anderson owned before he voted to end slavery. In 1850, the typical Kentucky slaveholder owned about five slaves. "Most slaves labored alongside their masters, contributing significantly to Kentucky's prosperity. But for the majority of slaves, day-to-day existence typically meant unrelieved poverty, limited movement, and subjugation to the will of owners with virtually no recourse in the law." Obviously, whites bought slaves to increase the profits of their farming or business enterprises. Therefore, slaveholders, almost without exception, minimally clothed, fed and housed their slaves. To do otherwise would reduce a slaveholder's profit margin. Most slaves were farm laborers who worked from dawn to dusk, or "can to can't." A few slaves were trained at carpentry, blacksmithing and other trades. Others were domestic servants, but only the wealthiest slaveholders could afford "house slaves."[48]

Anderson evidently lived comfortably, but it seems unlikely he was rich enough to own house servants. It is not known how he treated his slaves, but bondage itself sparked slave resistance. While they were powerless before the law and in society, slaves resisted in many ways. Running away was common, though the prospects for a successful escape were rare. Free states lay beyond the Ohio River. But many residents of southern Ohio, Indiana and Illinois were pro-slavery; a number were immigrants from Kentucky. They were happy to help slave catchers seize runaways and send them back to bondage to face punishment. Typically, runaway slaves were beaten. But sometimes their ears were clipped or their bodies branded to identify them as escapees. Some ran away expecting they would be caught. They considered a few days or weeks of precious freedom, especially at harvest time, worth the punishment that was sure to come.[49]

Doubtless, Anderson shared the fears of slave state whites, especially slave owners, that their chattels might rise up in revolt. He must have been aware of the 1831 Nat Turner Rebellion in Virginia, which whites brutally suppressed. Turner and most of his followers were hanged after they killed upwards of sixty whites. In the aftermath of Turner's revolt, white militia and mobs killed as many as two hundred slaves. Thus, slave revolts were few because slaves knew they amounted to suicide. Instead, most slaves turned to passive resistance and sabotage. Though aware they would be severely punished if they were caught, slaves engaged in work slowdowns, feigned illness or injury, damaged or destroyed the master's crops and mistreated his livestock. Slaves also burned barns or other buildings, although arson by a slave brought the death penalty. In some cases, slaves protested by mutilating themselves, such as cutting ankle or leg tendons, and they even committed suicide to escape punishment or being sold.[50]

Slaves played a crucial, but largely unrecognized role, in Kentucky's founding and development. Reflective of the anonymity of most slaves, the names of African Americans Anderson held in bondage will probably never be known. Few masters freed their slaves; before 1860, free blacks never comprised more than one percent of the state's population, and racism "condemned freemen to an inferior status in society." Very few slaves managed to escape to the free states or to Canada. "Those condemned to remain slaves found comfort in their families and hope through their religion, the two strongest institutions in Kentucky's slave community."[51]

Despite the growth of slavery in the Purchase, Lush's home region never overtook the Bluegrass as the state's major slave owning area. In 1860 in Woodford County, for example, slaves outnumbered whites; in Bourbon County, the number of whites exceeded the slave population by only 727. In Bourbon and in Fayette County, which including Lexington, slaves comprised approximately forty-six percent of the people. In 1860, the seven-county Purchase was home to 54,847 whites, 10,471 slaves and 189 free African Americans. Slaves made up about 19.5 percent of Kentucky's population, but approximately sixteen percent in the Purchase. Yet slavery was growing in the Purchase, while shrinking statewide. Between 1790 and 1830—the year of the first Purchase census—the slave percentage in Kentucky grew from 16.2 to 24 percent, the highest-ever percentage. In 1830, the Purchase numbered 1,706 slaves out of a total population of 14,173. Slaves were approximately 13.7 percent of the Purchase population. Between 1790 and 1830, the percentage of slaves in Kentucky's population expanded by nearly eight percent. Between 1830 and 1860, the percentage shrunk by 4.5 percent. By 1830, Kentucky had outgrown its frontier roots, but the Purchase, still thinly populated, had not. At any rate, in 1840, when the Purchase frontier was gone, slaves were almost thirteen percent of the region's population. Between 1850 and 1860, the number of slaves in the Purchase increased by 41 percent. The percentage of slaves was greatest in Fulton—20.3—followed by Ballard, 19.8, and Hickman, 17.8. Slaves comprised 17.5 percent of the population in Graves county, 15.9 in McCracken and 15 in Calloway. In Marshall County, the least prosperous section of the Purchase, slaves were only five percent of the population.[52]

In 1860, Lush's home county was home to 13,386 whites, two free African Americans and 2,845 slaves. Accounts of slavery in the county are rare. But a slave auction block stood at the corner of Broadway and Sixth Street, which would have been near the Anderson home. Armed and mounted men called "paterollers" watched over slaves at night, confining them to where they lived. The "paterollers" were a law unto themselves, often whipping slaves they judged to be "unruly" or "vagrant." Slaveholders also beat their chattels to punish them; in 1859, a Graves circuit court grand jury indicted as least one master for "cruel and inhuman" treatment of slaves. Of course, slavery was, by its very nature, cruel and inhuman, a distinction lost on almost all slave state whites.[53]

To be sure, slavery was not a wedge issue in the antebellum Kentucky of Lucian Anderson. White values were rooted in "white supremacy, or, more specifically, a belief that Western civilization was a product of characteristics unique to the white race and that all interracial relationships must protect the white race from subjugation or degradation by the black race." The foundation of border slave state thought was "the thirst for order in a region challenged by both abolitionism and secessionism.... It would trump all concerns about sectional honor in the ensuing crisis, revealing a population that embraced slavery and Union, or conservative unionism." Lush campaigned for congress and won on a platform with twin anti-abolition and anti-secession planks. In short, almost all white Kentuckians—including nearly every Unionist—supported slavery to one degree or another. The presidential election of 1860 would prove that; Lincoln, the candidate of what Anderson and nearly every white Kentuckian scorned as the "Black Republican" party, would receive a mere 1,364 votes in his native state and just ten votes in the Purchase. The Confederate states seceded because they feared Lincoln and the Republicans would abolish the South's peculiar institution.[54]

While cotton was king in the Deep South, Lush's Purchase was one of Kentucky's most important tobacco-producing regions. Between 1850 and 1860, production rose from three million to twelve million pounds. Landholdings and farm values also grew. Improved acreage in the Purchase grew from approximately 200,000 acres in 1850 to 300,000 in 1860. The cash value of farms rose from approximately three million dollars to more than twelve million dollars.[55]

Reminiscences of slaves in the Purchase are uncommon. But an account of slavery in Ballard County published in *Kentucky Slave Narratives: A Folk History of Slavery in Kentucky from Interviews with Former Slaves*, would likely be typical of the region:

> Buying and selling slaves was carried on at irregular intervals. The trading usually took place at the home of the slave owner. The prices paid for slaves was dependent upon certain conditions. In case of a full grown, robust negro boy the price was sometimes as high as one thousand dollars. The prices paid was varied according to age, the general health and other conditions of the individual.

The narrative goes on:

> At times pathetic scenes prevailed in the selling of slaves; namely, the separation of mother and child. Often, a boy or girl would be sold and taken away from his or her

mother. In many cases the parting would be permanent and the child and its mother would never see each other again.

Ballard County, like Graves County and the rest of the Purchase, was not plantation country. Genuine Taras, like the fictional Georgia plantation in the movie *Gone with The Wind*, were elsewhere in the South. In addition to tobacco, Purchase farmers raised corn, wheat, hay, hogs, horses and mules. The Purchase was just north of the cotton belt, which extended upward to northwestern Tennessee. Nonetheless, at least some cotton was grown in the southern part of the region. The port of Hickman exported 2,000 bales in 1845.[56]

While tobacco, not cotton, was the main cash crop for Purchase whites, most of them belonged to cotton state-style evangelical Protestant Christian denominations, notably Baptist and Methodist. Lush and the Cumberland Presbyterians were a distinct religious minority in Mayfield. Historian Alan Bearman convincingly argues that religion was crucial in underpinning Purchase support for slavery and secession.

> Repeatedly, historians have recognized how religious belief caused the South to view its cause as just. This was the case in the Purchase; its inhabitants believed they were on the side of God, and therefore chose secession with great confidence.... Purchase residents determined their identity as Southerners, in part, through their evangelism. Therefore, as the secession dispute became a religious battle they could, ultimately, only choose to support one side—the Confederacy.[57]

Anderson's denomination was apparently not as strong in supporting slavery as were the Southern Baptist and Southern Methodist churches, both of which had many congregants across Kentucky. Yet the orientation of Purchase Methodist and Baptist congregations was southward, toward Tennessee, not eastward toward the rest of Kentucky. In 1828, the Methodist Church permanently added the Purchase to the Memphis-based Tennessee Conference. Affiliation with the Tennessee Conference meant pastors assigned to Purchase churches would almost certainly be southerners. At the same time, Purchase Baptists were heavily influenced by deeply conservative Landmarkist theology debates over which centered in Nashville and its environs. Landmarkists claimed John the Baptist founded the Baptist Church. According to Bearman, "the geographical and cultural distance of Purchase Baptists from most of Kentucky made a fertile ground for Landmarkist ideology and further helped to tie them to Baptists in the South." Therefore, the historian maintains, "The dominant intellectual and spiritual ethos of the Purchase came not from the Bluegrass Region of Kentucky but from the South."[58]

Bearman also wrote that the exclusivism inherent in Landmarkist theology caused its adherents to condemn anti-slavery agitation as unjustified and, even more importantly, as an outside threat to their cultural identity.

Their honor and sense of distinctiveness meant that they were predisposed to defending their sense of being Southern when such attacks began. The Purchase culture was southern and to attack slavery would have meant, for evangelical churches, running the risk of becoming outsiders in their own communities.

Faith in Landmarkism caused Baptists to believe they were always right theologically, according to Bearman. "The evangelical leadership of the region was Southern in culture and could hardly contemplate a South without slavery; it was certainly unacceptable to have even suggested such a possibility publicly." Southern pastors used the Bible to claim slavery was heaven-blessed. They argued that the obvious presence of Christian slaves proved that human bondage was how God chose to bring Jesus to Africans.[59]

It is not known if pastors at Anderson's church preached pro-slavery sermons. But white Southern evangelical pastors also preached that slavery was a render-unto-Caesar issue. Unwilling to confront theological aspects of slavery, Purchase Methodists claimed human bondage was a secular issue. Bearman quoted Wadesboro and Murray District Methodists: "We believe that slavery is a civil institution, subject to the control of the civil powers alone, and whereas we believe that any interference of our Ecclesiastical tribunal with our civil rights and privileges is to be deprecated." He wrote that the statement represented a distinctly sectional approach in defense of slavery. The Methodists were "arguing that if slavery were legal within a particular state, then outside agitators should respect the rights of the residents of that region." He concluded, "the Southern tint to their argument is telling because it was a territory that profited in substantial fashion from slavery." Bearman concluded, "this attempt to declare slavery a civil institution, in all ways outside of the moral responsibility of the church, was a common Southern tactic."[60]

Like Purchase Methodists, Baptists in the region entertained

no thought of confronting the evils of slavery; to them it was a Biblically ordained and natural system. Their sole concern was to ensure ongoing efforts of proselytizing among the African-Americans of the region. The Southern belief structure that claimed that God had ordained slavery meant that the people of the Purchase became defenders of the right to own slaves.[61]

Almost all Kentucky whites, including future foe of slavery Lush Anderson, believed bondage was the "natural," if not "heaven-ordained" state for African Americans. On April 19, 1858, Anderson was a featured speaker at a pro-slavery Democratic rally in Mayfield. According to the Democratic and pro-slavery *Frankfort Yeoman*, he

arose and, in a few short and eloquent remarks, urged the people of the South to stand up to their rights, to indorse and sustain that patriotic statesman, [President] James Buchanan, who, in his course on [supporting a slave state Kansas] ... has proved himself

a friend to the South, a friend to the Union, and a relentless enemy to any sect or faction
which may seek to destroy that Union.

Of course, southern "rights" was a code word for slavery and the phrase
"any sect or faction" clearly meant northern, anti-slavery Republicans. The
meeting also endorsed "the principles of the Kansas-Nebraska act," praised
First District Democratic Congressman Henry C. Burnett and panned Senator John J. Crittenden. The Graves County Democrats said the senator
should resign unless he endorsed the admission of Kansas as a slave state.
Ultimately, Crittenden, an old guard Whig, and Anderson made common
cause in favor of the Union.[62]

On May 10, 1858, Anderson spoke at a similar pro-slavery Democratic mass
meeting in Benton, the seat of Marshall County, which adjoins Graves on the
east. The assemblage passed a resolution supporting the admission of Kansas
territory as a slave state "on an equal footing with the other States of the Union."
The *Yeoman* published an account of that meeting as well. The paper did not
quote Anderson but claimed he addressed the crowd "in a very able and
forceful manner." The conclave approved resolutions praising Burnett
"for his defence of Southern institutions" and calling on Crittenden to quit
the senate because of his "opposition to the admission of Kansas as a Slave
state."[63]

Anderson also went to the January 8, 1859, state Democratic convention
that nominated Beriah Magoffin of Harrodsburg for governor and Boyd for
lieutenant governor. Anderson cut a wide enough swath to get himself named
to the Committee for the State at Large from the First District. The other district committeeman was Edward Crossland, a Clinton lawyer and future Confederate colonel. Anderson also wound up on the First District Democratic
Committee.[64]

Besides fielding a Magoffin-Boyd ticket, the Democrats passed a series
of resolutions reaffirming their support for the party's 1856 presidential platform, which endorsed popular sovereignty and denied the federal government
had any right to interfere with slavery where it existed. The Bluegrass State
Democrats were confident in Buchanan's "ability, integrity, and patriotism,
and in his devotion to the constitutional rights of all sections of the Union."
Other resolutions favored the *Dred Scott* decision, called for the annexation
of Cuba and backhandedly denounced abolitionism by expressing the convention's "unfeigned abhorrence [at] the doctrine recently promulgated by
eminent agitators and sectionalists at the North, that the diverse system of
labor in the different States are incompatible with the harmonious continu-
ance of the Union." The Democrats also resolved their disgust with the Republicans for daring to appeal to southern Know-Nothings "to amalgamate with
the fanatics of the North, and sacrifice the dearest and most precious rights
of the slaveholding states for the spoils of office."[65]

**Beriah Magoffin (Library of Congress).**

Prospects for a Democratic triumph at the polls on August 1 seemed bright. The Opposition ran former congressman Joshua F. Bell of Danville for governor and Alfred Allen of Hardinsburg for lieutenant governor. Magoffin and Boyd won easily; the Democrats also gained control of the state House and Senate. Boyd was never sworn into office; he died at home on December 17 and was not replaced.[66]

Two months before, Southern whites' smoldering fear of slave uprisings blazed when John Brown, a fire-and-brimstone Kansas abolitionist, raided the U.S. arsenal at Harper's Ferry, Virginia, now West Virginia. Brown apparently hoped to arm local slaves, thus starting a slave rebellion that would spread across the South and border states, or possibly spark a war between North and South over slavery. Brown's attack failed; troops led by army Colonel Robert E. Lee overpowered Brown and his twenty followers—white and African American, killing and or capturing all but five who managed to escape. Brown was tried for treason in a state court and sentenced to be hanged. Though many anti-slavery northerners, Abraham Lincoln among them, called Brown a misguided fanatic, other northerners viewed Brown as a hero and martyr in the anti-slavery cause. Many white Southerners believed that "Brown loving" Republicans dominated the north.

Anderson's reaction to Brown's raid is not known. He was back in Frankfort shortly after the New Year as one of eight Graves County delegates to the annual state Democratic convention. If he spoke or played some other significant role at the gathering, the *Louisville Courier* did not mention it in its extensive coverage of the conclave. Most importantly, the delegates endorsed James Guthrie of Louisville for president. Pierce's treasury secretary, Guthrie was vice president of the Louisville & National Railroad from 1857 until 1860 when he became president of the line. Lush's friend, Circuit Judge Rufus King Williams of Mayfield, was elected an at-large delegate to the national convention set for Charleston in April.[67]

The Delaware-born Williams became one of Anderson's closest confidants. In 1826, ten-year-old Rufus King moved with his family to Wadesboro, then the Calloway County seat. At age nineteen, he and a half-brother opened a store, but King became a lawyer by studying at night. He succeeded as an attorney, ended up in Mayfield and was elected circuit judge in 1851. Though he was on the bench, he remained active in Democratic politics.[68]

One can only speculate about Anderson's view of the convention, its resolutions, and its support for Guthrie. Like Lush, Guthrie emerged as a leading Unionist in the secession crisis. Like Lush, Guthrie's ultimate choice for president was Douglas, the great promoter of popular sovereignty and the nominee of the Northern Democrats. Most Kentucky Democrats—and nearly every Graves County Democrat—would get behind Southern Democrat Breckinridge, whose principle campaign plank supported *Dred Scott*. In backing Douglas, Lush was starting down a path that would lead him far from his roots—ultimately to his country's capital where he would be part of what the *New-York Tribune* headlined "The Grandest Act Since the Declaration of Independence." It is not known if Anderson ever admired Henry David Thoreau, writer, abolitionist and practitioner of civil disobedience. But the western Kentuckian's journey would follow the gentle New Englander's famous admonition: "If a man does not keep pace with his companions, perhaps it is because he hears a different drummer. Let him step to the music which he hears, however measured or far away."[69]

# 3

# For Douglas
# and the Union

Thirty-six-year old Lush Anderson was one of Mayfield's leading citizens in 1860. His law practice and business ventures were evidently successful. He and Ann, had been blessed with four children: Harry, Nancy, Robert and Herbert. But faraway events would soon disrupt their apparently happy home.[1]

The presidential campaign of 1860 set Lush apart from most other Mayfield citizens, including his older sibling, Ervin. The election turned on the issue of slavery's expansion into the western territories. No election in American history was more fateful than this one. The Union itself hung in the balance. Reflecting the deep division in the country, four candidates ran: Abraham Lincoln of Illinois, Vice President John C. Breckinridge of Kentucky, Senator Stephen A. Douglas of Illinois and John Bell of Tennessee.

The Democrats met in convention in Charleston, South Carolina, in April. Lush was not part of the Kentucky delegation but Judge Williams was. Douglas seemed most likely to win the nomination; nicknamed "the Little Giant" and "a steam engine in britches," he was perhaps the most powerful lawmaker in Washington. Despite *Dred Scott,* Douglas clung tenaciously to "popular sovereignty."

Nonetheless, rabid pro-slavery cotton state delegates dubbed "fire eaters," stubbornly opposed Douglas and stormed out of the convention. They demanded nothing less than a candidate who stood foursquare behind *Dred Scott.* The Kentuckians pushed Guthrie as a compromise nominee but got nowhere. Neither did Douglas, who failed to muster the requisite two-thirds majority for nomination. The Democrats gave up but agreed to try to agree on a canidate in Baltimore in June.

The impasse continued. More slave state delegates, including nine from Kentucky, bolted the convention. Another nine supported Douglas, who finally won the nomination. Williams and five others stayed put but declined

**John C. Breckinridge (Library of Congress).**

to vote. The "seceders" met elsewhere in town and nominated Breckinridge on a pro–*Dred Scott* platform. Both the Douglas and Breckinridge factions claimed to be the true national "Democracy." But most history books label Douglas the "Northern Democrat" and Breckinridge the "Southern Democrat."[2]

Meanwhile, conservatives, most of them ex-Whigs and Know Nothings cobbled together the Constitutional Union party. Bell was their man. He scrupulously avoided the controversy over slavery's expansion and merely called for "the Constitution of the Country, the Union of the States and the enforcement of the laws." Republican Abraham Lincoln's platform demanded that slavery be excluded from the territories.

Lush was no fan of Lincoln or the Republicans in 1860. Precious few other Kentuckians lined up with the hated "Black Republicans." Lincoln had no chance to carry Kentucky, or even come close to winning the state, though he was born near Hodgenville in 1809. Lincoln only opposed slavery's expansion in 1860, but Republican abolitionists wanted slavery gone. Lush was a pro-slavery man in 1860, but ultimately Lincoln would get behind a

"Prominent candidates for the Democratic nomination at Charleston, S.C." (Library of Congress).

constitutional amendment to outlaw slavery, and Anderson would vote for it in Congress.

Douglas, Lincoln's fellow Illinoisan, also looked like a long shot in Kentucky. Many, if not most Bluegrass State citizens spurned "popular sovereignty" as an equivocation on the issue of slavery's expansion. On the other hand, Breckinridge was the state's rising political star. In 1859, the General Assembly elected him to the U.S. senate; he was to take office in 1861 at the end of his vice presidency.

At any rate, the election of 1860 seemed to boil down to Lincoln versus Douglas in the free states and Bell against Breckinridge in the slave states. Breckinridge could count on the Deep South, where slavery and support for the peculiar institution were strongest. On the other hand, the border states could swing to Bell or Breckinridge, or possibly Douglas. In Kentucky, the question was whether the state would return to its Whig roots or go with its Southern Democratic son.

Purchase politics was more like Deep South politics than Kentucky politics. The region titled sharply toward Breckinridge, though Bell seemed to have significant support in traditionally Whig McCracken County. Douglas had few supporters and Lincoln partisans could be counted on one hand, maybe two.

Lush, the Douglas man, must have cringed at the editorials in the brand new *Mayfield Southern Yeoman*. "In this portion of the State it is altogether a one-sided business," C.C. Coulter's paper blustered. "Only a few political croakers are heard to raise the Douglas note, and that sounds more like the dying wail of intriguing but thwarted demagoguery, than the clear notes of whole souled Democracy." The paper laid it on Lush's candidate: "Suffice it for the present for us to remark that we hold the nomination of Douglas, under the

John Bell (**Library of Congress**).

circumstances, as wholly out of order." The convention that nominated the Illinois senator was anything but "the *true* National Democratic Convention." Rather, the gathering was "a mere bogus affair, gotten up and 'packed' by the reckless friends of Judge Douglas for his own special benefit." The Douglas partisans were heedless of what was good for the party "and consequently the safety of this glorious confederacy." The last two words revealed how the soon-to-be rabidly secessionist *Yeoman* saw the Union. The paper claimed it "can very easily perceive that the only object Judge Douglas ever had, was and is, self-promotion." The Breckinridge boosters, not Lush and the Douglas disciples, represented "the true blue, Simon pure Democracy." The man of Kentucky was "the only candidate offered to the sovereigns of the Union who is free from sectionalism and conservative in his principles and his acts."[3]

Doubtless, Lush steered clear of a big Breckinridge rally in Feliciana in southern Graves County that featured a debate between George B. Hodge of Newport, a Breckinridge elector, and Bell elector W.H. Wadsworth of Mason County. Wadsworth leveled a charge against Breckinridge common among Bell and Douglas men: that Breckinridge was a dupe of the "fire-eaters" who were threatening secession if they did not get their way on the slavery issue. According to the *Louisville Courier*, which also published the *Southern*

*Yeoman* editorial, Hodge vanquished Wadsworth, refuting "the charge of disunion against the Breckinridge party" and passing "a high eulogy on our glorious candidates." He sat down "amidst loud cheers and enthusiastic shouts for Breckinridge and Lane." Hodge, the state's leading Breckinridge paper concluded, was "a glorious, eloquent speaker, logical, and ponderous in his vindication of truth, fearless and terrible in exposing error." Hodge became a Confederate general, but Lush and Wadsworth eventually crossed paths. They would serve together in Congress, Lush as an Unconditional Unionist allied with the Republicans and Wadsworth as a conservative Union Democrat.[4]

Meanwhile, Anderson had a hard time hunting up allies in Mayfield and Graves County. He finally found one in Williams, but not before a big Breckinridge meeting in Mayfield on July 16. After their party split, Kentucky Democrats gathered in county seats to endorse Breckinridge or Douglas. If the Breck loyalists expected Williams to champion their candidate, they went home disappointed. The party faithful "turned out in droves" for their candidate, according to a letter J.E. Anderson, a Graves County farmer apparently not related to Lush, wrote to County Judge A.R. Boone, a Breckinridge man. "It leaked out that [Williams] would not support the seceder's candidate," Anderson advised.

Immediately the secession wing took fright, and determined that Williams should not speak lest they could not ratify for as well you know the Democracy have ever opposed investigation, it being their true policy to keep the rank and file in ignorance.[5]

After local candidates spoke, Lush rose to tell "the unwashed that the Judge wanted to give an account of the [Democratic National] Convention." J.E, a Bell booster, said "the Douglas wing (though as you well know are not a whit more honest than the Breckenridge [sic] wing) were anxious for Williams to speak, believing it would make Douglas capital." The crowd wanted to hear the judge's account, but the "Breck leaders" did not, according to Anderson.[6]

"Then commenced a scene, the like of which old Mayfield's Courthouse never saw. Each Breck leader cried 'have let loose the dogs of war.' Bedlam seemed turned loose amongst us. Coats were flung in every direction, while 'he shall not speak' 'he shall not speak' 'take him out' etc. resounded from every side." Williams headed to the Market House, followed by two thirds of the crowd, while the Breckinridge men remained in the courthouse and "listened to a drunken speech from a Mr. Winn from Calloway—full of sound and fury, signifying nothing," Anderson reported. Boone's correspondent claimed that Williams, who refused to bolt for Breckinridge in Baltimore or vote to nominate Douglas, said neither "Breck nor Dug was worthy of our support."[7]

Anderson said as proof of the difference between disputatious Democrats and his party, "we (ie), the Union loving men had a ratification meeting here yesterday which was largely attended and passed off harmoniously.... It would have done your heart good to have seen the enthusiasm here exhibited for Bell & Everett." He recalled that J.T. Bolinger and Dick Hardin had a fight with "politics the cause—lie given and returned. Effect—Dick got a very black eye." Ultimately, Bolinger, Anderson and Williams emerged as a Unionist triumvirate and led the county's anti-Confederate minority.[8]

The pro-Douglas *Louisville Democrat*'s account of the meeting was silent about the fisticuffs and stuck to four resolutions the Douglas men approved. They "heartily" endorsed the presidential hopeful and his running mate, Herschel Vespasian Johnson of Georgia, recognizing the duo "as true men and the exponents of the Democratic party." The second resolution disdained the Southern Democratic standard bearers—Breckinridge and Joseph Lane of Oregon—declaring "we regard the nomination of Breckinridge and Lane, by a few bolters, as sectional, and the prominent and controlling elements that made said nominations were composed of Disunionists." Resolution three named Anderson and several other men to represent Graves County at the state Douglas convention in Louisville on August 11. The last resolution called for the Mayfield meeting to be publicized in the state Democratic papers.[9]

Anderson may have been disappointed that Williams was still on the fence at the county meeting. But Lush stumped western Kentucky for "the Little Giant" and Johnson. He was among several "distinguished gentlemen," including first district Douglas elector and Paducah lawyer Lawrence S. Trimble, who spoke at Douglas rallies. Allies in the Union cause in 1861, Lush and Trimble would end up bitter enemies during the Civil War and afterwards. At any rate, First District gatherings were set for Paducah, Mayfield, Columbus and Madisonville. By October, Williams was on the Douglas bandwagon. "We felt confident that he would not vote for Breckinridge; he saw too much at Charleston and Baltimore," the *Louisville Democrat* crowed. The paper published a letter from the judge in which he explained, "I am and have been for some time openly out for Douglas, having determined to stand by the National Democracy, and to keep company with those who are for a national party and the Union." Douglas was proud "to join that patriotic band, come whence they may, who are for maintaining the Union and the Constitution, and opposing all sectionalism and disunionism, whether it comes from the North or the South." The Republicans had not threatened to secede if Lincoln lost. But Williams, like Anderson and most other Kentuckians, viewed abolitionism and secessionism as equal threats to the Union.[10]

On November 4, Lincoln won the White House by sweeping the free state North. Breckinridge won the Deep South, plus border slave states Maryland and Delaware. Douglas managed only slave state Missouri, though he

Lawrence Trimble (National Archives and Records Administration).

shared free state New Jersey's electoral vote with Lincoln. Bell carried a trio of slave states: Virginia, Kentucky and Tennessee. In the Bluegrass State, Bell garnered 66,051 votes to 53,143 for Breckinridge. Douglas received 25,638 votes and Lincoln 1,364. The Purchase backed Breckinridge, who collected 4,547 votes to 2,885 for Bell, who won McCracken and Ballard counties. Douglas managed 1,089 votes. Lincoln pocketed ten, eight in McCracken and one each in Ballard and Hickman counties. Breckinridge claimed the other

Purchase counties; he carried Graves with 1,225 votes to 660 for Bell and 140 for Lush's man.[11]

Doubtless, Anderson was dismayed by the returns in Graves County, Kentucky and the nation. He might have agreed with William George Pirtle of Water Valley in southern Graves County who said Bell, Douglas and Breckinridge beat themselves. Had the Bell, Breckinridge and Douglas parties united behind "one man, they could have elected him easily, as the three parties poled [sic] more than three fourths of a million more votes than Lincoln did," he recorded his memoirs. "But every man would go for his man, or rather his own way." He remembered that after the election, "excitement became intence [sic], and increased every day in the south as the idea of the loss of their property in slaved [sic] did not set well." Pirtle ended up a Confederate officer.[12]

Led by the "fire eaters" and fearing "the loss of their property in slaved [sic]," cotton states, whites prepared to exit the Union over Lincoln's election. Most Kentuckians sorely regretted Lincoln's victory, but few considered his triumph, by itself, sufficient grounds for disunion. Speaking for most citizens, Editor George D. Prentice of the pro–Bell *Louisville Journal* pointed out that the Republicans would not control Congress or the courts, adding that Lincoln could be impeached if he abused his lawful powers. The president "could not infringe upon the Constitution if he would." He blamed "the ignorance and fanaticism of the Abolition party" for the national crisis, but said the Republicans were not the abolition party.[13]

Graves countian Eliza Gregory said Lincoln's victory caused a great stir in Dublin, southwest of Mayfield, where she lived and ran a store. "Nothing but uproar ... and talk of fighting in the Union," she said in a letter. "But I think the storm will soon be over and scarcely anybody hurt." The Civil War was America's bloodiest war, claiming approximately 752,000 lives on both sides.[14]

Kentucky's stand in the presidential election was deeply Unionist in that most voters considered Bell and Douglas the candidates most likely to preserve the Union. The great majority of citizens worried that Lincoln, who got less than one percent of the vote, really was an abolitionist who was willing to destroy the Union to end slavery. Likewise, they suspected Breckinridge was a tool of the "fire eaters" who was willing to sacrifice the Union to preserve slavery. Breckinridge hotly denied he was a disunionist, but most Kentucky voters evidently doubted him. He received only thirty-six percent of ballots cast in his home state.[15]

Magoffin was a pro–Southern, vehemently pro-slavery Breckinridge man, but he was not for immediate secession. After Lincoln's election was confirmed, he sent letters to the other fourteen slave state governors seeking their support for six proposals to save the Union, but on Southern pro-slavery terms. They included a constitutional amendment to enforce strongly the federal fugitive slave law and congressional action to make free states pay slaveholders for slaves not returned to them. In addition, Magoffin's plan required northern governors to extradite anybody indicted in a slave state "for stealing or enticing away a slave." Magoffin, also proposed three more constitutional amendments dividing the territories into slave and free sections along the thirty-seventh parallel, granting all states free access to the Mississippi River and permitting the South to safeguard itself in congress against "unconstitutional or oppressive" legislation against slavery.[16]

Throughout November, several Unionist mass meetings, usually without party distinction, were held statewide. The spontaneous gatherings suggested that most Kentuckians were disinclined to forsake the Union over Lincoln's victory. In the coming months, secessionism would prevail only in the Jackson Purchase, the state's sole Confederate-majority region, much to Lush Anderson's chagrin.

As Yuletide approached, Lush and many other Unionist Kentuckians pinned their hopes on Kentucky Senator John J. Crittenden's proposals to save the Union. On December 18, in true Clay fashion, Crittenden offered an ambitious compromise that centered on extending the old Missouri Compromise line (thirty-six degrees, thirty minutes latitude) to California with slavery guaranteed south of the line. In addition, he said future states should be allowed to decide on slavery as they came into the Union. Also, Congress could not ban slavery in the District of Columbia as long as slavery was legal in Maryland and Virginia. Further, he wanted slaveholders reimbursed if an escaped slave was not returned. Too, the compromise called for stricter enforcement of the fugitive slave law and for northern states to repeal their personal liberty laws that were passed to prevent slaveholders from retrieving their slaves. Southerners would not agree to Crittenden's proposals unless the Republicans approved them first, which they would not do. Undaunted, Crittenden, on January 3, 1861, tried to get his compromise submitted to the people in a national referendum. There was no precedent for such a vote and the Republicans refused to support it. The Crittenden Compromise generated scant support beyond Kentucky and the other border slave states, and it failed.[17]

The House also tried its hand at compromise, establishing a Committee of Thirty-Three with a representative of each state. Kentucky's man was Representative Francis Marion Bristow of Elkton, a future Unionist comrade of Lush Anderson. The committee proposed that the northern states repeal their personal liberty laws and that the fugitive slave law be enforced. The panel also endorsed a constitutional amendment forbidding Congress from ever interfering with slavery in the slave states. Congress passed the amendment, but the states never ratified it. At the same time, abolitionist

Republicans and die-hard secessionists denounced compromise.[18]

South Carolina withdrew from the Union on December 20 and asked the fourteen other slave states "to join us, in forming a Confederacy of Slaveholding States." The lower South seemed poised to accept the Palmetto State's invitation. Shortly afterwards, commissioners from Alabama and Mississippi met Magoffin in Frankfort and pressed him to lead Kentucky out of the Union. They stressed that the only way to preserve slavery and white supremacy was to found an independent Southern nation. Secessionists everywhere would make the same argument over and over. Stephen

John J. Crittenden (Library of Congress).

Fowler Hale, the commissioner from Alabama, was a western Kentucky native, born in Crittenden County, northeast of the Purchase. He wrote Magoffin a long letter on December 27, accusing the North of "waging an unrelenting and fanatical war" against slavery for the last twenty-five years. He praised slavery for cementing "not only the wealth and prosperity of the Southern people, but for their very existence as a political community." Lincoln, according to Hale, "stands forth as the representative of the fanaticism of the North" and of the Republican party, whose claims to popularity was based "upon the one dogma—the equality of the races, white and black." He said if the Republicans abolished the South's peculiar institution,

> the slave-holder and non-slave-holder must ultimately share the same fate; all be degraded to a position of equality with free negroes, stand side by side with them at the polls, and fraternize in all the social relations of life, or else there will be an eternal war of races, desolating the land with blood, and utterly wasting and destroying all the resources of the county.

The ex-Kentuckian demanded,

What Southern man, be he slave-holder or non-slave-holder, can without indignation and horror contemplate the triumph of negro equality, and see his own sons and daughters in the not distant future associating with free negroes upon terms of political and social equality, and the white man stripped by the heaven-daring hand of fanaticism of that title to superiority over the black race which God himself has bestowed?

Magoffin was sympathetic to the visitors' entreaties, but he was cool to the idea of state-by-state secession. Instead, he wanted a convention of all fifteen slave states, where common demands could be agreed upon and presented to Lincoln. If he rejected the proposals, the slave states could secede as a unit. When nothing came of his idea, Magoffin, on December 27, called for a special session of the legislature to convene on January 17.[19]

Worried that the legislature might put Kentucky out of the Union, the Unionists got organized. On January 8, 1861, leading supporters of Bell and Douglas met in separate conventions in Louisville and jointly resolved that Lincoln's election was insulting to the slave states but not cause for disunion. They endorsed the Crittenden Compromise and formed a ten-member Union State Central Committee to organize and coordinate Union sentiment across Kentucky.[20]

The committee found scant support among Bell and Douglas men in Lush Anderson's hometown or any place else in the Purchase. Nearly everybody who voted for the two candidates merged with the majority Breckinridge Democrats in the new Southern Rights, or secessionist, party. Lush, Williams, and Bolinger were conspicuous exceptions. Undoubtedly it pained them when the pro–Douglas *Hickman Courier* became one of the first—if not the first—newspapers in the state to endorse secession. "The South, therefore, who has considered herself aggrieved, who has been denied her rights in the Union, is bound, in order to have her rights, in order to maintain her honor, and the honor of her citizens, *to secede,*" the paper thundered. "Therefore, we say, all honor to the Southern Confederacy." Also reflective of regional sentiment, the other Purchase papers—the pro–Breckinridge *Yeoman, Paducah Tri-Weekly Herald* and *Columbus Crescent*—endorsed secession.[21]

Nonetheless, Anderson, Williams and Bolinger doggedly stuck with the Union. They attracted a small following, Dr. S. P. Cope and the Rev. William A. Dugger among them. On January 18, Cope spoke at a Union meeting in the Odd Fellows Hall at Feliciana. The physician had departed "the quietude of his rural home to canvass the county in defense of the Union," according to a letter the *Louisville Journal* published. The author said Cope warned the Feliciana faithful that secession was certain to bring "bankruptcy, war, rapine, and misery." The locals evidently agreed; they approved the Bell and Douglas convention resolutions by voting with their feet. The chair asked the "ayes" to repair to one side of the house, the "nays" to the other. "To the surprise of all, a very large majority ... indorsed them," the correspondent said. "The

Secessionists, seeing themselves in a slim minority, took to their heels." Interestingly, the writer described the Union Cope wanted to preserve as "our blood-bought Confederacy."[22]

Cope, Williams and Dugger teamed up for the Union for at a January 21 meeting in the Graves County courthouse in Mayfield. Lush must have been present, though he was not mentioned in any account of the gathering, chaired by John Eaker with William M. Cargill as secretary. The next day, the duo sent Senator Crittenden a report on the meeting which they said drew "from 800 to 1000 voters ... without distinction of party." The Graves Countians endorsed Crittenden's proposals "as a fair and honorable compromise" solution to "the present unhappy and perilous condition of the American Republic." They wanted the proposals put to a vote in Kentucky and nationwide. Also, the meeting supported a convention to determine the state's future, but agreed that the voters must approve whatever the gathering decided. They resolved that the convention should be held around the time similar gatherings were reportedly set for North Carolina, Virginia, Tennessee and Missouri. Kentucky could thus "act in concert with those states." Another resolution urged a convention of the fifteen slave states, or at least the border slave states, to take united action "to preserve their constitutional rights" and to submit "an ultimatum to the people of the North." The crowd, by voice vote, endorsed the resolutions "with only five or six" voting the other way. Williams wanted to verify the vote, so he asked those who favored the resolutions to "file to the right and those against the cause" to go to the left. "The entire mass save some six to ten persons moved to the right." Before heading out the door, the attendees urged Magoffin and state lawmakers to press Lincoln and the five seceded states—South Carolina, Mississippi, Florida, Alabama and Georgia—"to stay the hand of war until the people had time to act upon" Crittenden's compromise.[23]

Lazarus W. Powell (Library of Congress).

On January 23, Eaker wrote Crittenden and Kentucky's other senator, Lazarus W. Powell about the meeting, which he was sure reflected "the feeling of the people of the entire county of Graves." Eaker hoped Crittenden's resolutions would pass and that the two senators' "patriotic actions," would avert "the danger with which our beloved & once happy country is threatened." On the same day, Williams wrote Crittenden, also telling him about the meeting and praising the senator's "patriotic and wise counsel and conduct in this darkest hour of our country's peril." Yet he wondered, "Is it possible that the Republicans can act so stubborn and unwise as to drive true, loyal Kentucky from the Union?" Williams trusted "that some honorable compromise may yet be made that will save the further disintegration of the Union."

Turning to local politics, Williams said "we have no party here among the patriotic masses, and like myself the great majority having in times past been Democratic." Nonetheless, he and his fellow Unionists were ready to make common cause "with any patriotic party to save our Constitutional rights and the Union." He said the local press was not aiding their efforts. "Every news paper we now have in this Congressional District I believe are for disunion and their statements are all directed to that end." He said the papers were misrepresenting public opinion because "a very large majority of the common masses are for securing our rights and the preservation of the Union, the action of the Cotton States to the contrary notwithstanding." Williams told Crittenden that "steps are being taken to get up some conservative Union papers for securing and not destroying our rights." While Williams stuck by the Union, Eaker and Cargill ultimately embraced secession. Cargill joined the Confederate army.[24]

On January 28, Dugger was back on the road, traveling to Murray to address a Union meeting at the Calloway County courthouse where "a large number of the citizens ... of all parties" assembled. After Dugger's remarks, somebody suggested that crowd endorse the Bell and Douglas convention resolutions and Crittenden's constitutional amendments. "Thereupon the Disunionists ... raised as a big a yell as they could for one of their speakers to take the stand." To head off trouble, "four fifths of those present repaired to the large Baptist Church that was too small to contain them, and adopted the resolutions without a dissenting voice, and an adjournment took place amid the most enthusiastic cheers." The chair, secretary of the meeting "and others made eloquent Union speeches, interrupted with loud and frequent applause."[25]

Meanwhile, on January 17, the most momentous session of the General Assembly in Bluegrass State history opened in the capitol. Everyone knew that Breckinridge Democrats were leading the secession movement in the South. From Magoffin down, most Kentucky Democrats were Breckinridge men. In the legislature, the Democrats commanded a fifty-nine to forty-one

House majority over the Opposition. The Democrats enjoyed a twenty-four to fourteen edge in the Senate.[26]

When the legislature met, lawmakers divided into Union men and Southern Rightists. All five Purchase representatives and two of the region's three senators were Breckinridge Democrats. They all joined the Southern Rights side save one who could not bring himself to go all out for the Union or disunion. Naturally, friends of the Union feared that Magoffin and the legislature would wedge Kentucky into the Confederacy. South Carolina seceded by a sovereignty convention, and Unionists worried Kentucky might do likewise. Hence, their goal was to forestall a convention, and they succeeded. On February 11, the legislature adjourned until March 20 with Kentucky still under the Stars and Stripes.[27]

Yet two more states had abandoned the Union—Louisiana and Texas. On February 4 the seven seceded states formed the Confederate States of America with Montgomery, Alabama, as their capital and Kentucky-born Jefferson Davis of Mississippi as their president.

Eight slave states remained in the Union: Kentucky, Virginia, Maryland, Delaware, Missouri, Tennessee, North Carolina and Arkansas. While it spurned secession, the Kentucky legislature eagerly accepted Virginia's invitation to send delegates to a peace conference in Washington, which convened on the day the Confederacy was founded. Nothing came of the gathering, whose purpose was to pull the Union back together and avoid civil war.[28]

# 4

# The "straight-out" Union Man

When the legislature reconvened on March 20, the Unionists hoped for a replay of the previous session where they stymied every secessionist attempt to call a sovereignty convention. Still desperate to somehow to hold the Union together, the legislature, on April 3, called for a border slave state convention to meet in Frankfort on May 27.[1]

Lawmakers set May 4 as Election Day for Kentucky's delegates to the gathering. But on April 12, the telegraph in Frankfort tapped out news that Unionists feared might stampede Kentucky into the Confederacy. The rebels had fired on Fort Sumter in the harbor at Charleston, South Carolina, triggering the long dreaded Civil War. Major Robert Anderson, a Kentuckian, surrendered the brick bastion the next day.[2]

There is, of course, nothing in the Constitution about states leaving the Union or about what federal authorities could or should do about disunion. Nonetheless, Lincoln was swift to act, finding authority in a 1795 law "calling forth the militia to execute the laws of the Union" if they were resisted by "combinations too powerful to be suppressed by the ordinary course of judicial proceedings." Lincoln proclaimed that the laws of the Union were being resisted by the seven states calling themselves the Confederacy. Thus, on April 15, the president asked the other states for 75,000 militia troops to defeat the "combinations" and uphold the laws. He also called an emergency session of Congress to convene on July 4.[3]

Every free state governor responded with a flood of eager volunteers. Eight slave states were still in the Union. Among them, only the governors of Maryland and Delaware promised militiamen. The others, including Magoffin, sternly rebuked the president. "I say *emphatically*, Kentucky will furnish no troops for the wicked purpose of subduing her sister Southern States," he replied on April 15. The governor also declined a Confederate request for troops. In every other war, Kentuckians had rushed to volunteer. The Bluegrass State's sons fought the British and their Native American allies in the American Revolution and in the War of 1812. They soldiered in the Mexican-American War. But to them fighting fellow white Americans was different. Thus, Kentuckians hesitated, and Unionists among them begged the people to remain calm. Until Fort Sumter, most Kentuckians did not believe that Lincoln's election alone justified secession. But war between North and South was another matter; after all, Kentucky had been a slave state since it entered the Union in 1792. In a Lexington speech on April 17, Senator Crittenden, a War of 1812 veteran, besought the people to steer clear out of "the fratricidal war impending between the North and the South" and pleaded that they instead act as "a peaceful mediator, remonstrating with both sections against involving the nation in civil war, the fatal consequences of which no wisdom nor foresight could foretell."[4]

The next day, James Guthrie, John Young Brown, Archibald Dixon and William F. Bullock, all well-known Union men, and soon-to-be allies of Lush Anderson, spoke to a large gathering in Louisville. They vowed that Kentucky would not take up arms for either the North or the South and warned both sides to keep out of the state. Just after the meeting, the Union State Central Committee in an "Address to the People of the Commonwealth of Kentucky," essentially repeated what Guthrie, Brown, Dixon and Bullock said.[5]

Thus, the Unionists were sowing the seed of neutrality, but neutrality within the Union. Kentucky would remain in the fold but would not help prosecute the war against the South. Secessionists argued that such a position was untenable. They claimed that ultimately Lincoln would not permit Kentucky to stay in the Union and out of the war. Eventually, he would have to force the state's hand, they were sure. When that happened, Kentucky would secede, they predicted. The secessionists were wrong; Lincoln wisely left Kentucky alone. To be sure, Magoffin's rude rebuff of Lincoln's request for troops might have prompted a swift military response from a president less temperate than Lincoln was. But the president let it pass. He opted for patience over precipitate action toward the state of his birth, a course that would prove prudent. He believed that that the longer Kentucky stayed loyal, even as a non-combatant, the better his chances of holding the state in the Union, eventually as a full-fledged combatant against the rebellion.

Down the Ohio at Paducah, the *Herald* was predictably unimpressed with neutrality. Speaking for most Purchase citizens, Noble's paper sneered that all Dixon and Guthrie really said was that "it was foolish" for them to risk their houses and their slaves "for such things as the property, rights, liberty and lives of the Southern people; and that they did not care who went under, so that *their* dumplings boiled peacefully in the pot." Noble likened the secessionists to the patriots of the American Revolution, a comparison that would become common throughout the Confederacy. He concluded by quoting Patrick Henry's famous "reply to the dumpling men of that day ... 'give me Liberty or give me death!'"[6]

Lush would have sneered at any comparison between the Confederates and the patriots of 1776. But there is no record of how he and his hometown reacted to the news from Fort Sumter. Mayfield's response was probably similar to Paducah's. There, the townsfolk went "wild with excitement," lamented Unionist R.B.J. Twyman. "Men and women really seemed to go mad." He added that Lincoln's call for troops "increased the excitement and madness of the hour." Twyman recalled that "few, very few were able to withstand the tempest of excited public sentiment. The weak and wavering were irresistibly borne down and along with the great flood of secession fanaticism, scarcely knowing how or wherefore." Lush likely shared Twyman's sentiments. But both were determined to stand by the Stars and Stripes come what might.[7]

Fort Sumter put Virginia, North Carolina, Arkansas and Tennessee under the Confederacy's Stars and Bars flag. When those upper South states started to secede, the Kentucky Southern Rights party judged the border state convention futile and withdrew its candidates. Naturally, the result was a Unionist sweep. The Unionists almost certainly would have won nine of the state's ten congressional districts anyway, the First District, anchored by the Purchase, being the exception. At any rate, Williams was the district delegate to the convention. Besides the Kentuckians, only four representatives from Missouri and one from Tennessee showed up, so the gathering failed. Also in May, the Unionist legislature, not yet prepared to embrace the federal war effort, officially declared Kentucky's neutrality within the Union and Magoffin dutifully issued a neutrality proclamation. "Perhaps no party in the history of the state ever announced more nearly the general desires of the people than the Union men did at this time in their neutrality stand," E. Merton Coulter wrote in *The Civil War and Readjustment in Kentucky*.

Consciously or unconsciously the state had been advocating and living this doctrine since the secession of South Carolina.... So completely did the idea of neutrality permeate Kentucky thought, that the Southern Rights Party found it difficult to make headway in any plan by which it might be hoped to carry the state out of the Union.[8]

Only in Lush Anderson's native Jackson Purchase, and a few counties here and there, did neutrality not represent "the general desires of the people." Most Purchase citizens demanded secession. From the twenty-ninth to the thirty-first of May, a Southern Rights convention met in Mayfield, and delegates discussed forming a military alliance with soon-to-be Confederate Tennessee. In the end, convention-goers opted to stay in Kentucky, but only because they were sure the whole state would ultimately secede. They feared that splitting off deep western Kentucky would wreck the Confederate cause statewide. The Southern Rights men looked to the August elections for the state legislature, confident that secessionist candidates would win big and proceed to make Kentucky a Confederate state. Lush must have deplored the gathering, but Ervin was in the thick of it, serving as one of six secretaries. While minutes of the meeting evidently do not survive, J.N. Beadles, a Mayfield Unionist, wrote out a long account of the assembly, which the *Journal* published. Beadles, who witnessed the convention, was Lush's future brother-in-law.[9]

Meanwhile, Lincoln had called a special session of Congress to meet on July 4. In Kentucky, elections were set for June 20. So in other business, the Mayfield Convention nominated incumbent First District Congressman Henry C. Burnett, a Cadiz Democrat, on the Southern Rights ticket. His challenger was Lawrence Trimble of Paducah, Lush's friend, business partner and politically ally. Whatever help Anderson might have provided Trimble went for naught. In the election, Union candidates handily won every district except the First, where the Purchase carried Burnett to victory. He pocketed Graves County better than two-to-one, 1,270 to 620.[10]

As the summer wore on, hundreds of Confederate volunteers left Lush's home county and the Purchase for the Confederate army in Tennessee. Some stay-at-home secessionists, individually or in vigilante groups, terrorized their Unionist neighbors. They shot and hanged Union men and forced whole families to flee, notably from Milburn, a tiny Unionist community in Ballard County (now in Carlisle County).[11]

Such lawlessness was region-wide according to a letter Beadles dashed

**Henry C. Burnett (Library of Congress).**

off to the *Louisville Journal.* "These facts I hope you will not publish as having come from this point, as I am known to be your correspondent, and would expose me to the enraged mob or assassination," he begged.

> I was informed a few days since, by a gentleman of known valor and high standing and integrity, that he was afraid to write you the outrages perpetrated and threatened upon the Union men of his place (Paducah), as it would endanger his life to do so. This is the condition of things in the Purchase.

Civil War era papers routinely published letters signed with pseudonyms. But for whatever reason, the Journal stuck Beadles' name and a Mayfield dateline on his missive, which appeared in the July 15 edition.[12]

Beadles also wrote that "a lady friend" warned him that her husband's brother-in-law bragged that soon he "would be found hung up to a tree some where near Mayfield." He heard from "a reliable gentleman" that similar threats had been made against Bolinger and Anderson. Beadles said "such threats are but daily occurrences, and are only prevented from being put into execution by the strength and the valor of the Union men of our town." According to Beadles, "It would be dangerous for any one of the principal Union men to pass about in some portions of the county alone" and that everywhere Union men risked being mobbed.[13]

Beadles wrote the *Journal* in response to Elder J.R. Patterson's letter that the Louisville paper printed on July 6. Patterson, from Mayfield, wanted to move to Texas. He vowed that claims to the contrary, secessionists did not keep from voting for Trimble by threatening to send a letter to where he planned to settle, exposing him as a Unionist. Beadles said Patterson admitted to him that on election day that a local Confederate major ordered him to vote for Trimble or "it would be written to Texas on him and endanger him there." Patterson told Beadles that he shook his fist in the rebel's face and reminded him he was a free man and would do as he wished. If the officer "wanted to know where he was going he would give his county and post office address."[14]

Beadles said Patterson also complained to Anderson, Bolinger and others. "Indeed, he told it publicly in Bolinger's store, in the presence of sundry gentlemen." Beadles suspected that fear prompted Patterson to write the *Journal.* Beadles added that Patterson admitted to Anderson and others that he "received a letter from J.W. Kemble, a violent secession leader, in regard to the election, and that if it had not been for Kemble and others he should have voted for Trimble." Beadles concluded that the secessionists seemed "very anxious to make the impression abroad that there is no reign of terror in this part of the State, when they know it is false."[15]

Beadles conceded the election was fair in Mayfield and in most county precincts. Lynnville was an exception. Only Robert Cox dared vote for Trimble.

When he walked away from the polls, secessionists grabbed him, slapped him on the face, kicked him and brought him back where he was ordered "to look at his vote and was threatened to be hung." Local secessionists apologized and alibied that Confederate soldiers roughed up Cox. Beadles said they were army men from Graves County "sent back to vote for Burnett." He complained that "Union men are daily threatened by lawless scoundrels in all the counties west of the Tennessee River."[16]

Anderson evidently escaped physical harm, though one must wonder how much derision he had to endure. Because there is no record, we can only guess at the fate of an outspoken Union man in a rabidly rebel town. Did his law practice suffer accordingly? Or did the citizenry consider him such a good attorney that they overlooked his politics? Was he cursed and reviled as he walked the streets? Or was he such an affable fellow that most people looked past his "sins." Was he shunned by Southern sympathizing fellow congregants at the Cumberland Presbyterian church, where he, Ann and their children were faithful members? Or did a shared faith transcend politics?

Lush must have received news of the crucial August 5 elections for the state legislature with mixed emotions. The whole house and half the senate were up for election. Statewide, Lush's Union party swept to victory, claiming seventy-six House seats to twenty-four for the Southern Rightists. In the Senate, including holdovers, the Unionist edge grew to twenty-seven to eleven. There were no Senate contests in the Purchase. But the region sent six secessionists to the House; at least four, perhaps five, including Judge Boone of Graves County, had no opposition.[17]

The big Union victory did not ease the persecution of western Kentucky Unionists like Anderson. On August 20, the *Journal* ran a long article alleging months of multiple crimes against Union supporters. Among them was the reported murder of a Mr. Jones, a Calloway County man. A local vigilante group headquartered in Murray and led by "a violent, lawless secession Doctor of the name of Boggs," ordered Jones to clear out after he declined to join a group of local rebels bound for Camp Boone, Tennessee, the main recruit depot for Kentucky Confederate volunteers. Jones ultimately left, but four secessionists tracked him down and delivered him to the rebel camp at Union City, Tennessee. Evidently, Jones' captors figured the Confederates would want him. They did not and the quartet took him back to Kentucky. But close to Boydsville, "he was shot in three places and left to die in the road." Jones dragged himself to a nearby creek "where he got water and was found by a neighbor; he lingered two days and died, leaving a widow and two small children, entirely penniless, to mourn his death." On August 3, the *Journal* had printed a different version of Jones' death. That story said that the secessionists told two Unionist brothers named Jones to leave. The two were "the sons of a Methodist preacher, obscure, but honest and respectable." The siblings fled to a relative in Tennessee, but "several neighbors ... followed, forcibly seized the elder Jones, and took him to ... Union City." Brigadier General Benjamin F. Cheatham, the post commander, "would have nothing to do with" the Kentucky Unionman. "But the poor fellow only got a short distance from the encampment before he was shot through the head."[18]

On a visit to Louisville, Williams and Bolinger told the *Journal* that after Jones was abducted and murdered, "the most absurd and villainous falsehoods were put in circulation," including a claim that he had tipped off the Confederates at Union City that "a secret league" of 350 Union men led by Williams was scheming "to destroy secessionists and their property—murder and rob them." The paper also cited a mysterious letter purportedly written in Cairo and sent to a Graves County friend. The missive outlined a plot to free slaves owned by a trio of wealthy farmers and slaveholders. The letter suggested "Beadles, Anderson, and Bolinger were accomplices, who might be consulted and relied on." The *Journal* further claimed that the letter was "the work of a ready penman and scholar" whose "handwriting and spelling are disguised." The message was left close to where the rich farmers lived but had "neither envelope, postmark, address, nor signature." According to the *Journal*, the "villainry" happened soon after some local Confederate soldiers stole some nine hundred State Guard muskets and a six-gun artillery battery in Mayfield and sent them south.[19]

The purpose of implicating Williams in "the absurd and wicked report" was to draw attention away "from the foul murder of Jones, and to get up a mob and have the Judge murdered," the *Journal* claimed. The paper also said that Beadles, Anderson and Bolinger were "all pro-slavery men and slave-

**Benjamin Cheatham (Library of Congress).**

holders, and are prominent, respectable, responsible citizens" and thus the letter "did not even excite the suspicions of the community." The *Journal* said the man who authored "the foul forgery" was known and that "the high respectability of the slandered men and the confidence the community have in them, although Union men, were their security from violence. To this alone they were indebted for the defeat of the design of the forger." Perhaps the *Journal* story is a hint at why Lush escaped harm in the Civil War: he was a man of high standing and respectability who enjoyed public trust, however grudgingly given.[20]

A month after the state elections, Kentucky's fragile neutrality crumbled in the Purchase. Heretofore, both armies had steered clear of Kentucky. A Union invasion might have pushed Kentucky into the Confederates' welcoming arms. Likewise, a rebel advance into the state might have forced Kentucky to abandon neutrality and fight for the North. At the same time, Tennessee authorities liked the idea of Kentucky acting as a buffer between the Volunteer State and the North.

Nowhere along Kentucky's borders were the combatants closer than in Lush's Purchase. Soon after Fort Sumter, Union troops hurried to Cairo, Illinois, at the confluence of the Ohio and Mississippi rivers. The Confederates countered with a camp at Union City. Both sides coveted a trio of military prizes in deep western Kentucky. The Tennessee River flowed into the Ohio at Paducah. Likewise, the waters of the Cumberland merged with the Ohio at Smithland. Both rivers would be vital lines of supply and reinforcements for Confederate forces who might occupy Paducah and Smithland. Nashville, Tennessee's capital, was up the Cumberland from Smithland. At the same time, the Yankees could use the Tennessee and Cumberland to invade Rebeldom.

But the biggest prize was westward, at Columbus on the Mississippi. Here dirt bluffs a hundred feet tall loomed over the Father of Waters. An army could plant long-range cannons atop the bluffs and command the river for miles upstream and down. But throughout the spring and summer, political considerations outweighed military considerations, and both armies kept out of Kentucky.

The situation abruptly changed in early September. When it looked like the Yankees were poised to seize Columbus, the rebels advanced from Tennessee. They grabbed Hickman on September 3 and Columbus the next day. Grant, at Cairo, reckoned that the Confederates' next objectives would be Paducah and Smithland. So on September 6, he snagged Paducah and Smithland. Kentucky's hand was forced; before the month was out, the legislature ordered only the Confederates to leave. The Unionist majority asked the Federal government to help the state get rid of the rebels and named Robert Anderson commander of Kentucky Union volunteers.[21]

Perhaps emboldened by the arrival of the Confederates, local secessionists decided it was time to do more than threaten Lush's friend Bolinger. A "band of secessionist ruffians near Mayfield" kidnapped and dragged him away to the rebels at Columbus, the *Journal* reported in disgust. The enemy thus had "one of the truest and bravest men that ever lived." When Bolinger was in the Falls City," he "was strongly advised by Union men … not to return home, but he resolved to do so at all hazards, and the loss of his liberty if not his life is the sacrifice," the paper declared. "The best informed believe his life is in danger." The *Journal* added that "secessionists may rejoice at this outrage, but they cannot palliate it." The Confederate commander, Major General Leonidas Polk, had been an Episcopal bishop. "How dares that epauletted man of God … confine a man in his camp seized and taken to him under such circumstances? His doing so shows, that, while invading our soil, he sets all our laws and all other laws at defiance." Polk "has brought his army to Kentucky to establish over her the supremacy of his own will. He treats her free citizens as the serfs of a conquered province." The *Journal* warned: "But let the surpliced tyrant beware. If the life of Bolinger be sacrificed, a hundred lives will answer it."[22]

One wonders how Lush eluded capture; Bolinger was ultimately released. But with rebel soldiers prowling the Purchase and the Yankees ensconced in Paducah, Bolinger and Anderson concluded it was best to head for the McCracken County seat. But any relief they may have felt upon their arrival soon turned to deep displeasure with the post commander, Brigadier General Charles F. Smith, who took over from Brigadier General E.A. Paine. Anderson and Bolinger admired Paine, but they concluded that Smith, a career soldier who cared little for politics, was too soft on local rebels. On November 27,

**Ulysses S. Grant (Library of Congress).**

a disgruntled Anderson sent Major General Henry W. Halleck, the St. Louis-based commander of the Department of Missouri, a list of four grievances against Smith, "relative to the management and control of the Army of the US at his place." Afterwards, he and Bolinger went to St. Louis and complained in person to Smith's superior.[23]

First, Anderson charged that Smith's inaction cost the life of J.F. Conner, a Union man jailed in Mayfield for killing a secessionist who broke into his home. Conner allegedly shot John Milliken, Paducah's pro–Confederate postmaster who fled the Yankees. No sooner did Milliken arrive in Mayfield than he became "unscrupulous and

Leonidas Polk (Library of Congress).

unsparing in his persecution of every one who was loyal to his country," according to the *Journal*. The paper reported that on November 19 he stormed into the Conner home, vilifying J.F. and his brother, M.M. Conner, as "Black Republicans."[24]

"Having lashed himself into fury, he finally struck one of them," the paper recounted. "As quick as the thunder follows the lightning flash, the report of a musket was heard and the ruffian received its entire contents, killing him instantly." The *Journal* trusted that "this terrible retribution will … have the effect to deter others from the commission of similar outrages." Authorities took J.F. into custody.[25]

M.M. feared Confederate soldiers from nearby Columbus or Camp Beauregard, a rebel recruit center near Feliciana in southern Graves County, would murder his sibling. He went to Paducah and asked Smith to provide him "a force sufficient to protect his brother." Paine and Brigadier General Lew Wallace—who would become a general but achieve greater fame as the author of the novel *Ben Hur*—wanted to lead troops to Mayfield to save Conner from Confederate "murderers." Smith refused them, but granted Conner a pass to go back and help his sibling.[26]

Conner managed to round up some men, evidently civilians, and horses and he and his impromptu posse rode back to Mayfield. Meanwhile, John Eaker, now vehemently secessionist, allegedly sent word of Milliken's demise to Camp Beauregard, figuring soldiers would come and murder J.F., which they reputedly did an hour before M.M. and his band arrived. Anderson and Bolinger charged that Smith's failure to act on time led to the slaying of an "innocent man."[27]

Second, they claimed Smith was also slow to stop Ballard County men from selling wheat and hogs to the

**Charles F. Smith (Library of Congress).**

Confederates at Columbus. Paine told Smith about one man who lived near Lovelaceville. He said the man was buying wheat in bulk and grinding it into flour for the Columbus garrison. Smith refused to confiscate the hogs and the grain though Paine had an affidavit from a Unionist who swore the man was trading the enemy. Smith, according to Anderson and Bolinger, refused to act until "a true Union man" at Paducah confirmed the Ballard countian as a genuine Union sympathizer. After Paine got an endorsement, he was able to seize about 2,000 bushels of wheat and one hundred or so hogs. But had to leave another 2,000 bushels, which the rebels hauled away. Thirdly, the Mayfield men complained that Smith would not send soldiers to confiscate hogs in Union County, up the Ohio River from Paducah. Purportedly those porkers, too, were to become meat on rebel mess tables.[28]

The fourth complaint stemmed from Smith's alleged coddling of Robert Owen Woolfolk, "a wealthy old Rebel aristocrat," who defiantly flew a Confederate flag over his large, two story brick house in Paducah. Confederate Brigadier General Lloyd Tilghman and his family lived in the dwelling before he joined the rebels and his wife and children migrated south. After the Tlighmans left, the Woolfolks moved into what was supposedly "the finest house in town." (The two story brick home at 631 Kentucky Avenue is a local museum.)[29]

Smith ignored the enemy standard, but the flag and Woolfolk's penchant for cheering for Jefferson Davis were too much for Wallace. He sent his aide-de-camp and a squad of men to force Woolfolk to take down his flag. If he refused, they would replace the enemy banner with the Stars and Stripes. Aware that Smith outranked Wallace, Woolfolk would not budge. Wallace's aid lowered the rebel flag

Lew Wallace (Library of Congress).

and hoisted the national colors. When Woolfolk protested to Smith, the post commander dispatched his aide to order Wallace to remove the U.S. flag. Wallace's man slugged Smith's man, knocking him down, and the Stars and Stripes stayed put. Another account of the fracas had Wallace marching his whole regiment, the Eleventh Indiana Volunteer Infantry, to Woolfolk's house to rip down the offending flag and congratulating his soldiers after the deed was done. Also, a Missouri regiment reputedly "started with a fire-engine to wash out Gen. Smith's headquarters, which they were dissuaded from doing by Gen. Wallace." Thus, it seems that Anderson and Bolinger were not alone in their disdain for Smith. At any rate, Anderson and Bolinger summed up their complaints by charging that Smith pampered rebels while leaving Union men beyond his lines undefended against "the ravages of the Confederate troops." The duo warned, "Unless some changes are made here, bad results will certainly flow, for the soldiers here are almost prepared to rise against the policy which has thus far been pursued."[30]

Halleck sent a copy of the grievances to Smith for comment. He barely had time for a reply before northern newspapers started attacking him. The

*Chicago Tribune* accused Smith of "making an ass of himself, which is stating the case mildly." The paper said the general was "exceedingly unpopular both with the officers and the men. Worse, the paper said Smith was a rebel sympathizer who refused "to aid Union men who have been driven from their homes, and whose property has been plundered by the secesh." Doubtless, the editorializing pleased Lush and Bolinger.[31]

More pressing military matters delayed Smith's reply to Halleck. But in a letter to his superior on December 26, the general claimed that all of Lush's grievances were groundless. He said that when J.F. Conner came to him, he knew nothing of the shooting. After listening to Conner, Smith decided it was "a private broil" and declined "to send a large force (prudence ever forbid sending a small one) to Mayfield to take J.F. Conner from the hands of civil authority on a supposition." At some point, M.M. said he killed Milliken, but Smith countered that "subsequent events" showed J.F. shot him. To discredit M.M., Smith wrote that at some time before the shooting, Anderson and Bolinger appeared in civil court "to testify to Connor's [sic] character for truth and veracity," and both "made affidavit they would not believe him on oath," Smith also wrote.[32]

On the second grievance, Smith said he refused Paine's request to confiscate the hogs and wheat bound for Columbus until he "could get some proper grounds for action." He added that Paine spent too much time investigating the loyalties of Purchase citizens, thereby neglecting his military duties. Smith explained that he hesitated because many people Paine arrested had to be released for lack of evidence. Smith also said Paine failed to obey orders to destroy a mill, capture the flour and grain and bring the contraband to Paducah.[33]

Henry W. Halleck (Library of Congress).

Addressing the third grievance, Smith said he lacked sufficient cavalry to stop Union countians from selling their hogs to the enemy. Sending infantry to do the job would weaken his force at Paducah, he maintained.[34]

Finally, Smith claimed the downing of Woolfolk's rebel flag and the hoisting of the Stars and Stripes over his house was a sad affair "merely to annoy the family." The general hotly denied that he protected secessionists and not loyal citizens and turned the tables on Lush, questioning his patriotism. The general claimed that Anderson had "made violent and determined harangues against the government ... and proposed armed resistance to the passage of Federal forces through ... Kentucky." He dismissed Lush as "a shallow man" and "an ardent supporter of the Party in power be it Gov't or Rebellion." Without evidence, it is impossible to prove or disprove the general's allegations. However, after Fort Sumter, most Kentucky Unionists, while spurning secession, acquiesced in Magoffin's refusal to supply Kentucky soldiers to the president. Often, too, they denounced coercion of the seceded states. The Unionists feared that to come out too strongly for the Union would harm their cause in the long run.[35]

In the end, Halleck stood by his general, who rid himself of Paine. Smith sent him to command federal forces at Bird's Point, Missouri, across the Mississippi from Columbus. Smith called the remote post a "very hell hole." Smith would soon find himself back in the field, leading troops in the battle of Fort Donelson in February.[36]

Smith also got even with Bolinger after the Mayfield expatriate opened a store in Paducah. The general ordered his provost marshals to stop the shipment of goods from the city on Bolinger's recommendation, according to a letter from Paducah signed "Ky" and published in the *Democrat*. The author sharply criticized Smith, claiming that "the hearts of all true Union men are crushed with sorrow and shame at the course which has been pursued towards them by the General in command at this post." On the other hand, when Paine was in charge in Paducah, however briefly, "the worst and most rabid of the secesh left," afraid that the general, "who was known to be an enemy of that foul heresy, would give them their just deserts. Those that were left behind behaved themselves as long as Payne [sic] was in command."[37]

When the Yankees arrived in Paducah, the city "was as bad a secession hole as any in the United States, Charleston, South Carolina, not excepted," the letter said. Under Smith, "treason and traitors began to raise their heads" and they became "bolder and bolder, until to-day secesh in Paducah is as proud and defiant in its tones as it is at Columbus." The author asserted that it was widely known that Bolinger, the object of Smith's disaffection, "was driven from his home, robbed of his property by the Rebel army, and imprisoned at Columbus—all for the reason of his loyalty to the Government."[38]

Smith also went after Lush and Bolinger's ally, Judge Williams, who had stepped down from the bench to raise a Yankee regiment of First District Union men. He only managed to recruit a few companies, which were merged into the Twentieth Kentucky Infantry, most of whose soldiers came from the central part of the state. The letter writer claimed Smith told the newly-commissioned Colonel Williams that unless he "conducted himself better," he would lock him in the guardhouse. Perhaps Smith believed, or wanted to believe, an absurd charge that Williams made a secessionist speech in town. The accusation was known to be untrue

> by every loyal citizen in this part of the State; but the truth is the General has no doubt been listening to the statements of traitors here, and it seems, gives credence to their statements, and makes that a pretext for making war on men who are as good as he is and fully as true to the Government.

The writer added a postscript: "I have just been informed that General Smith's Provost Marshal, on yesterday, refused Bolinger the privilege of sending a letter to his wife, who is absent. Comment unnecessary."[39]

Meanwhile, Smith and his troops bolstered Paducah with an earthen bastion next to the Ohio. They dubbed the works, which surrounded the

A state historical marker at the approximate site of Fort Anderson commemorates the Eighth Artillery (Berry Craig).

Marine Hospital, Fort Anderson for Major Anderson, not Smith's nemesis Lush. The Yankees also ringed the city with outer works and spanned the Ohio with a pontoon bridge—said to be the longest floating bridge on record.[40]

Not to be outdone, the Confederates strongly fortified the bluffs at Columbus, using slaves to help dig trenches and build earthen forts atop them. The rebels emplaced cannons on and below the high ground and on rafts at the river's edge. They also sowed mines—called "torpedoes"—in the river—and blocked the waterway with a massive chain suspended on log rafts. They dubbed their strongpoint "the Gibraltar of the West" and dared the Yankees to attack them. On November 7, Grant led a small demonstration against the rebel outpost at Belmont, Missouri, opposite the Gibraltar. The Yankees captured the small camp, but soon found themselves pounded by Columbus's big guns and, surrounded by reinforcements, hurried across the river. Spurning surrender, Grant ordered his men to fight their way out of the trap, which they did.[41]

Eleven days after the battle of Belmont, Senator John M. Johnson and all six Purchase representatives gathered behind Confederate lines at Russellville and helped Burnett and a group of die-hard secessionists from across the state—most of them from pro–Union counties—organize a bogus Confederate "government" for Kentucky. As dubious as the proceedings were, they were enough to convince the Confederacy to admit Kentucky as its thirteenth "state" in December, 1861. (Missouri was the twelfth "state" by action of a similar extralegal government.)[42]

Congressman Burnett presided at the Russellville Convention, and he helped raise the Eighth Kentucky Confederate Infantry. Thus, it was only a matter of time until the House expelled him. On November 21, the *Louisville Democrat* endorsed Anderson, "that sterling Union man," to replace the "rebel Burnett." The Falls City paper declared that "no man in Western Kentucky deserves more at the hands of the loyal voters than" Lush.[43]

The *Democrat* claimed that Anderson had "never sought office, although frequently tendered." That was, perhaps, gilding the lily; he had been county attorney and a state representative, if only briefly. Anderson's

> energies have all been put forth for the good of his country, and without asking any other reward than that of the peace and quiet than a proper observance of the Constitution and the laws always brings. To the efforts of Anderson are the people of Kentucky largely indebted for the strong Union sentiments that now prevail in the First District, and to him are they mainly indebted for the breaking up of the infamous contraband trade that was carried on with the Rebels through that District.

Again, the *Democrat* was stretching the truth; Unionism was still the exception, not the rule, in the region, especially in Lush's hometown and the rest of the Purchase. The Louisville paper hoped Anderson would be elected unopposed.[44]

The Purchase was the only region of Kentucky that could claim its delegates to the Russellville Convention truly represented popular sentiment back home. Even so, the *Democrat* claimed the region was turning Unionist. The paper's assertion was wishful thinking and based on reports from anonymous Unionists in "the South Carolina of Kentucky." At any rate, the *Democrat* cited "a bitter Secessionist," who was arrested and hauled off to Paducah where the "kind treatment of the authorities" made him a Union man.[45]

The paper said the captive sent for Lush to make a speech in his county—but failed to name the Union man or his county. Even so, the man told the *Democrat* that Lush was just the speaker to convince secessionists "of their error." The informant also reported that "the change in the entire district has become so great, that only two counties sent any representatives to the bogus convention at Russellville and the people will elect Union legislators and send a Union man to Congress, in Burnett's place." While he was wrong about the region's representative at Russellville, he was right about the replacements for Burnett and the secessionist lawmakers. Unionists would indeed take their seats, but only because state and federal authorities would disenfranchise secessionists and Confederate soldiers as traitors and permit only men of unquestioned loyalty to vote. Yankee soldiers would enforce the proscription against rebels at the polls.[46]

Ultimately, Grant opted for an end run around the rebels' Gibraltar. In February, 1862, he led an army-navy expedition up the Tennessee and Cumberland rivers; on the sixth, he captured Fort Henry on the Tennessee. Ten days later, he bagged Fort Donelson on the Cumberland near Dover. As a result, the Confederates had no choice but to retreat from Columbus, Bowling Green and the rest of Kentucky.[47]

After the rebels forsook Columbus, Hickman and Camp Beauregard, the hard-pressed Purchase Unionists, now protected by Yankee soldiers, began to assert themselves as best they could. They were cheered by news from Washington where, on December 3, the House formally expelled Burnett for being "in open Rebellion against the Government of the United States." Lush surely would have relished the *New York Times* story about Burnett's ouster. According to the paper, Representative Charles A. Wickliffe of Bardstown blasted Burnett, explaining that he had intended to present the congressman's "obituary notice" but thought better of it since his "late colleague" was "now in armed Rebellion, at the head of a Provisional Government in Kentucky, and the chief of a revolutionary Convention." Wickliffe also flayed Kentucky State Guard chief-turned-rebel-general Simon Bolivar Buckner, claiming he was "much more wicked, than Simon Gerty [sic], who headed the Indian tribes in an attempt to conquer Kentucky in the days of her first settlement."[48]

Meanwhile, Burnett, according to Wickliffe, finagled "this Convention, composed of the young, and reckless, and desperate men who were already in arms under this man Buckner." Burnett opted for Richmond, Virginia, the new Confederate capital, over Washington. From February, 1862, to February, 1865, he was a senator from the Bluegrass State's rump Confederate government, which skedaddled from the state with the retreating rebels in early 1862.[49]

The vote to replace Burnett was set for January 20, but Lush was not the nominee. Trimble and Samuel L. Casey of the Union County community of Caseyville, apparently named for a member of his family, vied for the seat. Both ran as Union Democrats. The Union Democrats were conservative Unionists who supported war only to restore the Union, not to abolish slavery. Union County's name belied its majority sentiment; it leaned secessionist. At any rate, Casey was U.S. treasurer during President Franklin Pierce's administration. Compared to the June election, the vote was tiny and perhaps name recognition gave Casey the edge; he trimmed Trimble 541–442. In the Purchase, polls opened only in Calloway, Graves, Marshall and McCracken counties, which supplied Trimble 323 votes to Casey's 251. Trimble won his home county 297–70. It is evidently unknown whom Anderson backed in the election.[50]

The *Louisville Journal* reprinted the *Evansville Journal*'s alibi about the low turnout in Lush's neck of the woods. The Hoosier paper claimed that that few ballots were cast because "the secessionists did not recognize the election and the Union men were afraid to vote." The Louisville paper also reprinted a letter published in the Evansville paper that maintained the vote was skimpy because "the whole country where the Rebels have possession is full of guerrilla bands playing the devil generally." That may have been true in some parts of deep western Kentucky, but Paducah and McCracken County were firmly under Union military control. Indeed, the paucity of the vote suggests that the Union cause had a long way to go in the district. Two days after Union men sent Casey to Washington, secessionists elected Burnett to the rebel senate, though no record of the returns apparently exists. Willis B. Machen of Lyon County became the First District's representative in Richmond.[51]

Meanwhile, Purchase Union men organized mass meetings like the secessionists did before and during the Confederates' advent. Ballard County Unionists met in Blandville on March 24, 1862, and unanimously endorsed Colonel Williams for the Fourth Appellate District seat on the Kentucky Court of Appeals, then the state's highest court. Williams resigned his commission to run for the judgeship. The election was set for August 4, and delegates were to choose the nominee at a district Union convention in Henderson on May 1. The Ballard County Unionists agreed that if their delegates could not attend, the Graves County delegates would be their proxies.[52]

Five days later, Marshall County Unionists met at Flat Rock, endorsed Williams and appointed four delegates to the Henderson meeting. The county gathering resolved if none of the Marshall delegates could go, Anderson should cast the county's vote.[53]

On April 5, Lush attended a Mayfield meeting that endorsed Williams "with the full confidence that he will receive the nomination" because of his ten-year tenure on the bench and "his unqualified devotion to the Government although persecuted to an extent unparalleled...." The Unionists were sure Williams would win the nod from "men who are for the Union, the Constitution, and the enforcement of the laws." Anderson, Beadles and other Graves Countians were named as delegates.[54]

Williams faced a challenger when the convention met. Some counties in the eastern part of the district backed State Representative George H. Yeaman of Owensboro, who would join Lush in voting for the Thirteenth Amendment in 1865 and earn a brief portrayal in the 2012 Academy Award–winning film *Lincoln*. Yet he declined to run, and the convention unanimously nominated Williams after Anderson put forward his friend's name and "addressed the convention in a short but stirring speech." Lush's fellow Mayfield lawyer Richard Neal offered a resolution urging "every loyal man of this State to vote for no candidate for official station whose loyalty to the Federal Government and the State of Kentucky is not above suspicion." The proposal passed with no dissenting votes.[55]

Statewide, the Union Democrats looked to the August elections as their time to clean courthouses of the numerous secessionists who ran county governments. They also aimed to replace the secessionist lawmakers the legislature had expelled as traitors. In late 1861, the House booted five of the six Purchase representatives elected in August—A.R. Boone of Graves County, Daniel Matthewson of Calloway, George W. Silvertooth of Fulton and Hickman, Thomas A. Goheen of Marshall and John Quincy Adams King of McCracken. Facing expulsion, W.M. Coffee of Ballard County resigned. In early February, the senate stripped Johnson of his seat.[56]

On May 26, 1862, Ballard County Unionists again met in Blandville and endorsed Unionists for several local offices. They put up M.O. Hawthorne to succeed Coffee. In turn, they backed County Judge Charles S. Marshall to replace Williams as circuit judge. The meeting also passed a series of pro–Union resolutions, including two that reflected the stand of nearly every loyal Kentuckian—simultaneous support for the Union and for slavery. Subsequent Union meetings in Mayfield, Murray and again in Blandville passed similar resolutions.[57]

On June 16, Lush started the Mayfield meeting with a near two-hour speech "in his usual happy and impassioned style, and to an attentive and appreciative audience." Afterwards, the crowd named Lush's law partner

Mayes chairman and Neal secretary. The delegates backed Marshall for circuit judge and P.D. Yeiser of Paducah for commonwealth's attorney from the district. In addition, the Graves County Unionists endorsed "the Union, the Constitution, and the Enforcement of the Laws," and "the Constitution as it is and the Union as it was." They also agreed "that abolitionism, like secessionism, is unauthorized by the Constitution, and we regard them both as inimical to the free institutions of our country and destructive to the interests of the American people; a foul blot that should be eradicated from American politics." Further, the Unionists decried guerrilla warfare as a "violation of civilized warfare" that had "has been partially, and is likely to be generally, inaugurated by those in Rebellion." Too, they condemned guerrillas and their aiders and abettors as "outlaws" who "should be treated as banditti by the Government."[58]

Lush and the Graves County Unionists—like all Kentucky Union men—probably could not have been more pleased with the election results, though a Union victory was a foregone conclusion. Authorities closed the polls to all but proven Union men, a restriction Yankee soldiers enforced. Though the Union party swept to victory statewide, the vote was light. Marshall and Yeiser won handily. Marshall beat J.M. Bigger 2,014 to 839; Yeiser topped Thomas Corbett, 1,455 to 804. But Anderson might have been surprised and more than a little uncomfortable with the results. Though he was not a candidate, he beat "the regular nominee"—Mayes—by a vote of 466–280. Reportedly Unionists chose Anderson "because of some dissatisfaction about Mr. Mayes." While Lush won, Ervin lost the county clerk's job to Bolinger, which meant that for the first time in Graves County history, a non–Anderson would run the clerk's office. At any rate, the vote suggested that the Union cause had made little headway in the county; in the congressional election, Trimble managed only 610 votes to 1,270 for Burnett. Even so, the election wrought a sea change in the Purchase delegation in the state legislature. The new lawmakers were all Union Democrats; Neal would be heading to Frankfort to take Boone's seat.[59]

Nonetheless, Representative Neal, County Attorney Anderson and the other Graves County Unionists knew they were still a decided minority. Their disgust was mirrored in a long lament from an anonymous Mayfield Unionist the Louisville *Journal* published on January 14, 1863. The letter, signed "FAIR-PLAY," also was a look back to when the rebel army occupied Columbus, Hickman and Camp Beauregard. "FAIR-PLAY" was especially upset over the recently concluded circuit court term. Though Judge Marshall was a good Union man, "sixteen straight-out secessionists and disunionists" comprised the grand jury thanks to the machinations of the Southern-sympathizing sheriff, said "FAIR-PLAY," who, nonetheless, failed to name the lawman. He was most likely D.M. Galloway, who doubled as the county jailer.[60]

The correspondent said that the May, 1862, court term lasted approximately a week "owing to the then unsettled state of affair in this part of the State." Judge Williams, who was still on the bench, failed to name jury commissioners who were supposed to fill the grand and petit jury pools. Consequently, the sheriff got to choose the jurymen. He was a lame duck, having lost at the August election, but "smarting under his defeat" and seizing an "opportunity to gratify his petty spleen and malice on Union men," he packed the grand jury, whose foreman was staunch secessionist Eaker, a former state senator and representative. "FAIR-PLAY" might have been doubly vexed with Eaker because he supported the Union, at least conditionally, in early 1861.[61]

Eaker chaired that big January, 1861, Union meeting in Mayfield which almost certainly attracted Lush Anderson. At any rate, despite their known rebel sympathies, the grand jurymen swore the Union loyalty oath, according to the letter's author. He charged that Eaker had been part of "a secret conclave" to invite the rebels into the state "and signed a petition to that effect." Eaker cheered the Confederates and Jeff Davis when the troops arrived in town and he headed a "Safety Committee" organized to "*save Union men*" and prevent them from leaving without buying a ten cent pass from him. Worse, according to FAIR-PLAY," Eaker was, in effect, an accessory to murder in Conner's death because he sent word about the fight to the rebels at Camp Beauregard.[62]

Further, "FAIR-PLAY" vowed the grand jurymen knew their county contained "at least five hundred men who had committed treason against the State." He maintained that no less than fifty of these Confederate sympathizers, including Mayfield residents, helped steal the State Guards weapons and added that local men also helped burn bridges to thwart advancing Union troops. Even so, the grand jury did not indict any of the guilty parties, though Eaker and the rest knew who was culpable. Rather, they gratified "their damnable prejudices on Union men ... by indicting them for breaches of the peace, and for ... interfering in elections." "FAIR-PLAY" groused that two-thirds of the indictments were "for alleged minor offenses."[63]

Among those bound over for trial was "an old gray-headed Union man by the name of Cooper seven times charged with stealing guns, horses &c, and not a man on the Grand Jury who knew him believed him to be guilty." The panel also indicted three Union men over alleged irregularities in the January 20 special congressional election. They purposely did not hold "the election at the proper place of voting in the district." "FAIR-PLAY" lamented that the grand jury declined to indict secessionists who opened a polling station at the courthouse for the Confederate congressional election.[64]

He was confident the sixteen secessionists would get their comeuppance when the next grand jury convened. He expected they and other local Southern sympathizers would be jailed "to expiate for the treason and corruption they have been guilty of." He zeroed in on Eaker, challenging: "Let this old traitor ... wait for the wagon, which will pass along in due time; then we will all ride, not to the so-called Southern Confederacy, but to the Temple of Justice, erected by Kentucky, to try all traitors to her Constitution and laws."[65]

An angry Eaker replied to "FAIR-PLAY" in a January 23 letter the *Journal* printed eight days later. He signed his missive, which contained his pledge to vindicate himself and the rest of the grand jury from the "foul imputations" of "FAIR-PLAY." He called on "FAIR-PLAY" "to unmask himself" and "acknowledge the paternity of his literary offspring." If he declined, Eaker would "only leave him to the scorn and contempt of an honest community as a slanderer who uses publicly and vilely the names of others while ignominiously concealing his own to avoid exposure and personal responsibility."[66]

Eaker's Southern Rights party faded into near oblivion after Kentucky declared for the Union. But Lincoln's Emancipation Proclamation gave the party a new lease on life. Issued on September 22, 1862, it freed slaves in Confederate-held territory on January 1, 1863. Though the president's action obviously did not apply to Kentucky, nearly every white Kentuckian furiously denounced it, especially as it closely followed the Confiscation Act of July 12,

"The first reading of the Emancipation Proclamation before the cabinet" (Library of Congress).

which authorized the recruitment of African Americans. The idea of black men in blue uniforms appalled almost every white Kentuckian. At the same time, whites feared that if slaves could be freed in the rebel states, they could someday be liberated in Kentucky. From the start of the war, most Kentucky whites were wary of Lincoln's intentions toward slavery. They believed that in exchange for their loyalty, they would be allowed to keep their slaves.

On the other hand, secession would doom slavery, Unionists argued. The *Louisville Journal* claimed in May, 1861,

> In speaking of the many inevitable consequences of disunion in Kentucky, we have repeatedly mentioned the certain, the unquestionable fact, that, if this State should go out of the United States, thus cutting herself off from the operation of the fugitive slave law, her slaves, learning at once, as they of course would do, the condition of things, would strike by the thousands and tens of thousands for the Indiana, Ohio, and Illinois shores, and none of them would ever be sent back to us. This important truth we have considered as others have done, self-evident—beyond dispute—palpable to every man of common sense.

But Kentuckians' fears over slavery's future grew in July, 1862, when Lincoln proposed to pay slave owners up to $300 for each slave they set free. The majority of whites opposed compensated emancipation. They rejected the idea that they, as citizens of a loyal state, would be expected to give up their slaves while the rebellious states would remain unaffected. At the same time, Kentuckians were doubtful that the Republican-majority Congress would vote money to compensate slaveholders. When Lincoln issued the Emancipation Proclamation, whites in the Bluegrass State concluded that their faith in the federal government was woefully misplaced. Simply put, Kentucky Unionists made it plain they joined the war on the Union side to preserve the Union, not to get rid of slavery. In other words, they were for the Union, not Lincoln and his "Black Republican" party.[67]

Coincidentally, Confederate armies under Generals Braxton Bragg and Edmund Kirby Smith were in Kentucky when news of the Emancipation Proclamation reached the state. Despite widespread outrage against Lincoln, relatively few Kentuckians signed up to soldier with the rebel invaders, who even captured Frankfort and tried to establish a Confederate government before leaving the capital. On October 8, a Union army under Major General Don Carlos Buell fought Bragg to a standstill at the battle of Perryville, the bloodiest ever clash of arms on Kentucky soil. Strategically, the battle was a Union victory because the Confederates retreated from the state afterwards. Never again were the rebels able to return to Kentucky in force though the state was visited by cavalry raiders and plagued by Confederate guerillas to the end of the war.[68]

Meanwhile, the Southern Rights men figured they might be able to win over more disaffected Unionists if they changed the party's name. So they started calling themselves Democrats. After all, many Democrats in the northern states also opposed Lincoln, the war and the Emancipation Proclamation. Kentucky Democrats figured to make political hay off the proclamation and the growing public impatience with the rigors military occupation, which included Union soldiers arresting and jailing citizens accused of disloyalty. Thus, they called a state convention to nominate candidates for the August 3 elections in which Kentuckians would elect a governor, members of congress, state legislators and various local officials. They set the conclave for Frankfort on February 18.[69]

Unionists suspected the gathering was part of a scheme to yet pry Kentucky out of the Union, perhaps with assistance from rebel troops, including John Hunt Morgan and his cavalry raiders, who were wreaking havoc in parts of the state. When delegates assembled in the capital city, an Ohio colonel and his regiment stopped the convention.[70]

Nonetheless, the party refused to disband and became known as the "Peace Democrats." It became "the logical party for those to support who favored secession, if any there should be, for those who were looking for peace, and for those who wished to register their protest against the military regime and the various unpopular acts of the National administration," Coulter wrote. The Peace Democrats worried the pro–Union and pro-war—through not pro–Lincoln—"Union Democracy."[71]

Some leading Union Democrats, including Trimble, had defected to the Peace Democrats. The Union Democrats blasted everybody on the other side as "secessionists, Rebels and traitors, and even abolitionists—the Union Democrats using this last term to ward off as far as possible the use of the same term against themselves." Anderson was among those who flatly denied he was an abolitionist.[72]

Meanwhile, the Union Democrats prepared to battle the Peace Democrats at the polls. They held mass meetings across the state, including in the Purchase, in preparation for their convention, which was set for March 18 and 19 in Louisville. On February 28, "a large and enthusiastic meeting" of Graves County's "Union Democracy" met at the courthouse in Mayfield. Led by Lush, his uncle Crawford Anderson, W.A. Terrell and others, the Unionmen approved resolutions praising the breakup of the Frankfort convention and condemning secession and rebellion. They also condemned the Emancipation Proclamation "as wholly unconstitutional and an outrage on all the loyal men of the slave States" and again declaimed disunion and abolitionism with equal vehemence. Further, they denounced Eaker's grand jury and pledged their "unshaken faith in the conservatism and patriotism of the Northern people" as allies in saving "the Constitution as it is and the Union as it was." The Unionists also sympathized "with the masses of the seceded States," promising them a warm, brotherly welcome when they abandoned "their traitor leaders" and came home "to the old union under the ample folds of its Constitution." The Graves Union men did not ignore the elections and the possibility of the Peace Democrats triumphing. Thus, they resolved that only "straight-out" Union men who supported "putting down this infamous Rebellion" should be permitted to run for and hold office. They also declared that delegates to the state convention should favor "no man for office ... whose loyalty to the Government is not firm and unfaltering." "Straight-out" Union man Lucian Anderson was set to toss his hat in the ring for Congress. His challenger would be Lawrence Trimble, Peace Democrat.[73]

# 5

# Mr. Anderson
# Goes to Washington

The Emancipation Proclamation took effect on January 1, 1863, triggering a "storm of disapproval that … broke [which] had never been equalled up to that time. Virtually no one could be found to support Lincoln." Unionist Governor James F. Robinson, successor to Magoffin, who resigned under pressure in August, 1862, denounced the proclamation. He argued that Lincoln's action would only make the Confederates fight harder. The Unionist legislature, with just three "nay" votes, condemned the proclamation as "unwise, unconstitutional and void." The state's pro–Union press also scorned Lincoln's first step to end slavery, which Kentucky whites feared would cause freed slaves to flood the state. Consequently, the legislature banned African Americans "claiming or pretending to be free." Slaves who asserted their freedom were subject to arrest and jail. Emancipated slaves who came to Kentucky were seized and re-enslaved. Such open defiance of Washington deeply troubled Union military authorities in the state. Fearing the legislature was about to vote Kentucky out of the Union, they prepared to arrest lawmakers and judges. Additionally, some Kentucky army officers resigned after the proclamation took effect. Though the Purchase was Kentucky's only rebel region, the congressman who represented the First District supported the proclamation. Casey's endorsement raised eyebrows and hackles back home; many, if not most, Unionists disavowed him. "I live in Sam Casey's District, and voted for him, and I think he cannot find half a dozen men in his district who will endorse the President's Emancipation Proclamation," an irate Crittenden Countian wrote the *Journal*. "I never saw *one* myself." The Louisville paper accused Casey of cutting "as clean from his constituency as he has from the principles he once avowed." The *Journal* declared that "except in bare constitutional form, he is no more the representative of the First District in Kentucky, and no more a representative of Kentucky at large than Owen Lovejoy or George W. Julian or John A. Bingham is."[1]

On March 18–19, the Union Democrats congregated in the *Journal*'s hometown to nail together a platform and to name candidates for the August state elections. They nominated Joshua F. Bell of Lexington for governor, but he declined, and in May, the party central committee tapped ex-Major General Thomas E. Bramlette. At the convention, delegates approved the legislature's

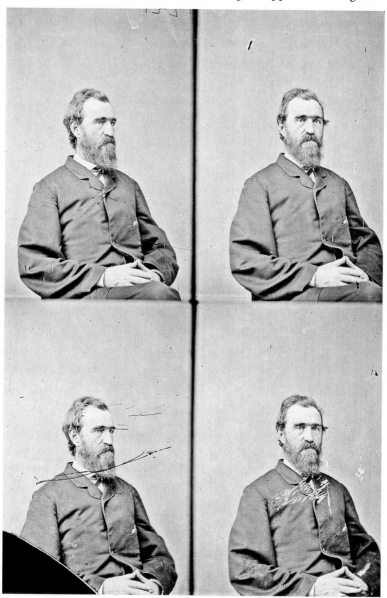

Thomas E. Bramlette (National Archives and Records Administration).

action in condemning the Emancipation Proclamation and hammered into their platform a plank supporting "the Union as it was and the Constitution as it is." In other words, the Union Democrats stood for the preservation of the Union and slavery.[2]

Based on his pro–Emancipation Proclamation stand, Casey was not a good bet for nomination. Besides, he was elected only to fill out the rest of Burnett's term. On June 18, 1863, First District Union Democrats gathered in Paducah, spurned Casey, and nominated Anderson for Congress. Unionist-turned-secessionist Q.Q. Quigley predictably was unimpressed. "I have not seen nor heard what character of resolutions they passed but from the character of [the] man they nominated, they endorsed the administration of Lincoln and a total destruction of States' rights," the lawyer griped. Quigley named Trimble and State Senator T.A. Duke, also of Paducah, as "independent candidates upon the platform of the Northern or Vanlandigham [sic] democracy." He added that as near as he could tell neither one was "in favor of the war as now conducted." Nonetheless, the *Frankfort Commonwealth* hailed Anderson as an "excellent" choice, adding that "the resolutions adopted by the convention are up to the very top-mark of loyalty and determination to prosecute the war vigorously." At their convention, the Peace Democrats tapped Charles A. Wickliffe of Bardstown for governor and Trimble for congress. Like Trimble, Wickliffe was a conservative Unionist who turned against the war and Lincoln after the Emancipation Proclamation and after the military started recruiting African American troops in Kentucky.[3]

Before officially announcing his candidacy, Trimble went to Mayfield and addressed "a large crowd of traitors," for two hours, according to a lengthy letter the *Journal* printed on June 4. The author, "CONSTITUTIONAL UNION," reported that Trimble said Lincoln wanted him to take on Burnett in 1861 and that the president promised him "slavery was not to be interfered with." Thus assured, Trimble added, he agreed to run on the Union ticket. He told the crowd that Lincoln had duped him and that secessionists were right that the war was being waged "for the destruction of slavery"; he called the conflict an "abolition war." Trimble also argued that the Confederates were justified in rebelling because "they were right in their belief that it was to be a war on slavery."[4]

The writer added that Trimble did not speak "against Jeff Davis and those engaged in this wicked rebellion," and that "he was repeatedly cheered by traitors who have taken the oath to support and defend this government against all enemies." CONSTITUTIONAL UNION advised that "all parties have regarded him as a secesh for eighteen months." When asked if he would vote "men and money to prosecute the war," Trimble evaded the question, but "was understood by all present that he would not." His reply, such as it was, prompted loud cheers from "the secesh" and hisses from the Union men.

Nonetheless, Trimble found his reception in the Graves County seat so "very satisfactory, that within a week" he tossed his hat in the ring.[5]

When Trimble made a campaign stop in Mayfield on June 1, county court day, Anderson turned up. Both candidates made speeches; Anderson prodded Trimble to clarify "his sentiments in regard to furnishing means for carrying on the war." Trimble hedged, notably vexing fathers of sons in the Union army. They demanded a straight answer. Trimble put his hand in his pocket, as if preparing to pull a pistol. Unfazed, Anderson said he was not looking for trouble; he merely wanted Trimble to answer his question, and pressed his opponent again. Trimble "writhed and twisted," hesitated, then confessed he "would vote neither men nor money." When Trimble exited the speaker's platform he vowed "as he went that he was as good a Union man as anybody."[6]

Anderson got off a parting shot, coaxing Trimble to endorse the actions of the March Union convention in Louisville and support its nominees. Trimble demurred, but Anderson promised the crowd "that he was for voting the last man and dollar for putting down the rebellion." Lush's rejoinder prompted "several traitors" to interrupt him. The jeerers included his brother Ervin. But when Circuit Judge Thomas S. Marshall banged his gavel, calm ensued. A Ballard County Union man, Marshall replaced Williams on the bench. "CONSTITUTIONAL UNION" added that "traitors" were going around claiming Trimble told them that he had the blessing of the Union military to run for Congress. The correspondent was skeptical because Trimble's speech represented the "last, meanest, and most cowardly phase of secession, and one that takes from the brave soldier in the field everything that sustains him."[7]

**Lucian Anderson (National Archives and Records Administration).**

If army commanders did acquiesce in Trimble's bid for Congress, they teamed up with Union Democratic civilian leaders to make sure he and every other Peace Democrat—especially Wickliffe—would lose. The Union Democrats accused the Peace Democrats of supporting secession and shielding traitors. They replied that the Union Democrats were Lincoln puppets, a charge they vehemently denied. On July 10, Robinson issued a proclamation reminding citizens that only loyal Kentuckians could vote, and an estimated one-third of potential voters were thus kept away from the polls. Fifteen days later, Brigadier General Jeremiah T. Boyle of Danville, commander of Union forces in Kentucky, warned that casting a ballot for Wickliffe was sufficient proof of disloyalty to warrant the seizure of a voter's property. On July 31, General Ambrose E. Burnside, commander of the Department of the Ohio, which included Kentucky, declaring martial law in the state "for the purpose only of protecting, if necessary, the rights of loyal citizens and the freedom of election." He explained that Kentucky had been invaded "by a Rebel force"—meaning Morgan's cavalry—whose "avowed intention" was "overawing the judges of elections … intimidating the loyal voters, keeping them from the polls, and forcing the election of disloyal candidates." Only the army could stop such perfidy, according to Burnside. Hence, the election's outcome was assured; the only question was the magnitude of the Union landslide.[8]

In many counties, officials removed Wickliffe's name from the ballot. Likewise, they struck Trimble's name off in several First District counties. Soldiers arrested him and kept him locked up until after the election.[9]

Perhaps nowhere were soldiers more zealous in damping down the Peace Democratic vote than in the Purchase, the northernmost part of Memphis-

Ambrose E. Burnside (National Archives and Records Administration).

based Major General Stephen Hurlbut's Sixteenth Corps command area. On July 14, the general issued Special Orders 159, which ordered his troops in the Columbus District to stop any man from voting or running for office who was "not avowedly and unconditionally for the Union and the suppression of the rebellion." His decree required civilian election officers to make suspected Southern sympathizers swear a loyalty oath. Anybody who refused could not vote. On July 15, Brigadier General Alexander Asboth, the Columbus commander, told Hurlbut he had passed the order to local civilian and army authorities, warning them that soldiers would arrest violators.[10]

Even before Burnside declared martial law statewide, Hurlbut had issued Special Orders 144, which put the Purchase under such a decree. On July 6, outgoing state senator Thomas A. Duke of Paducah wrote Lincoln, expressing his disapprobation with the general's action and seeking the president's help in improving his chances at the polls. Quigley's characterization aside, Duke was running as a Union Democrat. The candidate included a newspaper clipping of Hurlbut's order, obviously figured Anderson for the "avowedly and unconditionally" Unionist candidate Union authorities wanted. Duke pleaded that the order might "be abused and missunderstood [sic] and in several Counties may be used against me by preventing my friends from giving me their support." He promised the president he had always been "a union man," but said he, Representative Casey and other "union men & candidates" rejected the Paducah convention that nominated Anderson. "These gentlemen & myself are independent Candidates for Congress," he said. Duke felt honor-bound to bring Lincoln's "attention to an order so pregnant with danger to the elective franchise." He trusted the president might modify the order to "prevent its abuse." Duke said the that the Purchase had become quieter than any other part of the state and that "the people are at home sowing that they may reap—& they will continue to do so to the end of this rebellion." He said "Designing & bad men," an evident dig at Anderson and the Union Democrats who nominated him, had "poisoned the minds of the administration" against the Purchase "from motives of interest—Selfishness alone prompted them." Duke declared that Union commanders in the region, past and present, would "testify ... that there has not been a Rebel Soldier (except those who have voluntarily returned home) in any of the Counties west of the river for Sixteen months or more." Duke's letter revealed a coming split between the conservative Union Democrats and Republican-leaning "Unconditional Unionists," like Anderson. The Unconditional Unionists would form the core of Kentucky's budding Republican party.[11]

Duke's portrait of the Purchase was not exactly accurate. The Confederate army was long gone, but guerrilla bands, sustained, or at least tolerated, by the citizenry continued to harass Union troops. Thus, it is inconceivable that Union army commanders would have deemed the Purchase pacified. On July 29, Asboth wrote his own General Orders No. 47 to ensure there were no doubts "as to the intent and meaning of Special Orders, No. 159."[12]

His edict cautioned that "no person shall be permitted to be voted for or be a candidate for office who has been or is now under arrest or bonds, by proper authority, for uttering disloyal language or sentiments." Asboth instructed county judges to appoint only "avowedly and unconditionally" Union men as election judges and clerks. They were to sack judges and clerks "who are not such loyal persons." Also, election officials were forbidden "to place the name of any person upon the poll-books to be voted for … who is not avowedly and unconditionally for the Union and the suppression of the rebellion, or who may be opposed to furnishing men and money for the suppression of the rebellion." The latter proscription was pointed squarely at Trimble, as was part of the oath that Asboth mandated for voters and candidates: "I am unconditionally for the Union and the suppression of the Rebellion, and am willing to furnish men and money for the vigorous prosecution of the war against the rebellious league known as the Confederate States." Asboth's order also promised that any voter or election officer who did not obey his order "will be arrested and sent before a military commission as soon as the facts are substantiated."[13]

Asboth mentioned the election in a July 30 dispatch he sent to Hurlbut informing corps headquarters about his anti-guerrilla sweeps in the Purchase and adjacent West Tennessee. He told Hurlbut that Anderson campaigned in Columbus the day before. Asboth also included a copy of his General Orders No. 47, explaining that the measure was necessary because "the Rebel sympathizers will struggle to elect disloyal men." On the same day, Asboth inserted election instructions in a message he sent to Colonel George E. Waring, Junior, commander of the Fourth Missouri Cavalry. He and his Show Me State horsemen were hunting guerrillas and believed to be at Feliciana. Nearby was the site of Camp Beauregard, which had been decimated by a disease epidemic before the Confederates abandoned the hard-luck outpost in 1862. Asboth included his and Hurlbut's general orders and directed the colonel to "see that the ensuing election in your neighborhood is conducted and controlled in accordance to their provisions."[14]

Covering all of his bases, Hurlbut forwarded copies of both orders to Brigadier General Napoleon Bonaparte Buford, commander at Cairo, and told him to "send one discreet, well-posted, and firm commissioned officer, with ten men" to each of three evidently suspicious voting precincts in Ballard County: McChristian's, Thorp's and Fort Jefferson. The soldiers were to have Hurlbut's and Asboth's election orders. Hurlbut told Buford that his men must be at the polls by six a.m. and that "each officer should have the assistance of a well-posted citizen of known loyalty." Hurlbut also pointed Buford to an "unofficial but authentic newspaper report" of Burnside's declaration that was apparently included in the dispatch.[15]

Three days before the election, the *Columbus War Eagle*, the town's army newspaper, cried a warning to "traitors" who would "vote for Trimble, or any other man who has not publicly avowed himself as an unconditional Union man." They would hereafter "be treated as enemies, and as men deserving on their guilty heads all the punishment which the Government has in reserve for traitors." The paper advised,

> We tell the people of the District that their only safety and protection depends on voting the straight-out Union ticket. The issue is in your hand, and on your conduct [on Election Day] ... depends your future peace and protection. When you vote for traitors, you can of course expect no protection from the Federal Government.[16]

Naturally, "the straight-out Union ticket" won statewide on August 6. Union Democrats claimed all thirty-eight senate seats and ninety-seven of one hundred house seats. All nine Union Democratic congressional candidates won handily. Anderson defeated Trimble, 4,323 to 711. Lush carried Graves 682–0.[17]

Not surprisingly, the vote was way off statewide from 1861. In the First District, Burnett beat Trimble 8,998 to 6,225. In 1863, Anderson won with 1,902 fewer votes than Trimble managed in his loss. Though Kentuckians would go to the polls to elect a president in 1864, the next election for governor, the General Assembly and Congress would not come until August, 1865, after the war was over. Meanwhile, one must wonder how Anderson felt about his win. He must have known than he owed his victory to soldiers and state authorities who denied the ballot to all but Union men.

It would be fascinating to know if Anderson agreed that the "secesh" should have been disfranchised. Did he think that the imposition of martial law and loyalty oaths for voting in his election where justified? Presumably he would have agreed that the freer an election, the freer a country. But what if a country, a representative democracy like the United States, is threatened by armed rebellion?

Article III, Section 3 of the Constitution, sometimes called "the sheet anchor of the republic," defines treason and gives the government the right to indict, try, convict and punish traitors. The trick is, of course, balancing the right of free expression on the soapbox, in a newspaper or at the ballot box against the government's right to preserve itself. Such equilibrium was never more difficult to maintain than during the Civil War, especially in the loyal border states like Kentucky, where sentiment was nonetheless divided.

Kentucky's 1850 constitution, the state charter in effect during the Civil War, also contains a treason clause. Article VIII, Section 2, defines "treason against the Commonwealth" as consisting "only in levying war against it, or in adhering to its enemies, giving them aid and comfort."

Before the Civil War ended in 1865, thousands of United States soldiers, sailors and Marines lost their lives in what the North called the War of the Rebellion. They died of disease or in battle fighting soldiers engaged in armed insurrection against a lawfully-constituted, representative democracy whose constitution clearly defined their action as treason. Never before or since the Civil War was America so imperiled. Lincoln, his generals and officials of loyal state governments were desperate to save the Union in the midst of an unprecedented war—the most lethal war American has ever fought—and with almost nothing to guide their footsteps.

# 6

# "Sound on the goose"

Though Lush won on the Union Democratic ticket, some newspapers speculated that he might ally himself with the Republicans, who called themselves the Union Caucus. "But little has been said of the Hon. Lucien Anderson, elected to Congress from the First Congressional District of Kentucky," the Republican *Evansville Daily Journal* reported the day after the canvass. "For the comfort of the [Louisville] *Journal* and *Democrat* we will inform them that he is as 'sound on the goose' as Brutus J. Clay or Green Clay Smith," two more Bluegrass congressmen-elect. Clay, from Paris, was the nephew of fiery Kentucky emancipationist Cassius Marcellus Clay. Smith was a Yankee general-turned-politician from Covington. By "sound on the goose," the Hoosier paper meant that Anderson, Clay and Smith would likely join the Union Caucus. The *Journal* and *Democrat* supported the pro-slavery Union Democrats.[1]

"In the list of members of the 38th Congress, published in our columns a few days ago, Hon. Lucian Anderson, Representative from the Kentucky 1st Congressional District, was classed a Border State man, who would go into the caucus of neither party," the *Chicago Tribune* reported on October 28, 1863. Nonetheless, the Republican paper was happy to add that it had evidently erred. "The *Ogle County* (Ill) *Reporter* says this classification does injustice to Mr. Anderson."[2]

The *Tribune* said the *Reporter*, published in Oregon, Illinois, had "good authority for saying that Mr. Anderson is an Administration man, of the most radical stripe. He is in favor of all the measures of the Administration, and will vote with the Republicans for Speaker." The *Reporter* backed up its claim by quoting from a speech Anderson made at an October 20 meeting of Unconditional Unionists at the Union League headquarters in Paducah. The congressman-elect gave "the secessionists and their sympathizers some hard blows." When he finished, the gathering passed a trio of resolutions. The first noted that Almighty God was pleased

to arm the Union men of this country with principles as strong as the everlasting hills, to successfully meet that old traitor the Devil, who has in these modern times shown himself

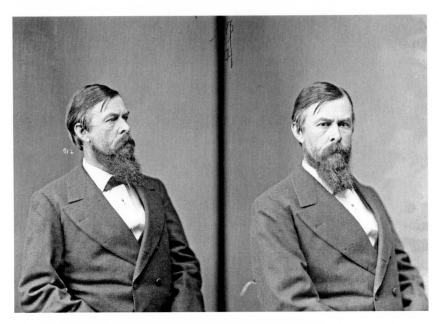

Green Clay Smith (Library of Congress).

true to his old character, to break up governments, destroy the happiness of communities and subvert free institutions.[3]

The second resolution congratulated the voters of Ohio, Pennsylvania and Iowa for defeating at the polls "Copperheadism, and all the other 'isms' combined, to destroy civil and religious liberty." Republicans commonly called anti-Lincoln and anti-war Democrats "Copperheads" for the poisonous snake. Lastly, "the true Union men of Paducah" promised to

stand by the Administration in its efforts to suppress the present unholy rebellion, and will give our support to no man who is not unconditionally for the preservation of the Union; and we now instruct our worthy Representative, Hon. L. Anderson, to vote for no man for office who is not in favor of appropriating all the means at the disposal of the Government to restore it to its former position among the nations of the earth.[4]

The *New York Times* had no doubt about the First District's congressman-to-be. "Lucian Anderson (all honor to him!) is an administration man 'up to the hub,'" the paper exulted. "He will as thoroughly sustain the war as Samuel Casey did in the last House. More, (and more honor to him!) he goes for the destruction of human Slavery, not only in his own noble State, but throughout the Republic. And Anderson will go into [the Union] caucus."[5]

Anderson probably wished he had gone to Washington sooner than November 2. Before dawn, rebel raiders galloped into Mayfield and surrounded his house close to the courthouse. The horsemen evidently were part of Colonel William Wallace Faulkner's Twelfth Kentucky Cavalry, according to the *New York Times*. The Yankee paper scorned them as "guerrillas," meaning outlaws, and claimed the host numbered "from 500 to 5,000." Five hundred was probably closer to the size of the force.[6]

If the raiders were from the Twelfth Kentucky, they were back home. Most of the horse soldiers were from the Purchase; several hailed from Graves County. At any rate, they made their presence known by torching a Mobile and Ohio railroad bridge between Columbus and Union City, Tennessee, before hitting Mayfield. While a hundred of them paid Lush an unwelcome visit, a like number called at the dwelling of a "Mr. Ballinger"—almost certainly Bolinger.[7]

The rebels abducted the congressman-elect, but Bolinger disguised himself and escaped into the darkness. After looting Mayfield of $18,000 worth of goods, the invaders demolished a construction train parked at the depot and cut the telegraph wires. Next, they concealed themselves in the woods along the railroad tracks, intending to ambush a passenger train expected at any minute from Paducah. When the train stopped at Hickory Grove Station, about six miles north of Mayfield, the conductor learned the enemy was in front of, and behind, his train. He ordered the train forward to Mayfield, but halted the locomotive and cars "several hundred yards from the depot."[8]

When the marauders surrounded the train, the conductor reportedly acquiesced in surrender. But a passenger made of sterner stuff managed to reach the locomotive. The fellow climbed into the cab, produced a pistol and threatened to shoot the engineer if he did not back up. The engineer threw the locomotive in reverse, pouring on "every pound of steam." The train chugged "with fearful rapidity down a steep grade, amid a perfect shower of musket-balls." The raiders had heaped crossties on the tracks two miles farther up the line. When the hindmost car crashed into the barricade, the whole train derailed and was "crushed into a wreck."[9]

Rebels waiting at the barrier let loose "a continuous fire" on the smashed up train. Edward Twyman, a local Union official, "received a buckshot in one leg, a large splinter was thrust through the other, and several pieces of timber fell across his body." The rebels refused him aid and would not permit anybody else to help him, the paper said. The man "remained several hours in this situation, suffering greatly from his wounds." Injured, too, were the conductor, a passenger, and the brakeman, an African American youth. In addition, the band stole $500 from a Dr. Humble, $600 from the Mayfield station agent and "robbed every one who came in their way, taking watches, money, breastpins and finger-rings."[10]

Two Union men, William H. Colley and Wesley H. Brinkley, ran away but the raiders used bloodhounds to track them down. Colley was "fearfully torn and mangled by the dogs." The rebels evidently killed Brinkley. While he tried to keep the hounds at bay, the invaders showed up and shot him, apparently fatally. Colley and Brinkley were among the few locals who donned Union blue. Colley was a private in the Paducah Battalion, First Regiment of the Capitol Guards, a home guard outfit. In April, Brinkley mustered out of the Fifteenth Kentucky Cavalry Regiment, whose men were from the Purchase and elsewhere in western Kentucky.[11]

Besides Anderson, the raiders kidnapped state Senator J.D. Landrum, a Mayfield physician, and for reasons not clear, Lush's secessionist big brother, Ervin. Surely, they knew he did not share Lush's sentiments. After suffering no casualties in the one-sided gunfight, "the miscreants" lingered around Mayfield until 8 p.m. when they rode away. They camped about eight miles from the Graves County seat before they "finally disappeared altogether."[12]

*The Times* subsequently accused the Confederates of "cooping up Anderson ... until after the organization of the House." But Bolinger thwarted their plans, according to the paper. No sooner was Anderson captured than Bolinger "went to work to effect the arrest of a squad of prominent Kentucky and Tennessee traitors," thus bringing Lush's captors "to terms." The rebels agreed to exchange Lush for Missouri Confederate Congressman Trusten Polk, whom the Yankees were holding on Johnson's Island in Lake Erie, near Sandusky, Ohio. "Consent to the swap was cheerfully given by our Government, and Luce [sic] Anderson was at Paducah [on November 22] ... on his way to Washington." The rebels apparently released Ervin and Landrum.[13]

The *Chicago Tribune* provided its readers an eyewitness account of the raid from a Mayfield merchant who fled to the Union army at Cairo, arriving on November 6. He said the "guerrillas" robbed him, adding that the foe, "five hundred in number, under Faulkner and Newsom," galloped into town about 4 a.m. They "surrounded the residences of Hon. Lucian Anderson, M.C. elect, and J.T. Bolinger, placing one hundred men around each place. Bolinger managed to escape but Anderson, less fortunate, fell into the hands of the enemy."[14]

The *Tribune* story paralleled the *Times* story, reporting that the invaders cut the telegraph wire, thus preventing "any knowledge of the raid reaching Paducah." Afterwards, the Confederates sacked the town. "Every store ... was broken open, and goods to the value of $18,000 stolen." Either some of the attackers were local men who knew where Unionist families lived, or Mayfield secessionists pointed out Unionist dwellings because the paper said "the houses of Union men were entered and plundered of all their valuables, and many indignities offered unresisting citizens." The storekeeper also told about the train wreck, in which several passengers were badly hurt. "While endeavoring to extricate themselves ... marauders came upon them, presenting pistols to their heads, and compelling them to give up money, watches, &c." The

*Tribune* also said Twyman suffered "a buckshot wound in the leg," according to the merchant who claimed that when the train wrecked, "a large splinter was thrust through the other leg, and several pieces of timber fell upon him." Though Twyman was seriously injured, the Confederates "prevented aid from being rendered him, and he remained several hours in this situation, suffering greatly from his wounds." The rebels relieved the station agent of $600 and Humble of $500.[15]

The rebels stayed in town until 3 p.m., when they rode off toward Paducah. They were back in Mayfield at 10 p.m., before departing and camping for the night eight miles north of the county seat. The merchant said that several of the rebels came from Ballard and McCracken counties and that some were "sons of residents of Paducah." They left Mayfield and headed south through Henry and Carroll counties in Tennessee. "They had with them a pack of blood-hounds, and used them on the march to hunt up Union men, whom they inhumanely murdered when they caught them." The storekeeper said that besides Lush, the raiders also grabbed Ervin and Landrum. The merchant said he heard that the rebels planned to exchange Anderson for Polk.[16]

Word of Lush's abduction spread as far as Union-occupied New Orleans. The *Times-Picayune* published a dispatch from its Cairo correspondent who wrote that military authorities permitted attorney William R. Corbitt to go and seek the release of Anderson and Landrum. (The rebels evidently had already released Ervin.) The lawyer "and a few friends" met Faulkner under a flag of truce at McLemoresville, Tennessee. "The interview was successful, and he returned under escort of fifty rebels, some arrangements to be completed." The paper added that the hostages were freed on November 15. The *New Orleans True Delta* published a similar story filed from Cairo, but it said the hostages the Yankees took included Faulkner's brother and brother-in-law.[17]

The *Evansville Journal* published Anderson's account of his capture. Presumably, he was on his way to Washington and spoke to a reporter when the Ohio River steamboat he was riding stopped at the Hoosier State's southernmost city. On November 30, he gave a local scribe "some interesting particulars of his late capture." Anderson confirmed that Faulkner led the raiders and that they carried him, Landrum and some other prisoners as far south as Jackson, Tennessee. Anderson said his abductors "were divided into several predatory bands, numbered in all about 3,000 men, many of whom were poorly armed and some without arms." He said Faulkner's force lacked artillery. "It was their policy to avoid a fight, unless they outnumber their opponents eight or ten to one," the paper maintained, adding that their mission was to conscript "peaceable citizens" into Confederate service and rob civilians. "They appeared to be apt practitioners in their profession."[18]

The Confederates treated their prisoners "with all respect until Faulkner ascertained that his own father-in-law and other prominent secessionists had been seized by the Union authorities and confirmed as hostages for the safe return of Mr. Anderson and party." Afterwards, the captives "were treated with more severity," though the colonel said "it gave him great pain to use them ill." Yet he felt "compelled to retaliate on them" because of "the usage his friends were receiving at the hands of the Federal authorities." Anderson thought "the retaliation dodge" a bit odd since "Faulkner had commenced the game of seizing civilians."[19]

The congressman-elect confirmed that the Confederates—the Evansville paper also called them "guerrillas"—used bloodhounds to hunt Union sympathizers "for the purpose of forcing them into the Rebel army." Anderson said he spoke to "conscripts who had been chased, caught and lacerated by them, their wounds being yet unhealed." According to the Hoosier paper, "it is enough to freeze one's blood to read of such atrocity." Nonetheless, at one point, Faulkner allowed Anderson to walk freely about the Confederate camp. "He made no concealment of his views, but talked to the men plainly of their rebellion against the best Government the world ever saw, and pointed out to them how the thing was likely to end," the paper said.[20]

The *Journal* claimed "the men listened to him patiently, and seemed to be impressed with the truth of his statements." A lieutenant even invited Anderson to give the men a pro–Union speech. Lush agreed, but only with Faulkner's blessing. When the junior officer sough the colonel's permission, "Faulkner became greatly enraged, and placed the lieutenant under arrest, and revoked Mr. Anderson's parole."[21]

Anderson's release also made the *Cincinnati Gazette* of November 19. One of the paper's Paducah correspondents was happy to pass on "the gratifying intelligence of" Lush's early release.

> A telegram was received here on yesterday from Gen. A.S. Smith at Columbus, Ky., commanding this military district, ordering the release of several well known and prominent Rebel sympathizers, who had been arrested, and were held as hostages for Mr. Anderson, in view of his release by the Rebels holding him at Poplar Corners, Madison county, Tenn., [Jackson is the seat].... The news was confirmed this morning by Union citizens direct from Columbus, Ky.

The writer said soldiers at Columbus, Paducah and Union City, Tennessee, were rounding up "Rebels and Rebel sympathizers so fast, as hostages for him, that it alarmed the Rebels, and 'brought them to their milk.'" He added that the Confederates were warned "that if they did not release Anderson it would cause one-third of the citizens of Graves county, Ky. (Mr. Anderson's county) to be arrested and held as hostages for him."[22]

Anderson's trip to the capital was evidently uneventful. He likely continued on by steamboat to Pittsburgh, where he probably caught a train to Washington. The papers did not say if Ann and the children were with him.

While the other papers praised Lush, the *Cairo Democrat* pilloried

Bolinger, claiming the purported patriot was smuggling medicine to the rebels. The paper also implied that he was in cahoots with Anderson. The Louisville *Democrat*—now a "Peace Democrat" paper—gleefully reprinted the story on December 3, prefacing it with a swipe at the congressman-elect:

It seems the patriots down in Lucien Anderson's district are well rewarded; and it is hinted the Hon. "Lush" himself is not exempt from those delicate failings of frail mortality which in the general deluge of all things find the Treasury plank the safest one to ride on into quiet waters.[23]

The *Democrat* quoted the article extensively. The paper apparently published Bolinger's denial, mocking, "No doubt, most infamous John, you gloat and brood over the idea of that 'good time coming' when you, Lush. Anderson and the like, shall have undisputed sway." The Louisville paper added,

That is what we call neat and not at all gaudy. We might almost call it personal. But there is more of it, and it rejoices us to give more of this refreshing language. After defending the loyalty of the citizens of Paducah, and declaring that its citizens should not suffer, the [Cairo Democrat] ... continues to address Mr. Bolinger " [and his] cowardly slanders upon those who, like ourself, were serving the Government in good faith—our only sin being, perhaps, that we considered the rules and regulations of the Government made for the observance of all loyal citizens, and not for the exclusive benefit of such men as you, Lush. Anderson, and others who wish to make this wretched war the stepping-stone to fortune; who substitute gain for patriotism; who are continually talking war, but never laying their shoulder to a wheel; good *money-making patriots*, who profess to believe that their pretended Unionism entitles them to disregard all laws that stand in their way to preferment, and to denounce all who are governed by such old fogy institutions as statute laws as "d——d traitors!"[24]

The paper found it "strange that there are other good money-making patriots in other quarters beside that garden spot touched by the river Ohio, and curtained by the blue skies of Paducah. Even up our way we learn there are some." After declaring that Bolinger moved from "Virginia for Virginia's good," the Cairo paper lowered the boom on Anderson's ally. "...We never charged that you smuggled quinine in a dry-goods box. We charged that you had smuggled two hundred ounces of quinine into Paducah, and, of course, smuggled it out again." The paper repeated its accusation and demanded an investigation."[25]

Bolinger evidently claimed he got a shipping permit from Warren Thornberry, apparently a local Union official. "Mr. T. authorizes us to say that he never gave a permit to any person for such an amount of quinine to Paducah or elsewhere," the *Cairo Democrat* countered.

We learn that the veracious John exhibits a bill of purchase from some Philadelphia house, for two hundred ounces of quinine, twenty five ounces of morphine, and twenty-five pounds of iodine of potash. Now who recommended you, John, for this purchase?[26]

Obviously, the Cairo paper insinuated that the goods were destined for the Confederacy, where they were in short supply and vital to the war effort. Quinine was used to treat malaria. Morphine was a potent painkiller and iodine an antiseptic for treating wounds. The idea that Bolinger was trading with the enemy seems absurd. After all, the rebels had imprisoned him in Columbus earlier in the war. The fact that the *Louisville Democrat* republished what were almost certainly false charges against Bolinger suggests that the paper would stop at nothing to discredit him and Lush.[27]

The *Cairo Democrat* maintained that Bolinger knew

> what the rule has been in such cases since the occupation of Paducah by the Federal forces. Who was it, John? John, what did you want with two hundred ounces of Quinine? For the largest drug store in Paducah one hundred ounces at a time is an extra large amount. Ten ounces of morphine and ten pounds of iodine of potash is also a large bill for a Paducah wholesale drug house to make at one time. What are you doing with such articles, John Thomas?[28]

The Cairo paper claimed "there were two drug stores in Mayfield, which it is fair to presume supplied the legitimate demand for all such articles. But these drug stores were compelled to deposit all their supplies of contraband articles in Paducah, and only take to Mayfield ten ounces of quinine and other contraband articles in proportion." In connection with this Philadelphia purchase order, the paper claimed Bolinger had a permit from Thornberry to take a half-barrel of whiskey and three boxes of drugs from Paducah to Mayfield. "The books of the customhouse show no such shipment of quinine, morphine, &c.," the paper claimed. "But we do not wish to be considered as defending or excusing Mr. Thornberry. He is amply able to explain his official acts, and to defend himself. We certainly have no incentive to do either for him."[29]

The *Cairo Democrat* was prepared to inform Bolinger that it knew

> when fifty ounces of quinine was sold by his house in Mayfield, the larger portion of which is yet in the possession of the purchaser—but it is no fault of yours, *patriotic* John, that it was not long since in Rebeldom. Do call for that *strict investigation* you threaten, John! We are anxious for it. With this we bid you "good evening," John.[30]

The *Louisville Democrat* poured on the sarcasm. The editors were curious

> about that quinine ourselves. We are stricken with alarm at the awful prevalence of the chills and fever in Lucien Anderson's district. Until it is explained we are seriously afraid that no steamer ought to leave Paducah without a clear bill of health. How do we know but it was used to allay the dreadful visitations of the yellow fever or some other fearful contagious disease? We would not be understood as believing all of these grave charges with all of data and facts given to support them.[31]

The *Democrat* conceded that

> we have heard only one side so far. But we boldly assume that, if Mr. Bolinger has made a profit by his loyalty even by smuggling contraband goods South, he was right. In the first

place, he is understood to be a loyal man of the pure Administration stripe, and if the patriots are not to have the profits, we ask who are to be rewarded? It is as plain as the old Connecticut fathers, who resolved—first, the land and the fullness thereof belongs to the saints; second, we are the saints.

The paper hoped to learn more about the controversy. "There is a downrightness about the way in which both sides fling out hard words worthy of commendation in these days of courtesy and sham, and we wish to hear further that the golden, or greenback, shower is falling upon the chosen of Israel."[32]

While Bolinger was catching heat back home, Lush was settling in at Washington. The guessing over how he would line up ended on the night of December 5 when he arrived at a meeting of the Union Caucus. He was among a handful of border state lawmakers, including Green Clay Smith, at the gathering which attracted seventy-two freshmen and re-elected House members. Brutus J. Clay and fellow Kentucky freshmen George H. Yeaman of Owensboro and William H. Randall of London, were absent. But they were "regarded as strong Unionists" who apparently could be "counted on as being certain to sustain the proposed Union and Administration organization," according to the *Washington Evening Star*. The paper did not know "what kept the rest of the Kentucky delegation away, elected as they all were, upon an emphatic Union platform." The *Star* reported that freshman Robert Mallory of New Castle, Kentucky, "the border state whig—not Democrat" was reportedly "the opposition" choice for speaker. "The certainty that [Indiana Republican] Schuyler Colfax will receive the support of the large array of border State members we name above, however, makes it sure that there can be no other than a filibustering opposition to his election."[33]

On December 7, the day Congress convened, Anderson voted for Colfax, who easily won the job. Brutus Junius Clay of Paris, Cassius Clay's brother,

**Robert Mallory (Library of Congress).**

Randall and Smith also backed Colfax, who fended off seven challengers, including Mallory, who won on the Union Democrat ticket. Kentucky's other four representatives—freshman Yeaman and second-termers, Benjamin Grider of Bowling Green and William H. Wadsworth of Maysville and Aaron Harding of Greensburg, voted for Mallory, who did not vote.[34]

Predictably, the *Louisville Journal* and *Louisville Democrat* disdained the Kentucky backers of Colfax, a staunch abolitionist. The *Journal* argued that Anderson, Randall and Smith ran on a platform with a resolution denouncing the Emancipation Proclamation as "unwise, unconstitutional, and void." The paper charged that "Anderson and Randall were nominated expressly on this platform while Smith and Clay expressly and formally indorsed the platform subsequently to their nomination." All four were "elected on a distinct and solemn pledge that they would act in Congress against the radicals and not with them." None of the freshmen congressmen "could have been elected without giving such a pledge tacitly or expressly."[35]

The *Journal* deemed "further remark … painful as well as unnecessary" and was willing to "hand over the delinquents to the tender mercies of their constituents and of the public." In the meantime, the paper warned that "all are not conservative Unionists who profess to be, and that a sterner and more searching test of political character must be applied hereafter if we would not be deceived in the future as we have been in the past."[36]

The *Democrat* chimed in on the *Journal*'s side, singling out Anderson, Clay and Smith for ridicule. "We see 'Lush' Anderson voted for the Republican candidate for Speaker," the paper reported. "If the Cairo Democrat is right, he is on a fair way for a 'Lushious' time." After Clay's vote, "Kentucky may well exclaim, '*Et tu, brute!*,'" according to the *Democrat*. The paper also scorned Smith, claiming "such a contradictory name as that, where the Smith can't mold the Green Clay, or the Clay make anything of the Green Smith, or anything Green grow out of Clay, but such a vote a different course could not be expected."[37]

The *Democrat* also collectively denounced the pro–Colfax quartet, claiming they were really Republicans.

> If these four representatives in Congress from this State had told their people that they intended to act with the Republican party as they have done, they might have been elected, for ought we know, by the means employed at the last August election; but we do not believe they represent a majority of their districts.

The paper figured their votes surprised their allies elsewhere in the state. "If we had foretold what they would do, and which we thought they were as likely to do as not, we should have been written down as a slanderer of the faithful." According to the *Democrat*, "the Republicans claimed the Union party of Kentucky, and rejoiced over the signs of the times, as they understood them. We believed they were not altogether mistaken, and the result shows they were not."[38]

The Louisville paper argued, "The fact is, there is a Republican party in Kentucky, and they have four out of the nine representatives in Congress; and it is not to be disguised that they represent a considerable party at home." The *Democrat* would not

> deny any man's right to entertain, discuss and vote any opinions he pleases; but we insist upon it that he is bound to say out what he means; not to leave people in doubt, or take them by surprise. That is the meanest kind of treason. It produces nothing but complications, embarrassment and difficulty. This thing of putting platforms before the world, and then stultifying the people by spitting on their own professions of principle![39]

The *Democrat* kept hammering away at the four lawmakers the paper considered turncoats to Kentucky.

> Who would expect that a man, who had solemnly adopted the resolutions of the Union party in this State, should signalize his advent to power by giving his first vote for the Speaker of a party radically opposed to every sentiment of that platform? What faith is to be put in politicians who play such tricks?[40]

The *Democrat* conceded that Anderson, Clay, Randall and Smith possibly "know their constituents better than we do." The implication, of course, was that the *Democrat* really knew best. The paper challenged the four, "Why can't they say what they are—that they are Republicans? What are they afraid of? After this vote, we presume, they will be understood, and they had as well begin now to be honest."[41]

Seven days later, the Democratic *Cincinnati Enquirer* linked Anderson, Clay, Randall and Smith to abolitionism. "It is a fact considerably commented on here, that Kentucky has in Congress four abolitionists ... as was evinced by their vote for Colfax."[42]

Nonetheless, Anderson's vote earned him some good press in the *Cleveland Morning Leader*. The Buckeye State paper pilloried the *Louisville Journal* for scorning Lush and the other Kentuckians who supported Colfax. "It is the whirlwind blast of free thought, dashing to earth the proud superstructure of an insolent oligarchy, that tells Clay and Smith, Randall and Anderson" and other border state Unconditional Unionists "that in standing by the side of freedom they listen to the tumultuous beatings of the great popular heart of the Border States." These men

> know what demon it is that has wrought such ruin manifold upon the South wherever the scourging terrors of war have gone. They know that a union reconstructed with the virus of slavery yet residing in its life, would only renew the devastation and bloodshed it has brought upon the land.

The border state Unionists

have no soft words or gentle feelings for the men who have plunged the fair heritage of their State into this wretched civil war. We prophesy that it will really be refreshing to anti-slavery men in the North, to see a zeal of "new converts," as the journal styles them, which will be but the ushering in of a bright millennial morn to all that border land where freedom is to realize her proudest triumphs.[43]

Likewise, the *Chicago Tribune,* lauded Lush and other border state Unionists in a long article. The Republican paper praised "Winter Davis, and Gratz Brown, and Lucien Anderson, and the men who, with them, are coming out of the prison-house of bondage, having shaken their garments clear of all its defilements and are bending their energies to pull down the whole accursed fabric of oppression." In 1863, Maryland voters elected Henry Winter Davis to the House and the Missouri legislature sent Benjamin Gratz Brown, a Kentucky native, to the U.S. Senate.[44]

The *Tribune* told its readers that for three years it had been accustomed to viewing border state politicians like Anderson "as a distinct class, having interests and aims considerably different from any other party." Other Republican organs probably shared the Chicago paper's opinion, that the border state men

occupied a post which might well enough be designated as the Half-way house to Rebellion. They opposed secession, to be sure; but then they wanted to hold onto that which was the life and soul of Secession. Their God was slavery; but they preferred slavery in the Union—as who but one stark mad, as the Rebels *are,* would not?[45]

The simultaneously pro–Union and pro-slavery men "have constituted, in fact, a sort of Slavery Protection Society," the *Tribune* charged. "Their natural allies have been our Northern Copperheads, from whom they scarcely differ by a single shade." Borderland parties like the Union Democrats were "natural enough in the beginning of the war. Nothing was more natural than that the Border States should cherish the hope of being able to hold onto slavery. Their interests—or supposed interests—blinded them to the fact that slavery was the cause of all the trouble." Or the border state leaders realized slavery "did provoke the war." But "they cherished a selfish hope of being able to get through the war and keep the institution tolerably safe."[46]

The *Tribune* said the border states

have been the stamping ground of the war.... The people have seen—are seeing—that to keep old things through such eras of change is simply impossible. The antediluvians might have well have thought to save their sugar through Noah's flood. You cannot set up a foundry in a powder-house without some risk to one institution at least. The result is that our Border State men, as such, are evaporating.... The Border State party will disappear.[47]

The paper predicted that some "benighted" border state citizens would elect candidates who would become Democrats. "But, in the main, it can scarcely be doubted, that the Border States will be found with the party of progress; and their men, instead of holding on to the caudal end of it, and thus being pulled along, will be in the advance and lead it." In other words, men like Davis, Anderson and Brown would steer states like Maryland, Kentucky and Missouri to the Republican party.[48]

"What we see beginning in Maryland, in Missouri, in Tennessee, and even in Kentucky, will go on," the *Tribune* argued.

> Slavery being dead, there will be haste to bury it quickly out of sight, as so much carrion, offensive both to the eye and olfaction. To our Northern conservatives, such men will seem dreadfully radical. Their idea would be, to keep the dead carcass as long as possible, to look at and smell of; as it were so much rosewater. But those who live in the neighborhood know better. Let the earth cover it, and the grass will grow all the greener, and the flowers more plenty and gorgeous for its burial.[49]

By backing Colfax, Anderson found at least one friend in the press back home. The army paper at Columbus lauded Lush. "Again we say, Bully for Anderson!" The *War Eagle* exclaimed on December 12. On Christmas Eve, the *New York Times* quoted the Frankfort correspondent of the *Cincinnati Commercial*: "A majority of the members from Hon. Lucien Anderson's district have signed a statement that his cooperation with the Republicans, and his vote for Colfax is not inconsistent with his principles and professions at home, and will meet the approval of his constituents." Neither *The Times* nor the *Commercial* provided details of the "statement." Given the political proclivities of the district, it seems doubtful the story was true. The *Times* and *Commercial* were ardently Republican. Civil War newspapers North and South were given to stretching the truth to suit their side.[50]

On December 30, Lush offered more proof of how far he had strayed from the conservative Democratic flock. He addressed the Union League and "emphatically indorsed the President's emancipation policy." Headquartered in Washington, the league was essentially an auxiliary of the Republican party with branches throughout the north. In several states, the Republicans were calling themselves the Union party, implying that the Democrats were the disunion party. At any rate, Anderson "made a witty, patriotic, and highly interesting speech" to a large crowd in the capital city. Green Clay Smith spoke after Lush and "fully indorsed all that his colleague had uttered."[51]

In concluding his remarks, Lush said "there was no peace he would regard as peace, until the dark spot, the black institution of slavery, was wiped from every state of this government," reported the *Orleans Independent Standard* of Irasburg, Vermont. "He was not willing either that the great mass of the people of the South found in arms should exercise the same political power with the Union men, and he was in favor that all those should be served as the sinners are at the Methodist camp meeting, that they should take the back seats." Speaking of his home state, Anderson "could only say that when the voice of the people was unbridled, then would her sons be found standing side by side with those of the States of the North." The *Independent Standard* characterized Lush's address as "an emphatic endorsement of the president's emancipation policy, and the humor of it was only exceeded by its patriotism."[52]

Anderson also got a boost from the *Belmont Chronicle*, published in St. Clairesville, Ohio.

> The law of Kentucky regards every black man within her borders as a slave until the contrary is proved.... This is a beautiful system, which would enslave a freeman simply on account of his color. A few such occurrences at this time, when thousands of black men are fighting to save Kentucky from the devastating march of her enemies, will create such a whirlpool of public sentiment against the accursed institution that the efforts of Kentucky's noble son, Anderson, and his coadjutors, to sweep the blot from the State will be crowned with success at a very early day.[53]

Lush, Smith and Randall were Union Democrats in name only. By their actions and boldness, the trio had cleared a path for everybody who wanted to break with the party. In each of their home counties, men organized themselves into groups that would form the vanguard of the Unconditional Unionist Party. Such a band huddled at Lush's house on New Year's Day.[54]

Not surprisingly, the *Journal,* still straining to dig Anderson's political grave, ridiculed the meeting in a long story published on January 14. The state's chief Union Democratic organ reminded its readers that "Mr. Anderson's first act as a Representative was to go into the abolition caucus at Washington; and his second act was to vote for the abolition candidate for the Speakership." According to the paper, Lush "has been acting with the abolitionists ever since." The *Journal* claimed that

> he is now confessedly a regular abolitionist in particularly good standing. The last time we heard of him, he was under engagement to address one of the abolition conclaves, styled Loyal Leagues; and we have no doubt, that, more faithful to his new allies than to his constituents, he redeemed his engagement. Apostates, in the first flush of their apostasy, are seldom wanting in eagerness.[55]

The *Journal* story kept after Anderson, lampooned the January 1 meeting in which the paper claimed "The Six Radicals of Graves" professed their "abiding confidence" in Anderson's "patriotism" and pledged to "sustain him in the best and most practicable mode of subduing the Rebellion and sustaining the Government." The paper reminded its readers of the resolutions the state Union Democratic convention approved in March, 1863, notably the one that endorsed the legislature's denunciation of the Emancipation Proclamation "unwise, unconstitutional, and void."[56]

The *Journal* also quoted Lush who, two days after his nomination, declared

I am opposed to the policy of the Administration.... The President and his advisers are not the government; the term of office is of short duration; and the time will come, if we are true to ourselves, when their places will be filled with other men,—when a conservative Executive and Congress, under the Constitution as still the supreme law of the land, will annul all unconstitutional legislation, illegal edicts and proclamations.

The paper remembered that First District Union Democrats nominated him as a candidate who was "neither contaminated with secessionism or abolitionism." The paper charged that after he made common cause with the Republicans, two of "his associates in apostasy" attempted to organize a meeting in Mayfield "to endorse his conduct." After "privately beating up for attendants some ten or fifteen days in all parts of the county, this brace of enterprising radicals succeeded finally" in organizing the January 1 gathering.[57]

Between twenty and twenty-five Union men showed up but only a half-dozen participated "in the proceedings, and, of these six, one refused to vote for the resolution in question," according to the *Journal*. The paper reported that right before the pro–Anderson resolutions were to be voted on, a man wanted to know if they were meant "to represent the sentiment of the Union men of Graves." Lush, "the master-spirit," explained, "No, they are intended to represent only this meeting." Forthwith, "the meeting of six" adopted the resolutions. "And yet this sexangular concern has had the effrontery to put forth its proceedings in the name of the Union men of Graves." The *Journal* sneered

When the Three Tailors of Tooley Street met and resolved in the name of the people of England, the thing was very generally looked upon as rather brazen; and so it was no doubt for that age and clime. "But," as Gregory says to Sir Jasper in the farce of The Mock Doctor, "we have changed all that." The Three Tailors of Tooley Street would be accounted very unassuming craftsmen in our time and country. Compared with the Six Radicals of Graves, the Three Tailors of Tooley Street were not only modest but shy and shamefaced.[58]

The pro–Union *Frankfort Tri-Weekly Commonwealth* also reported on the January 1 meeting but spared the vitriol. Lawyer J.S. Lindsey chaired the gathering and W.A. Turner took notes as secretary. Judge Williams spoke to the assemblage, confessing, "it had been a time honored custom in Kentucky, for those occupying judicial stations, to refrain from commingling in political strifes, and nothing but the gravest reasons would justify a departure from this custom." Nonetheless, Williams argued that

when a question of the existence of the Government was forced on the country by a Rebellion of vast magnitude, a departure was not only justified, but emperiously demanded of every citizen, especially of every officer ... to use every legitimate exertion, publicly and privately, to sustain that government.[59]

After Williams denounced the rebellion, James B. Happy, another Anderson ally, offered five resolutions, all of which passed unanimously except the third one, which prompted a single nay vote. The first resolution declared that "it is the paramount duty of every citizen to give the Government an unconditional loyalty." The second one urged the legislature to wait until after the 1864 presidential election to elect a U.S. senator. Resolution three praised Bramlette and expressed pleasure at the prospect of his being "elevated to the United States senate." The fourth resolution expressed "an abiding confidence in the patriotism of our Representative in Congress, the Hon. L. Anderson, and we shall sustain him in the best and most practical mode in subduing the Rebellion and sustaining the Government." The last resolution asked the *Journal* and the *Cincinnati Gazette* and *Cincinnati Commercial* "to publish these proceedings." The *Commonwealth* did not refer to the size of the gathering, simply describing it as "a meeting of the Union men of Graves County, Kentucky."[60]

Thus, the First District's Union Democrats dumped the Republican-leaning Casey for the "conservative" Anderson, who had turned out to be an anti-slavery man. It doubly ironic; another Republican sympathizer was representing the Purchase, the "South Carolina of Kentucky" in Washington. Perhaps the *Journal* was especially hard on Anderson because he had been one of the paper's favorites—one of the few courageous Unionists in the traitorous Purchase. Yet Anderson the fearless had made himself Anderson the feckless, according to the January 14 *Journal*. Less than three months earlier, the paper had rushed to Lush's defense when a rumor spread that the congressman would vote for Colfax over Mallory. The *Journal* claimed the rumor was untrue, reminding its readers that Anderson "was expressly nominated on the platform of the Union party of Kentucky."[61]

Lush endorsed the platform with its anti–Emancipation Proclamation plank and stood on it for the campaign, according to the Louisville paper. "We indeed have never seen any declaration of political opinion from Mr. Anderson wherein he did not equally denounce the abolitionists and the secessionists," the *Journal* said, dismissing the claim that Anderson would support Colfax over Mallory as "a gross insult not merely to Mr. Anderson but to every Kentuckian." Yet when Anderson voted for Colfax, he made the *Journal* into his avowed enemy.[62]

Meanwhile, Anderson claimed Uncle Sam was unwittingly helping the rebel enemy by removing trade restrictions on Kentucky. On January 8, the treasury department announced "that all products and goods might be 'freely taken into and transplanted within the state as in time of peace.'" The move seemed to make sense. By 1864, the major battles and campaigns were miles away from Kentucky. Thus, it seemed to be safe to return free trade to the Bluegrass State. Anderson disagreed in a January 29 letter he wrote to Secretary of the Treasury Secretary Salmon P. Chase. The congressman argued that the change in policy was bound to dash "the hopes of the Union men, especially in my district." He claimed free trade was "what the Rebels want." Lush maintained that without trade restrictions, "the Rebels will be supplied with every thing they desire, which will go into the houses of Rebels in their army."[63]

Before January was over, Lush was lambasted again in newsprint, this time in *The Congressional Globe.* A face-to-face confrontation followed. Anderson never would have admitted it in public but he surely knew he owed his election to Union troops who, with the blessing of the state's Unionist government, kept many Southern sympathizers, real and suspected, from voting. Representative William J. Allen, a Tennessee-born, anti-war southern Illinois Democrat from Marion, unabashedly challenged the legitimacy of Anderson's election.[64]

Only the width of the Ohio River separated the southernmost counties in Allen's district, which was dubbed "Egypt" for reasons not certain. But the two lawmakers were not friendly neighbors. In a January 26 speech printed in the *Globe*, Allen insulted Anderson, dismissing him as "one of the president's military appointees." Anderson said he was ailing, abed and was not in the House chamber when the southern Illinoisan delivered his remarks.

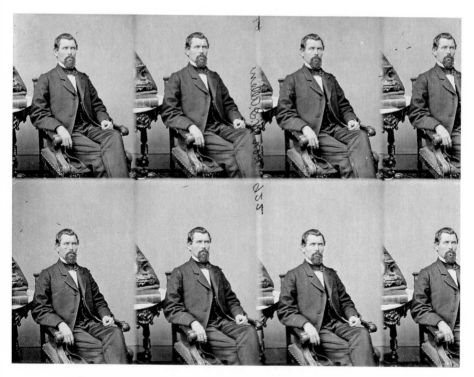

William J. Allen (National Archives and Records Administration).

But on February 2, the western Kentuckian had recovered enough to rebuke Allen on the House floor. Anderson said he was "totally unacquainted with" Allen but decried his comments "as false and slanderous, without any foundation in fact." Anderson insisted he

> was elected by ... true, unflinching, sturdy Union men ... not professed Union men, but Union men who have been tried by the fires of persecution, Union men who have come of this rebellion with unspotted garments ... Union men who have been robbed and plundered, who have been imprisoned, Union men who have been hunted with hellhound ferocity by the rebels in arms against this Government, and who seem to have an apologist upon this floor to-day in the person of the gentleman from Illinois.[65]

Lush said Allen knew that in January, 1862, First District secessionists elected Burnett to the Confederate congress. Unionists spurned the election as treasonous, Anderson added. He said the same men who voted for Burnett returned the polls in 1863 "to send a rebel and traitor to the Congress of the United States" but were kept from voting because they were disloyal. Thus, First District "Union men ... have secured the indignation of the gentleman from Illinois," Anderson said. "They were denounced simply because those rebels and traitors were not permitted to go to the ballot-box side-by-side with the Union men."[66]

Furthermore, Anderson argued, the Kentucky Court of Appeals upheld the legality of his election. "The gentleman from Illinois pretends to the friend of Union men in the border States," Lush challenged. "He makes the declaration that he is an unconditional Union man." The House—at least the Republican side—laughed when Anderson proposed, "If it had not been for that declaration, made over and over again by the gentleman in his speech, I would have thought that it was one made in the so-called confederate congress in Richmond." More laughter followed when Anderson declared that Allen, not satisfied with declaiming western Kentucky Unionists, also castigated a trio of Tennessee Unionists—Military governor Andrew Johnson, attorney general Horace Maynard and newspaper editor "Parson" William G. Brownlow—and scorned Andrew Jackson Hamilton, Texas' military governor whose office was in Union-occupied New Orleans. "Why, sir, they stand in loyalty as far above the gentleman from Illinois as heaven is above hell."[67]

Allen's temper flared; so did Anderson's. Lush kept on insinuating that Allen was less than loyal. Allen stuck to his charge that Lush's election was fraudulent. The former challenged the latter to deny that Trimble was under military arrest until after the election because "he was a candidate in opposition to" Anderson. When Anderson tried to explain, Allen said he could have the floor after he was through. Lush demurred and awaited his chance.[68]

"He says that the Union people of southern Kentucky elected him," Allen jeered, "The Union people! The bayonets were the Union people that elected him." Allen admitted he had not seen the election returns. But he "would be somewhat curious to see how many votes the member received, although his chief competitor was held in bonds, surrounded by a guard." Allen, alluding to Anderson's kidnapping and release by the rebels, jabbed that the congressman

> has had some experience of the kind, and that it is to the good offices of a system of exchange that he owes the opportunity of being able to circulate freely in this Hall to-day and maintain his subserviency to his masters and his contempt for the popular will of his district.

Allen asserted that throughout Egypt, "it is well known that the election in Kentucky was a mere farce; everybody so speaks of it, especially in that *Union portion* of Kentucky the member hails from." Even though Anderson was a Colfax ally, the speaker stopped the feud before Anderson could reply to Allen. Yet the Kentuckian did fire a parting shot: "I did not intend to carry the war to Africa, but only into Egypt, from which the gentleman from Illinois comes."[69]

# 7

# Denouncer of Democrats

Though Lush Anderson quickly allied himself with the Republicans in Congress, his shift toward abolitionism was gradual, much like Lincoln's. Both men tried to balance their principles with what they considered practical politics. The Emancipation Proclamation did not end slavery in the border states or in Union-controlled Confederate territory on January 1, 1863. The president worried that if he wiped out slavery everywhere and all at once, he would antagonize the border slave states and possibly spark rebellion in them. He was deeply unpopular in Kentucky. Likewise, Anderson understood that he owed his election to Union men who had slaves and to non-slaveholding Unionists who were pro-slavery. Almost certainly, the majority of Unionists in the First District were conservative, pro-war and pro-slavery Union Democrats. At the same time, Lush must have known all too well that most of his constituents were Peace Democrats or outright secessionists, with the latter group holding sway in the Purchase. Surely, he understood, too, that he alienated even more voters when he joined the Republican caucus.

Anderson believed slavery would not survive the war, but at first he tried to safeguard the interests of slaveholding Union Democrats. So he endorsed compensated emancipation, but only for loyal slaveholders and only if the Kentucky legislature abolished slavery. On January 25, he introduced a resolution directing the House Committee on Emancipation "to inquire into the expediency of providing for compensation to loyal owners of slaves in [Kentucky] ... in the event a system of emancipation be adopted by the people thereof, and that said committee report by bill or otherwise." Anderson's proposal recognized that Lincoln had "heretofore recommended that Congress make an appropriation to compensate the loyal owners of slaves in the State of Kentucky in the event the people of that State should adopt a system of emancipation." The resolution noted that the Kentucky legislature was in session and that

it is believed the institution of slavery in said State has become so endangered and precarious in consequence of the present war, forced on the Government of the United States by the disunionists and traitors of the South [and] ... that it would be to the interest of the people of Kentucky to accept compensated emancipation.

It is inconceivable that the General Assembly would have agreed to any proposal leading to slavery's demise. Lush's proposal went for naught.[1]

Not surprisingly, Anderson's growing opposition to slavery further angered the homefolks, even Union men. On February 26, the *Journal* boasted that "a club of subscribers from Mayfield" had sent a letter denouncing Lush. "Whatever a few radicals may say or do in the way of endorsing and whitewashing Lucian Anderson, he is repudiated by the mass of the truly loyal men of this county, and the position of your noble Journal approved," wrote "J." The author wished the paper "God speed you in your noble work."[2]

Yet few days before, a big Union meeting at city hall in Covington mentioned Anderson favorably. The attendees mostly praised Smith, their congressman, in a series of resolutions. But one approved "the conduct and votes of the Hon. Brutus J. Clay, Lucien Anderson and W.H. Randall, at the present session of Congress."[3]

On February 11, Anderson came out against drafting slaves held by

**Brutus J. Clay (National Archives and Records Administration).**

Unionists. He was afraid they would get little or no compensation if the military took their slaves. But Lush was for conscripting "the slaves of rebels in Kentucky, and of rebel sympathizers." He explained that because so many young men were in the Confederate army, his district failed to meet its draft quota, adding that in the upcoming draft, his constituency "will owe the Government something near seven thousand men."[4]

Anderson pleaded that

> unless the slaves of rebels who have cheated the Government out of the young men it was entitled to, unless they are taken, every poor Union man who is capable of bearing arms will be sent off, torn away from his wife and children, while those who have been guilty of inducing the young men to go into the armies of the rebellion will be permitted to stay at home in peace and quiet with their families and slaves.

Apparently, Lush was fine with African Americans risking life and limb for the Union cause so pro–Union whites disinclined to fight could stay out of harm's way.[5]

At the same time, Lush also protested drafting the slaves belonging to Union men because "they have suffered already sufficiently in consequence of this rebellion." Slaves, of course, had suffered bondage all their lives. Further, Anderson pleaded, First District Union men did not have the money—he put the figure at one million dollars—for commutation in lieu of military service that draftees provided. On the other hand, Anderson said it was the government's duty "to take the slaves of these men who induced and persuaded our young men to go into the rebel army." Anderson was willing for Uncle Sam's representatives to draft "all of the slaves of the rebels that they can reach." Ultimately, Lush relented and voted for the enlistment of Unionists' slaves as well. The bill called for a slaveholder to receive $100 for each drafted slave and a maximum of $300 for each slave who volunteered.[6]

Meanwhile, Anderson became embroiled in the controversial case of William Yokum, an Illinois soldier who was in charge of contrabands at Cairo. "Contraband" was the military term for escaped slaves who worked for the government for pay. Yokum was sent to prison for abducting Morris McComb, one of his workers, and trying to sell him back into slavery in Kentucky. Congressmen Anderson, Clay, Randall and Smith—plus former Congressman Casey—petitioned Lincoln to pardon Yokum. Their request raised suspicions in Washington, prompted Senate and House inquiries and led Lincoln to ultimately cancel the pardon.[7]

On or about August 14, 1863, Yokum allegedly lured McComb out of town and handed him over at gunpoint to Joseph K. Gant, who gave Yokum fifty dollars. The army arrested Yokum and charged him with kidnapping. Yokum claimed he was innocent, but on December 31, 1863, a military court in Washington found him guilty and sentenced him to five years imprisonment at hard labor in the penitentiary at Albany, New York, or elsewhere at the secretary of war's pleasure.[8]

A report by Judge Advocate General Joseph Holt of Kentucky provided more details of the abduction. Yokum enticed McComb to go with him to the Ohio River bank under the pretense of looking for "secesh cows," according to Holt. When they met Gant, he pulled a pistol on McComb and threatened to shoot him if he tried to escape. After Yokum left, Gant tied McComb up and flagged down a Paducah-bound steamboat, forced McComb aboard and confined him in a stateroom. But after the boat stopped at Paducah, Lieutenant R.D. Cunningham of the Second Illinois Artillery foiled Gant and Yokum's plan. He had both of them arrested and sent McComb back to Cairo, a free man again. "The plot appears to have been previously well arranged, and but for the vigilant and commendable action of Lieutenant Cunningham would have been successfully carried out," Holt wrote. He added that Yokum "proved previous good character and efficiency in the discharge of his duties in superintending and caring for the fugitive slaves under his charge." Further, Yokum "denied that money was an inducement to his action" and claimed that "he simply returned the slave as an accommodation to the owner (who was proved to be a loyal man), without intending to commit a wrong, or violate law or military orders." The loyal slaveholder was not Gant, according to the report.[9]

On January 8, 1864, Secretary of War Edwin M. Stanton approved Yokum's sentence and seventeen days later, he was sent to the state prison at New York's capital. On February 16, Lincoln endorsed a pardon for Yocum based on a petition from Anderson, Clay, Casey, Randall and Smith. But after receiving the case records from Stanton, Lincoln suspended the pardon on June 13. Yokum stayed behind bars and the House and Senate moved on to other matters.[10]

In the president's home state, nearly every white person—even ardent Unionists—ferociously opposed making soldiers of slaves, though doing so would greatly aid the war effort.

At first, Lincoln proposed enlisting only free blacks, but

**Joseph Holt (Library of Congress).**

opposition was so strong that action was delayed until February, 1864, when the army ordered the enrollment of all African Americans, slave or free. Enrollment was the first step toward enlistment.[11]

In Congress, Anderson, Randall and Smith joined the Republicans in supporting legislation authorizing the enrollment of African Americans and establishing a commission to provide at least minimal compensation to loyal holders of slaves who volunteered. Union Democrats in Kentucky denounced the enrollment bill as a threat to slavery.[12]

In Lush Anderson's district, the enlistment of African Americans provided needed reinforcements to hard-pressed white troops in their seemingly endless fight against elusive guerrillas. Despite strong opposition from Governor Bramlette and the legislature, black recruiting began in Kentucky. The First District "camp of reception" opened in Paducah. Other African American volunteers, including soldiers of the Fourth United States Heavy Artillery (colored), were trained at Columbus, second only to Camp Nelson in Jessamine County as the largest recruit center for black troops in Kentucky.[13]

Almost all white Kentuckians were horrified at the flood of black enlistments, which, "at the very least ... threatened a calamitous breakdown in social order" of long-established white supremacy. Even more dangerous in white imaginations, was "the suddenness of the black enlistment stampede," which "heralded the sort of disorderly racial catastrophe befitting the onset of a slave uprising." Further, "African Americans in their midst had become a powerful political force, and unbeknownst to the master class, the newly militarized black population, drew energy and organization from decades of kin and social networks built during slavery."[14]

J.L. Seaton of Smithland was one of the few Kentucky whites anywhere in the state who supported making soldiers of slaves. In February, he approvingly wrote Anderson that Lieutenant Cunningham, who was white, had "mustered in about 200 colored men" into a heavy artillery regiment he was raising in Paducah. Like Anderson, Seaton was a devout Union man in rebel country; he disparaged his hometown as a "Rank *Secesh Hole*." Seaton informed Anderson that Cunningham was authorized to enlist soldiers only in "Paducah and Vicinity" but that the captain wanted to seek soldiers over a wider area. Seaton believed African Americans should be signed up district-wide, although he acknowledged such a move would cause pro-slavery Unionists to "cry out and say it is a great violation of the CONSTITUTION of K*ai*ntucky," though "in their hearts they sigh for Jeff. Davis and his hellish crew, to win, so as to save their" slaves. Seaton vowed that "the true unconditional me[n], who had the honer, to work for your Election, will now, Stand up for you, and we wish you to assist us in having the order Extended, through the 1st District." He also advised

that the Kentucky Conservative Copperheads [Union Democrats] had made up a purse, and hired some weak kneed, Union man to go to Washington & endeavor to have the order of Sect. Stantons [authorizing the raising of black troops], revoked, so that no more Negroes, should be mustered or conscripted in Kentucky.

He concluded

Now as your friend and the friend of the Government I ask is it not right that Rebel sympathizers negroes, should be taken to put Down this infernal rebellion and restore the Government to its former Dignity & power. Therefore I would respectfully ask you to assist the true Union men of your district in having the order of Sect. Stanton to Extend over this whole Congressional District, as I am informed there are many men anxious to recruit Colored Regiments, if they can get the Authority to do so.[15]

Initially, the army designated Cunningham's men the First Kentucky Heavy Artillery (Colored). Because state political leaders so vehemently objected to applying "Kentucky" to African American outfits, the regiment became the Seventh United States Colored Artillery (Heavy) and finally the Eighth United States Colored Artillery (Heavy). Colonel Henry W. Barry, who was white, was the commander. Whites commanded African American units during the war.[16]

Seaton's opinions were rare as July blizzards in Kentucky. Simmering white opposition to African American enlistments in Paducah boiled over into bloodshed on March 21 when some of Cunningham's soldiers tried to draft African American crewmen off the steamboat *Carrie Jacobs*. The white officers and crew resisted and asked white soldiers for help. A "bloody fight" broke out between the white and black troops "and several were badly wounded on each side." Nonetheless, recruiting continued and five days later, the soldiers stood as comrades-in-arms in the battle of Paducah, holding the city's earthen Fort Anderson against an attack by Major General Nathan Bedford Forrest's cavalry. Forrest sent part of his force against the fort while his other troops burned a supply boat and seized union supplies. Had the assault on the fort succeeded, historians say it is likely the Confederates would have massacred the black troops.[17]

Meanwhile, on February 22, guerrillas struck Mayfield, again terrorizing Unionists. The outlaws also murdered pro–Union James B. Happy, Anderson's friend and neighbor. The raiders evidently were not the ones who had rampaged through town and kidnapped Lush in November. Determined to stop the guerrillas, Colonel Stephen G. Hicks, commander at Paducah, dispatched Cunningham and two hundred of his African American artillerymen to the Graves County seat. They arrived too late. The guerrillas were gone, but before departing, they also tied up and abducted the Rev. W.W. Dugger, "robbed three stores (all belonging to Union men), took all the goods they wanted, and destroyed the rest." Hicks ordered his men to stay in Mayfield pending further orders.[18]

On February 29, the *Journal* published a detailed account of the raid, citing a letter the paper received. The correspondent praised Happy as "one of the most prominent and respectable citizens and business men of the town." He said the guerrillas gunned him down "without cause or provocation—they meeting with no resistance whatever." The brigands pillaged several stores and homes "of their most valuable contents, and then ... departed with their ill-gotten gains, and the life blood of one of the most gentlemanly and magnanimous citizens of the town upon their hands." Mayfield was "an unlucky place," the *Journal* said. "It has had so many raids from guerrillas that it must be pretty well used up by this time." The paper guessed that the town's "location must be bad, and we would advise what is left of the Mayfieldites to gather into their haversacks what they have left of the place, and go to some more congenial clime—Cairo for instance."[19]

The news from Mayfield, especially of Happy's brutal slaying, surely saddened Anderson. At the same time, it may have hardened his attitude toward the Democrats, his old party. Before the war, Lush was one of Graves County's staunchest party men. He voted Democratic, albeit for the Northerner Douglas, in the presidential election of 1860. By early 1864, he was thoroughly disgusted with his former party. Democrats who backed Breckinridge in 1860 formed the nucleus of the Southern Rights or secessionist party. The Union Democrats were pro-war, but also pro-slavery. Peace Democrats opposed the war and supported slavery. All Democrats detested Lincoln and his "Black Republican Party."

Schuyler Colfax (Library of Congress).

On March 5, Anderson took the House floor to flay the Democrats in a long oration in which he also defended his vote for Colfax. Lush started by noting that while the state legislature condemed "startling usurpations of power by the Executive," it also recognized "that our institutions are assailed by an armed Rebellion ... which can only be met by the sword." Lush cited four of Kentucky's Union Democratic congressmen— Robert Mallory, William H.

Wadsworth, Aaron Harding and Henry Grider—recalling that they voted against tabling a proposal by anti-war Democratic Congressman Fernando Wood of New York City to start peace talks with the Confederates. Anderson scorched the "Copperhead" Wood as "that impersonation of peace disloyal Democracy" and sneered that Mallory, Wadsworth, Harding and Grider tried to keep alive a proposal that would "humble the nation and disgrace our gallant Army by begging for peace." In doing so, they "abandoned this cardinal idea that our institutions are assailed by an armed Rebellion that can only be met by the sword." He continued with "a short retrospect" of Kentucky Democratic history he said proved that the party's fealty to the Union was always absent "in its actions, and only occasionally its professions." His whole address equated Democrats with disloyalty, drawing no distinction between Union Democrats like George D. Prentice and "the Southern Rights alias Democratic party" which dominated Purchase politics. Lush's history lesson began with events of 1861, including the crucial elections for the border slave state convention, Congress and the state legislature.[20]

Anderson said the "pseudo Democracy of Kentucky," facing almost certain defeat, "and the time not having arrived when by force and fraud they could carry Kentucky into the maelstrom of Rebellion," pulled its candidates out of the May border state convention contest. Even so, the party stooped to "many ... fraudulent devices" to sabotage the vote. Early on Election Day, Graves County Democrats dispatched runners to the polls "with the lying information that both tickets were withdrawn, and no election was to be held," Lush charged. He claimed that "in a majority of the precincts of my county no polls were opened; in some of the Democratic counties of my district no election was held." The Union side polled a big vote statewide anyway. Anderson bragged that in the June congressional elections, "nine Union men were elected and one Democrat, that notorious traitor, Henry C. Burnett." He also crowed over the even more important Union landslide in the August legislative election. "Thus Kentucky had, from May to August, pronounced by overwhelming majorities that her people would abide in the Union."[21]

Though their party was "thrice defeated by such imposing numbers," the Democratic traitors resorted to "violent lawlessness and disregard of decency unparalleled," according to Anderson. "In most of my district all law and order was broken down; no man who professed Union principles was permitted to exercise the functions of his office." He said Judge Williams was prevented from holding court. "Had he attempted to do so, an excited populace would have taken his life by the most brutal means."[22]

At the same time, Lush recounted, "committees were regularly organized, and constant communication kept up with the rebel military authorities at Memphis and elsewhere in Tennessee; these were constantly urging the Rebels to possess Kentucky, especially that part of it where I reside." He said the local "State's attorney" went to Montgomery, Alabama, then the Confederate capital, seeking "guns to put in the hands of ... disloyal" citizens, who "openly boasted that that if they could obtain twenty-five thousand stand of arms, they would take Kentucky out of the Union in twenty-five days." The prosecutor evidently was Lush's brother-in-law, Albert P. Thompson of Paducah; he was commonwealth attorney when he joined the Confederate army.[23]

Anderson also recalled the July theft of State Guard muskets and artillery from Mayfield. "A disloyal Governor, through a disloyal inspector general, had the State arms distributed among disloyal State guards, most of whom went into the rebel service and took with them the State arms." He said

> twelve hundred muskets and a battery of six cannon and caissons were sent to a disloyal colonel of State guards at Paducah, who shipped them out to my town, placed them under the care of a disloyal captain of State guards; and this within thirty miles of the rebel encampment at Union City, in Tennessee.

Anderson claimed that, "as was intended," the firepower "fell into the hands of the rebels; they made a raid one night and got the guns without resistance." Again, Anderson did not name names, but he meant, of course, Governor Magoffin, Inspector General Buckner, Colonel Tilghman and Captain Andrew R. Boone.[24]

Additionally, Anderson charged that Paducah was ruled "by a mob" and that in the Purchase's largest town there was "no law or order, no guarantee to Union men; these were mobbed and driven off, and sometimes murdered." He said the railroad was used to ship contraband to the Confederates "while the packages of citizens who were Union men were violently opened and searched." Worse, Anderson declared, "the lives of Union men were daily and openly threatened because of their sentiments, and more than twenty murders occurred within a circle of twenty miles of my town, of citizens, before either side had taken military possession." Anderson said the Confederate army "openly and defiantly" signed up soldiers in the Purchase "with the avowed purpose of possessing Kentucky and subjugating her free people" while the citizenry frequently held "large meetings ... at which the most treasonable sentiments were uttered." Meanwhile, "a disloyal Governor had twice called the legislature together to get it to call a 'sovereignty convention,' but it persistently refused."[25]

Lush heaped on the scorn: "Having failed to accomplish their wicked designs, through the firmness and patriotism of the people and Legislature, they resorted to means which, although more wicked, was more promising." The secessionists tried a statewide petition drive for a convention and gained thousands of signatures. The *Louisville Courier,* the state's leading Confederate paper; and the *Paducah Herald* endorsed "this great abomination," yet "the loyal men in various ways made it known to the Governor that his life would be the forfeit of any such wickedness." Anderson cited the Mayfield convention, which he said fathered the November, 1861, Russellville convention:

> All their nefarious projects having miscarried, these *par excellent*, patriotic, and much-oppressed Democrats of the first congressional district—a part of the people of which I have the honor to represent, the others being represented by one Willis B. Machen in the rebel congress, placed there by their votes openly and notoriously given at a public election—called a convention, to meet at my town, Mayfield, for the purpose of making a military alliance with the then seceded State of Tennessee, and separating the entire first congressional district from the State of Kentucky. The address that called forth that immense convention—the largest ever held in my district—was one of the most treasonable documents ever put forth by the most unblushing traitor. It was signed by three now prominent Democrats of my section. The bold and treasonable utterances of that convention were not excelled by South Carolina. Who were chief actors in that traitorous conclave? Without stopping to rehearse their names, I will say they embrace almost every prominent Democrat in my district at this time. In this nest of rebels and conspirators was hatched that most infamous of pretended governments, the provisional government of Kentucky.

The trio of "traitors" was Oscar Turner of Ballard, Mayfield attorney William R. Bradley and Anderson's brother, Ervin.[26]

Lush claimed the Russellville convention attracted a "motley crew of traitors, bankrupts, in principle as well as personal and political." He exulted in the demise of the state's rump secesh government—"this unworthy betrayal of the State and its people." Presently, according to Lush, the elders of "the Southern Rights, alias Democratic party," were "at home, enjoying the protection of the Government, complaining of the 'unconstitutional' acts of the President" even as "their sons were in the rebel army, fighting against the State that gave them birth."[27]

He praised the Union victories at Fort Henry, Fort Donelson, Shiloh, and Perryville and was grateful "to the gallant men from the great Northwest" who drove Bragg from Kentucky. He panned Wickliffe and the Peace Democrats, charging that "to-day nine-tenths of this Democratic party of Kentucky would hail with delight the 'stars and bars'—the ensign of treason—and rejoice to see it waving from every hill-top and turret of Kentucky." He said nothing would gladden Democrats more than to see General Robert E. Lee and his Confederate army "possess and plunder the northern cities and people, and be able to dictate terms of peace from that venerable and sacred edifice, the Hall of Independence, in Philadelphia."[28]

Anderson applauded the Union troops that dispersed the Democratic convention in Frankfort and chastised the state's Democratic press and its editorializing on the 1863 election. He claimed many Democratic sheets denounced the election … as a fraud on the great Democratic party of Kentucky; and in almost every Democratic convention held since that election they have denounced it in like offensive terms—not in particular districts, but throughout the whole State—when in fact the Union State ticket received a majority of the legal votes of the State.[29]

Anderson also denied he was obliged to stand on the Union Democratic platform and he refused to disavow his vote for Colfax. Lush maintained that he, Clay, Randall and Smith

had either to act with the Union men of the North, and give them the organization of the House, or act with the Democracy, and give them the organization; in other words, to give the power to *those known* to be in favor of destroying the rebellion by force of arms, or to place the power in the hands of those who were opposed to furnishing the means necessary to speedily end this war by military force.

Lush protested that "for this I have been charged with a violation of the platform of my party in the State of Kentucky. Not only so, but have been denounced as an abolitionist by that *loyal sheet* and would-be organ of the Union party of Kentucky, the Louisville Journal." He laid into editor Prentice, scoffing that

the idea of the Journal charging this Representative on this floor from Kentucky, who voted for the honorable gentleman from Indiana for Speaker, as being abolitionist is simply ridiculous, especially when it is known that the editor of that paper has been charged by the Democratic party with abolitionism for the last twenty years; and they have further charged that before that gentleman left the land of steady habits, the State of Connecticut, he wrote a book, in which he appeared to be so anxious for the abolition of slavery in the United States that he wanted "*the Lord* to meet them in the *air* to free them." Prentice came to Kentucky from his native New England in 1830 to write a campaign biography of Henry Clay but stayed to become editor of the *Journal*, the state's leading Whig organ until the party collapsed. Afterwards, the paper endorsed the Know-Nothings. Anderson knew "of no party in this country to-day who propose to go *as high up for this purpose*." He vowed that "this charge of being an abolitionist, Mr. Chairman, cannot deter or drive me from a full discharge of my duty." Anderson said he was a lifelong Kentuckian who had always been identified with slavery and still owned slaves. Nonetheless, he pledged that "my slaves, nor all the slaves in Kentucky, cannot make me disloyal or traitorous to my country. If slavery is being destroyed it is the result of this wicked rebellion; and my judgment is that when the rebellion is destroyed this institution will go with it."[30]

Still rolling, Anderson admitted that

to be a Union man in a slave State is no easy task; he suffers the taunts and jeers of those who are ignorant, led on by designing demagogues, who too cowardly to fight remain at home with an oath on their conscience, protected by the Government, but on all occasions are talking about the Constitution and its violation by the President and those aiding him in crushing the rebellion. These are the men in my State who call themselves Democrats.

He blamed them and their supporters, "the so-called Democrats of the North," for "prolonging the war."[31]

Lush likened the Unionists of the 1860s to the patriots of the American Revolution and to President Andrew Jackson,

> the hero of New Orleans [who] crushed nullification in South Carolina in 1832 [and] ... was sustained by the patriotism of men such as Clay and [Daniel] Webster.... Let the lesson taught by their example and precepts prevail over the dishonoring suggestions of degenerate sons of the present day, who profess to belong to the Democratic party, but who malign and traduce the name of those who were true to the flag and interests of this country, one and indivisible.

He ended with a flourish: "The true Union men of this country will protect it from foreign despots and domestic traitors: 'One country, one Constitution, one destiny.' Let this be the rallying cry of the Union men in the coming contest for political power." Soon, Lush would be in the contest, not for his reelection but for Lincoln's. He would be a Kentucky delegate to the National Union Convention in Baltimore that would endorse Lincoln for a second term, and he would stump the First District for the president.[32]

# 8

# Lush the Lincoln Man

Lush Anderson, Captain Thomas J. Gregory and Brigadier General Eleazer A. Paine were the unholy trinity to Jackson Purchase Confederate sympathizers. It is hard to say which one the secessionists loathed most. A Mayfield Confederate veteran denounced Gregory and his men as a gang "of robbers and murderers." Lewis and Richard Collins' 1874 *History of Kentucky* accused Paine of masterminding "a fifty-one days' reign of violence, terror, rapine, extortion, oppression, bribery, and military murders." Anderson was linked to Paine's alleged misdeeds.[1]

Local secesh might have expected Paine's purported perfidy. He was an Ohio-born, Illinois Yankee. But Anderson and Gregory were sons of the Purchase. During the post–Civil War Reconstruction era, Southern white supremacists denounced men like Paine as "carpetbaggers." Yet their hatred burned hotter for the likes of Gregory and Anderson. Unrepentant rebels scorned them as "scalawags," meaning fellow white Southerners who became Republicans or who supported the bi-racial Republican governments in the old Confederate states. The die-hard Confederates doubly despised "scalawags," claiming they were traitors to their race and region.

In local Confederate lore, Gregory is a Civil War version of Simon Girty, the much-feared and detested "great renegade" of frontier Kentucky during the Revolutionary War. Girty went down in history as the Bluegrass State's meanest villain, though his alleged misdeeds were almost certainly exaggerated. Likewise, it seems Gregory was far from the monster rebel sympathizers claimed he was.

The pro–British Girty preferred the company of Native Americans to whites. Thus, Kentucky whites cursed him as a turncoat to his "kind." Southern sympathizers passed the same sort of judgment on Anderson and Gregory, reviling them as disloyal to their kith and kin. At any rate, Gregory's deep disdain for the Confederacy might have been as personal as it was political. When the war broke out, he and his younger brother were Union, though almost all of their neighbors in the Dublin community were secession. "Being high-spirited men, they could not hear treason uttered without rebuking it, and this obtained for them the ill will of their neighbors, who threatened their lives."[2]

The threats were real. In the fall of 1861, when the rebel army was close by at Columbus, Southern sympathizers "determined to 'root out' the brothers, and to make examples of them." About a hundred armed went to the Gregory home, aiming to hang the siblings. Expecting the unwelcome visitors, the brothers barricaded themselves inside the house where they "calmly awaited the coming of their chivalric neighbors."[3]

E.A. Paine (Murray State University).

The band opened fire, bullets rattling "like hail around the house." The Gregorys shot back, purportedly killing three assailants and wounding several more. "Finding the game somewhat hazardous," the attackers retreated, "leaving the Gregorys master of the situation." Even so, the brothers knew the intruders would be back. So they prudently fled their dwelling, which the secessionists burned.[4]

In January, 1862, Gregory joined Williams' Twentieth Kentucky and was commissioned a first lieutenant. He signed up for three years but resigned after about a month. Military records do not reveal why, but Gregory may have decided to go back home and raise a Home Guard company. At any rate, on September 12, 1862, Gregory and fourteen of his recruits stopped "a robbing guerrilla band" from plundering Bolinger's store. Gregory's group got the drop on the marauders, whose leader was "Dr. Hart, of Boydsville." They killed one of Hart's men, fatally wounded the physician's brother, dispersed the guerrillas and captured most of their horses. Gregory became a hero to local Unionists and an arch villain to the secesh.[5]

After the battle of Paducah, Gregory and his men nearly bagged Colonel Edward Crossland, one of Forrest's most trusted officers. Wounded in the assault on Fort Anderson, Crossland spent the night in a Confederate sympathizer's house near Mayfield. From Clinton, the Hickman County seat, Crossland took command of the Third Kentucky after Colonel Albert P. Thompson, Lush's brother-in-law, was killed while overseeing the rebel assault

on Fort Anderson. The
Home Guards surprised
Crossland and his small
escort, killing or wounding
some of the rebels. But the
colonel, helped by one of
his men, managed to escape
in the darkness.[6]
  Reportedly, a Yankee
cannonball tore Thompson
to pieces. Because none of
Anderson's personal papers
evidently survive, one is left
to speculate on how he and
Ann received the news of
Thompson's death. He was
family, yet an enemy soldier
engaged in armed rebellion
against the government
Lush was part of in Wash-
ington. Ann's sympathies
are unknown, though pre-
sumably she sided with her
spouse.[7]

Thomas J. Gregory's hometown today (Berry Craig).

  The Lincolns found
themselves in the same dif-
ficult situation as the Andersons. Confederate Brigadier General Ben Hardin
Helm was married to Emily Todd, Mary Todd Lincoln's half-sister. He was
killed in the battle of Chickamauga in September, 1863. Lincoln was fond of
Helm, though Helm voted for Breckinridge for president in 1860 and declined
the president's offer of a Union army commission as a paymaster in Washington. The Lincolns hoped Ben and Emily might live in the White House
with them. Lincoln was grief-stricken when he learned of Helm's death. "I
feel as David of old did when told of the death of Absalom," the president
confided to his aide, David Davis. After Helm's death, Emily, an ardent secessionist like her slain husband, briefly stayed in the White House with the
First Family.[8]
  Meanwhile, Thompson's brother-in-law was looking more like a Republican. So was Judge Williams. The presidential election was, of course, the
main political event in 1864. Most Union Democrats did not consider their
party pro–Lincoln. So they decided to participate in the Democratic National
Convention in Chicago, set for August 29 through 31. To that end, the central

committee, dominated by Prentice and Guthrie, called a state convention for May 25 in Louisville. Lush, Williams and the rest of the Unconditional Unionists, who were more a faction than a party, preferred a different destination—the Republicans' National Union Convention in Baltimore on June 7 and 8. By dropping "Republican" and calling the gathering the "National Union Convention," the president's party hoped to win over pro-war, if not anti-slavery, northern and border state Democrats and perhaps some southern Unionists.[9]

By early 1864, pro–Lincoln Kentuckians were sorely in need of a boost. They got it from a group of anti-slavery Missourians who organized a "Slave States Freedom Convention" in Louisville on February 22 and 23. On February 9, "friends of the Union and Emancipation" in Louisville and Jefferson County met in the Falls City, organized a local Unconditional Union party and called for the prompt organization of a statewide party. James Speed, Lincoln's friend, presided over the gathering which thanked Anderson, Clay, Randall and Smith for backing Colfax for speaker and for "supporting the Administration in all measures necessary for the suppression of the rebellion, and thereby reflecting the true sentiments of the great majority of their constituents." The resolution was a stretch in the First District; Unconditional Unionism was the rare exception.[10]

While Missourians apparently dominated the February 22 meeting, Speed and the other local emancipationists made their presence felt. They and anti-slavery men from five other Kentucky counties—none from Lush's constituency—met separately on February 23 and urged their friends in the state "who are in favor of the suppression of the present Rebellion, of the eradication of its great cause—slavery—throughout the land, and of the restoration of the Union upon the firm and permanent basis of universal freedom," to come to Louisville on May 9 to elect delegates to the National Union Convention and name eleven presidential electors.[11]

Meanwhile, the *Journal* was unimpressed with the anti-slavery gathering and accused the out-of-staters of stirring up strife in Kentucky:

> So the apple of discord, which the Union men of Kentucky have studiously excluded from the State, and which the Jacobins and Jayhawkers of Missouri, as if envious of the comparative peace and prosperity that still reigns in our borders, have with devilish malevolence thrown into the midst of us, is seized eagerly by kindred spirits here, and is borne on through the ranks of the people.

The *Journal* predicted, "This is the beginning" and trumpeted,

> Whatever the end may be, the Missouri anarchists can at least cherish the consciousness that they have done their part. Such infernal exultation is theirs as swelled the heart of the Goddess of Discord when she threw the golden apple into the assembly of the gods.... Let the Union men of Kentucky prepare to bury this revolutionary party at the polls so deep that the hand of resurrection stretched out from Missouri or from any other place

will never reach it. Let us bury it in the same grave with the secession party. Until we do, our pledge of devotion to the Union and the Constitution, so solemnly declared and so often repeated, is but half redeemed.[12]

Not surprisingly, the *Democrat* was equally uncharitable toward the convention. The Louisville paper noted that the Cincinnati papers were "delighted with the novelty of an Abolition Convention in Louisville. How times have improved. Three years ago such a body could not have assembled in in this State. A great change has taken place." But the *Democrat* chided the Queen City papers for not noticing "another novelty, unlike anything that ever took place before in this State. This Convention was attended by a guard of soldiers from the opening to the close." To the *Democrat*, it looked "very much like the Convention felt conscious that they were surrounded by enemies and needed protection." The paper recalled that fifteen years earlier, an emancipation convention was held in Louisville without armed guards.

> And after the fight was over there was nobody killed, wounded on missing.... The truth is many of these delegates came out of the hot-bed of Missouri and Kansas strife, where they kill each other on the slightest political differences, and they seem in coming here to be "Kurnelling up" a fight, when the fact was, the people of this city regarded the whole thing with indifference. The sentiments uttered in this Convention will not make many converts in this State.[13]

The *Democrat* offered a proposition to the "radicals" who "are making great progress, they say." Their movement "is like the ocean-tide, and all efforts to stop it are as silly as the old woman's who tried to sweep out the waves of the ocean" with her broom.

> If that be so, let us have free elections and free conventions. Show us you believe what you say, by dropping this logic of force. Otherwise, we beg leave to distrust your sincerity; your honesty, loyalty—all. You do not believe what you say. You feel conscious that you can't produce conviction, and, therefore, must *force* assent.[14]

The *Democrat* said the convention offered Kentuckians "an inside view of the doings of the radicals" who "are entirely emancipated from the shackles of the Constitution, and, like a locomotive which has flown the track, go pitching around, destroying dwellings generally, and everything else that comes in their way." The paper sneeringly reported that one of the delegates suggested "a convention of the blacks of the State to settle the slavery question and all applauded it. Doubtless seeing how incompetent they are themselves to settle the question, they prefer to trusting the government of the country to former slaves."[15]

When the Unconditional Unionists broke away from the Union Democrats they did not want to appear merely as a disaffected splinter group. So they claimed to represent the genuine Union men of Kentucky and as such moved the date of their convention to coincide with the Union Democratic gathering. Led by the Reverend Robert J. Breckinridge, Anderson and others, they elected delegates to the National Union Convention. The Unconditional Unionists declared that their convention would promote "harmony and unity of action among all true Union men in the State...." The *Louisville Democrat* naturally put a different spin on the conclave: "They protest against being sold, and to counter this sinister action of the [Union Democratic] committee, they propose getting up, in an irregular and revolutionary manner, another convention, which shall consider the matter and send delegates to some other Convention."[16]

The Unconditional Union convention drew 256 delegates from twenty-six counties. Anderson, Bolinger and Williams represented Graves County. Lush served on the resolutions committee that reported only one resolution of principle, which passed unanimously: "That the Union men of Kentucky, in convention assembled, are for the preservation and maintenance of the Union, the supremacy of the National Constitution, and the destruction of the rebellion, without any regard to what these objects may cost." Of course, the implication was that "cost" would include the end of slavery. Indeed, "a manifest Pro-Lincoln and Anti-Slavery spirit pervaded the body." The Unconditional Unionists also instructed their delegates to the national convention, including Lush, Bolinger and Williams, "to cast a unanimous vote for Lincoln."[17]

Again, the irony is inescapable. Lush, Bolinger and Williams came from one of the most Southern-sympathizing towns in Kentucky, a community where, in late May, 1861, delegates from far western Kentucky discussed forming a pro–Confederate military alliance with Tennessee, a move which would have been almost the same as secession. At the same time, Anderson, Bolinger and Williams must have known that they did not represent majority sentiment back home and that almost every white resident of the Graves County seat hated Lincoln and the "Black Republicans." In Baltimore, they would be among kindred spirits. There is no doubt the three Graves Countians had the courage of their convictions, but they must have worried about their homecoming to Mayfield, the center of "the South Carolina of Kentucky." After all, Rebels had kidnapped Lush and Bolinger. They and Williams had received death threats.

At any rate, the three Mayfield men were among twenty-two Kentucky delegates at the National Union Convention on June 7 and 8. Williams was a delegate-at-large and he chaired the Kentucky delegation. Lush and Bolinger were First District delegates. Though Kentucky gave Lincoln only 1,364 votes in 1860, Breckinridge was named president pro tem when the convention began. Editor of the *Danville Quarterly Review* and a staunch Unconditional Unionist, he addressed the gathering, prompting "great applause" when he asked, "Does any man doubt that this Convention intends to say that Abraham

Lincoln shall be the nominee? What I wish, however, to call your attention to, is the grandeur of the mission upon which you are met, and therefore the dignity and solemnity, earnestness and conscientiousness with which, representing one of the greatest, and certainly one of the first people of the world, you ought to discharge these duties."[18]

When the time came to ratify Lincoln's nomination, Williams declared, "Kentucky casts her twenty-two votes for Abraham Lincoln, and will ratify that nomination in November." Not surprisingly, delegates responded with "great applause." The Kentuckians also seemed pleased with Lincoln's running mate, Andrew Johnson of Tennessee. When the Volunteer State seceded, Johnson refused to relinquish his senate seat. To many in the North, he became the embodiment of heroic Southern Unionism. After Union soldiers conquered Tennessee in 1862, Lincoln named Johnson the state's military governor. Lincoln and Johnson campaigned on the National Union ticket.[19]

Meanwhile, the Louisville Union Democratic Convention had proclaimed the war a fight to preserve the Union, not to abolish slavery. The delegates—said to be 518 in number from sixty-three counties— made plain their "unqualified condemnation of the policy of enlisting negroes in the armies of the United States, as unjust to our soldiers, degrading to our armies, humiliating to the nation, and contrary to the usage of civilized nations." In addition, the Union Democrats elected delegates to the national convention. They were to vote for Major General George B. McClellan for president and Governor Bramlette for vice president. "The tone of [the convention] ... speakers was decidedly Anti-Lincoln and Pro-Slavery."[20]

Even though they were all but wiped out in the 1863 elections, the Peace Democrats, many of them secessionist in 1861, were enough of a growing force in the state to hold their own convention in Louisville on June 28. The delegates resolved that "the revocation of all unconstitutional edicts and pretended laws, an immediate armistice, a national convention for the adjustment of our difficulties, are the only means for saving our nation from unlimited calamity and ruin." The delegates also resolved

> that all assailants and enemies, either of the people or of their government, are traitors alike, whether their treason be manifested by joining a foreign foe or by fomenting civil war, by suppressing free elections, by chaining the press, by establishing political bastilles, and by ridiculing or repudiating the observance of oaths and constitutions.

Though they wielded no power in Kentucky's government, the Peace Democrats claimed they were the state's true Democrats and thus voted to dispatch delegates to the Chicago convention, too.[21]

Despite what he said when he cast Kentucky's vote for Lincoln, Williams surely knew he, Lush and the rest of the Unconditional Unionists would have a hard time selling the Bluegrass State on the president's re-election. True, his running mate was a Southerner and they were paired as Union men, not Republicans. But most Kentuckians seemed dead set against the duo.

Anderson and Williams believed a strong hand was needed to rule the "South Carolina of Kentucky." Anderson and Bolinger had moved to Paducah, presumably to escape guerrilla groups and Confederate raiders like Forrest's cavalry. Bolinger left his hometown about June 2, but he continued to act as county clerk through his deputy. On June 2, 1865, he announced his resignation effective August 2. He and Anderson gave Paducah as their residence when they attended the National Union Convention. In 1861, Bolinger had taken refuge in the city after rebels seized and briefly confined him. Williams evidently stayed put in Mayfield, though Forrest rode through town going and coming to Paducah. On June 18, Anderson and Williams went to Lincoln in Washington to plead their case for sterner measures in the Purchase. They claimed the region was still unrepentantly rebel. Hence, they urged Lincoln to reinstate punitive tax assessments on Southern sympathizers and bring back the no-nonsense Paine as commander in the region. Anderson and Williams might have figured they had some extra leverage with Lincoln; after all, they had just helped renominate him, though that eventuality was a foregone conclusion. The president supported the tax on Confederate sympathizers and the return of Paine. "Do both these things for them unless you know some reason to the contrary," he wrote Secretary Stanton. "I personally know Gen. Paine to be a good man, having a West Point education; but I do not know much of his military ability."[22]

While Lush's pro-war credentials were peerless, the Raleigh, North Carolina, *Daily Conservative* bizarrely reported on July 16 that

> a Tupelo correspondent of the Mobile *Advertiser* says, letters have been received from Washington, one at Mayfield, Ky., from Lucien Anderson, Congressman from that district, and the other at Dresden, Tenn., from the notorious Emerson Etheridge, saying that hostilities would cease next month; or, at all events, that an armistice would be proposed, and begging their respective friends to use their utmost endeavors to have those States go with the North.

According to the Tarheel State capital paper, Etheridge said, "We are whipped," while Lush declared "that 'the present Congress will recognize the Confederacy.'" The *Conservative*, whose story was headlined, "Getting Weak In The Knees," surmised "If reports be true, all the South has to do to establish her independence firmly, in a brief space of time, is to persevere in her present habit of whipping the Yankees." After Etheridge's third term ended in March, 1861, he was elected clerk of the House, a position he held until December, 1863. The story was false, of course. Lush was gravitating toward the Republicans. Etheridge, though he had broken with the president over emancipation, was still anti–Confederate. Besides, the war turned in the Union's favor after Vicksburg and Gettysburg.[23]

Even before Paine showed up in the Purchase on July 19, Memphis-based Major General Cadwallader C. Washburn was running out of patience with the Purchase, which was part of his command area. Citizens continued to provide aid and comfort to guerrillas and Confederate raiders. In June, Washburn, in effect, declared economic war:

> The people of that disloyal region, Western Ky., will not be allowed to sell their cotton and tobacco, or purchase supplies, until they show some friendship for the U.S. government, by driving out the guerrillas and irregular bands of regular Confederate soldiers who pay them frequent visits.

Lincoln was also troubled by "the prevalence of Confederate and guerrilla raids" into his home state. On July 5, he suspended the writ of *habeas corpus* and proclaimed martial law in Kentucky.[24]

By the summer of 1864, the pro–Republican Union League, or Loyal League, had spread to some Kentucky towns, including Paducah. On July 11, the Paducah officers sent a letter to Washburn, endorsing his order. In addition, President pro tempore William H. Kidd, State Representative Thomas Barchett, who was the league vice president; and secretary John Perkins, were glad to hear "our old and true friend, General Paine," was evidently returning to Paducah. Meanwhile, they groused that that "Rebels are doing all the business, and they are reaping all the advantages of trade." Yet they expected "to obtain relief" from Paine. The Unionists also informed Washburn that "large quantities of goods of all descriptions are going from this post to the interior, and of course the articles find their way into the hands of rebels." They were sure that Paine, "being somewhat acquainted with the people here, will be able to protect Union men, and give traitors and secret Southern sympathizers their just dues." Kidd, Barchett and Perkins concluded with an entreaty: "We have stood by our Union through weal and woe for the past three years of this terrible struggle, and we earnestly hope the military authorities will give us the protection we need and respectfully ask."[25]

Gregory was doing his best to protect Unionists. But on the night of July 17, a band of guerrilla "traitors" bested him in "a sharp and severe contest" somewhere along Mayfield Creek. The guerrillas killed about nine of Gregory's men and wounded several more before the captain ordered a retreat to Paducah. Gregory's little band had become Company A, the Paducah Battalion, of the Capital Guards. Several of them, like their captain, were also Graves countians "hunted from their homes because of their attachment to the government."[26]

Two days later, Paine arrived in Paducah. His tenure would represent the high water mark of the Union crackdown against the Purchase's unregenerate rebel populace. To the long-suffering Unionist minority, he seemed just the man to "give traitors and secret Southern sympathizers their just dues."[27]

Almost all Purchase historians have demonized Paine. One claimed that "at least forty-three persons in the District fell victim to the oppressive commander's firing squad during his fifty-one–day 'reign of terror.'" Nonetheless, no records evidently survive to back up charges that Paine orchestrated wholesale executions, according to Kentucky historian Patricia Ann Hoskins. "While an argument could be made that the names of the victims were conveniently lost ... no private letters or diaries, local histories, or newspapers contain a list of the supposed victim's names," she wrote. Records detail only eleven executions during Paine's purported "Reign of Terror." Four men were shot on Paine's order; seven were sent to their deaths by one of his subordinates, Colonel Waters W. McChesney, commander of the 134th Illinois. According to Paine, McChesney and Purchase Unionists, all eleven men were guerrillas who deserved their fate. Locals also accused of Paine of being a crook, as well as a tyrant and named Lush and Bolinger as his partners-in-crime.[28]

In any event Anderson and Bolinger's hometown continued to be a frequent target for guerrilla raiders. Mayfield seemed to be an easy mark for the marauders. The nearest Union troop concentrations were about thirty miles north at Paducah and a like distance west at Columbus. So Paine decided the Graves County seat needed a fort built around the courthouse, the highest spot in the town.

Most Purchase historians claim the earthworks were of no military value and that the general really built it to show the rebel town who was boss. But in various raids, guerrilla groups murdered J.B. Happy, kidnapped Lush and others, shot up and plundered the town and even derailed a train. Forrest rode through Mayfield to and from Paducah.

Construction on the fort began in August, and Paine dispatched the 134th Illinois and other soldiers to garrison the town. Gregory's company sometimes operated out of Mayfield as well. Paine needed laborers, so he drafted several citizens—many of them Confederate sympathizers. In 1861, armed Confederates had pressed hundreds of slaves, overseen by rebel soldiers, into building their fortifications at Columbus. Now white men had to make the dirt fly, guarded by ex-slaves in Union uniforms.[29]

On August 15, Lush and Bolinger delivered Union addresses in town that especially pleased Private Hawley V. Needham of the 134th Illinois. "These men are tried and true and are objects of bitter hatred to the Rebs," Needham penned. "It was expected that General Paine would be here and make a speech as he had given an invitation to all to come in today and there was a big crowd." Needham claimed that "many prominent guerrillas" were supposedly present, apparently in anticipation of Paine's advent. The general failed to appear, and Bolinger spoke for Paine. He warned that "the people must submit peaceably if they would, forcibly if need be. One hundred Rebel families must be banished from the U.S. and the county must pay $250,000." Too, slaves of military age would by necessity become soldiers, according to Bolinger. "Bully for Paine," Needham exulted. "That is my ticket every time."[30]

Almost every other Graves County citizen preferred another ticket. But the *Evansville Journal* was ready to welcome Anderson to the Hoosier State's southernmost town. "Hon. Lucien Anderson has promised to make our people a Union speech at any early day," the paper advised its readers on August 1. "He is a Union man of the right sort, and can make the wool fly from the rebels and Copperheads in a way that is delightful to witness." The *Journal* added, "Would that Kentucky had ten thousand more Union men like him. She would be 'redeemed, regenerated and disenthralled.'" The paper promised to provide due notice of Lush's speech. "He is now in Paducah—his home, Mayfield, being 'unhealthy' for Union men."[31]

Meanwhile, the Unconditional Unionists were working hard for the Lincoln-Johnson ticket in Kentucky. Their task seemed mission impossible; the Democrats had the momentum in Kentucky. They hoped to capitalize on war weariness in the North, where, it seemed, many people were wondering if the conflict was worth the cost in blood and treasure. The Democratic convention nominated McClellan but not Bramlette. George H. Pendleton, an anti-war Ohio Democrat, was "Little Mac's" running mate. Still in uniform, McClellan was for continuing the war and restoring the Union but not for ending slavery. Even so, the party platform called for an armistice and a negotiated peace settlement with the Confederacy. Though McClellan repudiated the peace plank, many people saw him as the anti-war candidate of the anti-war party. In the Bluegrass State, the Union Democrats and Peace Democrats reconciled and unified behind McClellan. Lush stumped the First District for Lincoln, giving speeches for the president and Johnson.[32]

They had a steep hill to climb in western Kentucky. Paine's rule was not winning hearts and minds for the president either. He hounded guerrillas and smugglers with equal fervor. He showed no leniency to those who aided and abetted guerrillas and traffickers in contraband. While General Smith went easy on the region in hopes of winning converts to the Union cause, Paine did not. Paine believed the Purchase was irredeemably rebel and acted accordingly. Union Democrats complained to Bramlette, one of their own. They charged Paine with multiple misdeeds from mass executions to extortion. The conservative Bramlette appeared ready to believe any accusation against Paine, a Republican, abolitionist and friend of Lincoln. On September 2, he wrote Lincoln, claiming the general, Anderson and Bolinger apparently "were confederates in the system of oppression and plundering instituted in that part of Kentucky—sharing the spoils iniquitously extorted from the citizens." He charged all three with abusing Paine's position "to oppress unjustly and extort corruptly money and property from the citizens for their own private gain, and to the disgrace of the service and injury of the public interest." The governor maintained that "the extent and character of the oppressions and plundering carried on by these men, as related to me by persons cognizant of the facts, is astounding." Therefore, Bramlette pleaded "in behalf of that people, of justice, the honor of our country, that a military commission, composed of good, brave, just, and fearless men, be appointed to inquire into the conduct of these men." The governor concluded by assuring the president that he had "forborne to complain until I could be assured of the verity of these charges."[33]

Heretofore, Kentucky Unionist politicians seemed to have had no problem with Union army commanders lording it over the rebellious Purchase. So why did Bramlette now take up for the state's only Confederate region? Was the governor playing politics? Did Bramlette see a chance to rid himself of three enemies at once: The Republican Paine and virtual Republicans Anderson and Bolinger? On September 6, Grant ordered the Kentucky military commander, Major General Stephen G. Burbridge, to fire Paine. His replacement was North Carolina-born Brigadier General Solomon Meredith of Indiana, who turned out to be far more agreeable to the Purchase secesh than his predecessor.[34]

Stephen G. Burbridge (National Archives and Records Administration).

Anderson was at home in Mayfield when he learned Paine got sacked. The news stunned the congressman; Lincoln had told Lush a few weeks earlier in Washington that Paine would stay in command. Anderson dashed to the depot and hopped a train to Paducah on September 9. He was determined to save his general. Anderson found Paine ill, in bed and unable physically to defend himself, so lawyer Anderson took the general's case, evidently *pro bono* and immediately protested to Stanton and Lincoln. "General Paine was ordered here by the President to collect assessments on Rebel sympathizers," Anderson telegraphed the secretary. "Union men all indorse his policy. If sent away the Union men in this end of the State will all leave. All is lost. Have the order of Grant revoked. Telegraph me." Anderson included a copy of Paine's dismissal order. The next day, Anderson wrote Lincoln, appealing to the president's political side. Lush argued that Paine's "removal will destroy all our prospects for success in this end of the State & all I have promised the Union men here turns out to be false. He

Solomon Meredith (National Archives and Records Administration).

pledged, "I will do the best I can no matter who is in command" but begged the president to allow Paine to stay in Paducah for sixty days. Such an extension would keep the general in charge of the Purchase through the election. No doubt Paine would command his soldiers to make sure only men of unquestioned loyalty voted and thus enable Lincoln to squeeze a few more votes out of the corner of Kentucky most hostile to his presidency. Anderson also dispatched telegrams and mailed letters to his political allies in Washington asking them to lobby Lincoln to keep Paine in Paducah. He encouraged his friend Green Adams of Barbourville to meet with the president and urge him not to fire Paine. Adams was the Treasury Department's auditor. Lincoln was unmoved. "I will write no more I am too damn mad," a disgusted Anderson penned Adams.[35]

Possibly fueling Anderson's anger was the fact that several people had connected him to Paine's alleged crimes. John M. Mackenzie, a U.S. Customs agent at Paducah warned the president that that "the Honr L. Anderson is implicated in the maladministration of Genl Paine who is a monomaniac— Let nothing that he the said Anderson may say to you, induce you to interfere with Genl Grants removing Genl Paine from this command."[36]

Bramlette was granted his commission of enquiry. On September 9, Burbridge named Brigadier General Speed S. Fry of Danville and Colonel John Mason Brown of Frankfort to investigate Paine, Anderson, Bolinger and their military and civilian associates. Paine was gone by the time the duo, along with Lieutenant Colonel J.J. Craddock of Hart County, arrived in Paducah on September 13. Based on his letter to Lincoln, Bramlette clearly wanted the heads of Paine, Anderson and Bolinger; Fry, Brown and Craddock seemed just the officers to deliver them. All three shared the governor's conservative Unionism. A Mexican-American War veteran, Fry joined the Union Army early in the war and, in August, 1861, helped establish Camp Dick Robinson in Garrard County, the first recruit training center for Union soldiers in Kentucky. Fry fought in the battle of Mill Springs, Kentucky, on January 19, 1862, and supposedly shot and killed Confederate General Felix K. Zollicoffer. Afterwards, Fry was promoted to commander of the Eastern Division of Kentucky and he established his headquarters at Camp Nelson. Fry was also the Camp Nelson commander when Burbridge tapped him to help bring down Paine, Anderson and Bolinger. Like almost all white Kentuckians, Fry opposed blacks serving in the military and considered them inferior to white troops. While in charge at Camp Nelson, he refused to feed and shelter the families of African American recruits, almost all of them ex-slaves. In addition, he issued orders to whip refugees found in the camp and to return escaped slaves to their masters. Bramlette was also deeply racist, warning Lincoln in a follow up letter on September 3, "We are for preserving the rights and liberties of our own race and upholding the character and dignity of our position. We are not willing to sacrifice a single life or imperil the smallest right of free of white men for the sake of the negro."[37]

Brown was on temporary assignment at Military District of Kentucky headquarters in Lexington when Burbridge appointed him to assist Fry. Brown was a Yale graduate and an attorney who had practiced law in St. Louis and Louisville before the war. He was the son of James Brown, Kentucky's first U.S. senator and a half-brother of Senator Benjamin Gratz Brown of Missouri. He enlisted early in the war and combat as a cavalry and infantry commander in Kentucky, Tennessee and Virginia.[38]

Craddock was second in command of the "Capital Guards" at Frankfort when Burbridge called on him. He, too, was a combat veteran, having served as a cavalry officer at the battles of Shiloh, Perryville and Chickamauga. He, Fry and Brown appeared in Paducah with what seemed to be a clear, if unspoken, agenda: get Paine, Anderson and Bolinger.[39]

Doubtless, Paducah secesh and conservative Unionists alike were glad to see Fry and Brown in town. The officers began their inquiry on September 14 and concluded ten days later. They pored over records, heard testimony and took depositions, including from Lush and Bolinger. After they finished, Fry and Brown wrote a lengthy report and sent it to Bramlette who was doubtless happy to share it with the legislature. They listed eight parties they claimed were "most culpable." Lush was first on the list, followed by Bolinger;

Paine was last. Nonetheless, most of the report pilloried Paine, claiming the general flagrantly misused his power. The report accused him of corruption and cruelty, and all but called him a murderer. Paine's "violence of manner was of a character to very much alarm the citizens," even Unionists who helped defend Paducah against Forrest and "were terrified into leaving their homes," according to Fry and Brown. Paine continually made "the most sanguinary and brutal threats" against the citizens "and the execution of some guerrillas (or persons charged with that crime) gave such color to his threats as to alarm the entire country." Of course, the word in parentheses were calculated to imply Paine ordered or countenanced the shooting of innocent civilians.[40]

Fry and Brown professed to be impartial. The officers said they had a hard time "*procuring* information from official sources" because Paine and Captain Phelps Paine, his son and assistant adjutant general, had decamped before they arrived. The duo took with them or ordered away "every clerk who was familiar with the office business of Headquarters." The implication, of course, was that Paine was guilty or he would not have fled. Fry and Brown commended Meredith, hardly a Paine supporter, for showing them the records he had. But the commissioners pronounced them "so incomplete and irregularly kept, that they proved of little service in the investigation." In prefacing their findings, the two officers took great pains to portray themselves as unbiased judges of Paine's tenure, promising "it was the constant aim of your committee to elicit, as nearly as practicable, the actual charges, and the palliating circumstances which might exist." Fry and Brown said the records they compiled "were open to the reception of any matters of complaint or defense relevant to the subject-matter of investigation." The duo said they also made it plain "that any person complained of, might, if he desired, read the affidavits against him, and file rebutting proof." Though "irregular," such a course "was judged, under all the circumstances, to be necessary and expedient" and, thus, "enables us to make the following report of facts, about which, we think, there can be but little controversy."[41]

The report found Paine culpable of corruption, extortion, unjust taxation, fencing stolen goods, banishing allegedly innocent civilians to Canada, cursing in public and even countenancing immorality. The commissioners lamented, "It would be endless to enumerate the indignities, wrongs and outrages that the citizens of Paducah, without distinction of political faith, have endured." Even so, Fry and Brown tried to catalog Paine's alleged misdeeds in their lengthy report. They also accused Anderson and Bolinger of "corruption, bribery, and malfeasance in office."[42]

The most serious charges against Paine centered on the executions. Fry and Brown admitted they could not accurately determine how many people faced firing squads during Paine's tenure. The general's order books "gave no clue to the matter," nor did guardhouse records. Fry and Brown did report that at Mayfield, McChesney had seven men shot. But the investigators conceded they had no way of knowing if they were guilty or innocent. Yet based on "vague and uncertain evidence," they estimated that between five and forty-three people suffered the ultimate punishment.[43]

In wrapping up, Fry and Brown dropped all pretenses of objectivity. They could not hide their "feelings of indignation and disgust which their investigation of the conduct of affairs in Western Kentucky has inspired with them." The commissioners obviously knew their history, concluding that "the administration of Verres and Warren Hastings may be safely challenged to show a parallel to the fifty-one days of terror and rapine that measured the duration of General Paine's authority."[44]

The two officers heaped more scorn on the general.

> Well may we blush for the tarnish attached to the national uniform when debased to such ignoble uses by an officer whose only glory seems to have been oppression of non-combatants, and a loud-mouth denunciation of his superior officers as "cowards and scoundrels." Such were the epithets repeatedly attached to General Halleck's name by General Paine.

Paine perhaps had not forgiven Halleck, chief of staff of the all Union armies in 1864, for siding with Smith, and not him and Wallace, in Paducah in 1861. By "healthy contrast," Fry and Brown held up Meredith as a "firm, judicious, and effectual" administrator. The commissioners said they could attest to the Meredith administration's "justice ... energy, and its vivifying effect on the drooping Union sentiment of the Western District of Kentucky." They thanked Meredith and his staff and Craddock for helping with the investigation. In concluding their report, they recommended "most respectfully ... that Brigadier General Meredith be instructed to consider General Paine's administration as a nullity, and that he be relieved from the accumulated enormities of the late rule in Western Kentucky."[45]

Fry and Brown's investigation made headlines across the northern and border states. How the story was played naturally depended on the politics of the paper. The Democratic *Portsmouth*, Ohio, *Daily Times* and *Daily Milwaukee News* sided with Fry and Brown. "This is the ending of the tyrant Payne [sic], and we confess we shall not be surprised of any rascality that he is not capable of being the principal or accomplice," the *Times* predicted. The *News* zeroed in on Paine's purported accomplices. The paper claimed that at three different locales, Lush and Bolinger warned the citizens "if they did not vote for Lincoln, they would not be allowed to trade, their property would be taken, and they would be reduced to beggary and a starving condition. Every possible effort was made to exasperate the people in order to have a pretext to seize their property." The paper charged that McChesney ruled "Mayfield with an iron hand," adding that "he nearly destroyed the beautiful town by cutting down the shade trees and erecting a fortification around the courthouse on the public square." The *News* poured it on: "On this work all citizens were required to labor, neither sickness nor age exempting a man from duty." Those refusing to toil were "assessed a fine of from $50 to $300." According to the paper, "the fortification was a useless piece of work, as many of the hills surrounding the town commanded the square. The commission think it was simply done to exasperate the people and serve as a pretext to assess heavy fines on them."[46]

No hills surround the court square, which crowns a rise. Doubtless, the widow Happy and her children wished Mayfield had a fort guarded by soldiers when guerrillas murdered her husband within a stone's throw from were Paine had the earthworks built.

# 9

# Lush and "an epoch in the history of the country"

Perhaps nobody was happier at Paine's ouster than Editor Prentice of the *Louisville Journal*. The paper chose not to wait for Fry and Brown to issue a public report to declaim Paine, Anderson, Bolinger and others connected with the general. Craddock was the source.[1]

The long story, published on September 27, claimed Paine and his son fled to Illinois while the general's "subordinate officers also took 'French leave,' knowing their conduct would not bear investigation." The *Journal* lauded Meredith who, "with the feeling of a true soldier … afforded every facility in his power" to assist Fry and Brown in their investigation, meaning, of course, to help them do in Paine and his associates.[2]

The *Journal* said Craddock prompted the investigation into Paine's alleged machinations. The colonel went to the Purchase on business and "by close observation he became convinced that Gen. Paine and his subordinates were exercising the iron rule of despots" and "persecuting and robbing the people under various flimsy pretexts" while "the worst corruption prevailed in his office and characterized all of his official acts." Purportedly, Paine had a special loyalty test—his soldiers would ask citizens what paper they read. If they answered the *Louisville Journal*, "the parties were denounced as d——d Rebels of the meanest kind."[3]

After leaving Paducah, Craddock saw Burbridge at the general's Lexington headquarters and made his case against Paine, according to the *Journal*. Burbridge responded in disbelief; the colonel swore he was telling the truth. As a result, he accompanied Fry and Brown to Paducah. Paine was supposed to stay in town to face the music but was gone when the investigators showed up, the story said.[4]

The *Journal* cited several examples of Paine's alleged cruelty, notably the firing squads. "Prisoners were executed without a hearing, and often without any definite charge being preferred against them." The paper claimed forty-three graves of Paine victims "were counted at Paducah." The *Journal* did not say where the burials were in town or who totaled them. Even so, the paper charged that among those put to death "were two men, named Nolin and Taylor, of well-known loyalty, who" somehow offended the general. The paper said it had a statement from Hiram R. Enoch, quartermaster of the 132nd Illinois Infantry, in which he said "he heard of four citizens being executed without a shadow of a trial—Kesterson, Taylor, Mathey and Hess." Enoch added that about September 1, McChesney told him "he had shot seven men at Mayfield, and had one more in the guard-house that he intended to execute the next day." Paine ordered McChesney to Mayfield, and the colonel acted under the general's instructions, according to Enoch. The quartermaster said McChesney admitted that he condemned all of the men without a trial "and boasted that one of the prisoners was shot and covered up in his grave in forty-five minutes from the time that he was" brought before the colonel.[5]

The story named Lush and Bolinger as aiders and abettors "with Gen. Paine in his swindling transactions." Bolinger was "still at large, but Gen. Meredith is making arrangements to effect his arrest," according to the *Journal*. Lush and Bolinger's misconduct included giving speeches in which they warned citizens "that, if they did not vote for Lincoln, they would be granted no privileges, would not be allowed to trade, their property would be taken, and they would be reduced to beggary and a starving condition." The *Journal* also complained that in Paducah, Paine's soldiers seized the homes of whites and gave them "to negro families for occupation." Elsewhere, the story denounced Paine for exiling citizens, including "two old widow ladies, their hair silvered by more than sixty winters," who "were torn from their comfortable houses and sent to Canada under a guard of negro soldiers."[6]

The *Journal* concluded that "from various sources, it is estimated that Gen. Paine swindled the people and the Government out of not less than $150,000." The paper did not name any of the sources. Nor did the *Journal* offer any proof of its charges against Paine, Anderson, Bolinger or anybody else. Enoch's accusations against McChesney, who was supposed to be arrested and returned to Paducah, were hearsay. Craddock did not talk to the *Journal* in an official capacity. If he provided evidence, the paper did not cite it. Though the story was clearly slanted against Paine and his associates, the *Journal* concluded that "the facts speak plainly enough for themselves. No word of comment is needed from us." The whole story was commentary, of course.[7]

On September 28, the *Journal* followed up with a story that focused the paper's fire on Lush. The *Journal* was "not surprised" that Fry and Brown named "the Hon. (how that term is prostituted!) Lucien Anderson ... among the persons who were 'guilty of corruption and were sharers with General Paine in his swindling transactions.'" The editorial let loose on Lush: "Ever since Lucien Anderson got himself elected to Congress upon strong conservative pledges, and, on arriving at Washington, turned abolitionist and voted in all instances for abolition men and abolition measures, we have known him to be a scoundrel." The *Journal* had "felt assured that he was guilty of corruption in that case, and that he could consequently be corrupted in any case, if indeed what is thoroughly corrupt admits of being corrupted." The paper maintained that "undoubtedly the corruption just brought to light, including the sharing of the booty of an official robber and swindler, is no worse than the corruption which induced him to prove a base breaker of his plighted faith and the perfidious betrayer of his constituents and of the sacred cause of the nation." The paper challenged, "Let the abolition organs, which have hitherto defended him so warmly, defend him hotly now it if suits their worthy purposes." The *Journal* said those papers had failed to print "a word against the myriads of corruptions of their political friends, and why shouldn't they not defend poor Anderson?"[8]

Prentice's paper claimed it had learned that instead of appearing before Fry and Brown, Anderson "skulked away somewhere, and at the last dates was skulking still." The *Journal* suspected "that he can venture to come in. It doesn't seem to us that he need fear punishment for his crimes." Anderson's "friends in Washington … wouldn't like to see so useful a friend martyred," the paper mocked. "Come in out of the cold Lucien [sic]."[9]

Lush shot back a letter that the *Louisville Daily Union Press*, one of the *Journal*'s "abolition organs," published on October 24. Lush explained that he wrote his response while he was ill and in bed, but his rejoinder was lawyerly; he attempted to debunk the editorial point by point, first challenging its credibility. "Of course the editors of the Journal did not then, nor do not now know what the decision of the commission is," he challenged. Nor were they in command of Union troops in Kentucky, "nor does any *United States* officer report to them," a dig at Craddock. Anderson argued that Paine was "fully able to defend himself," but Lush was confident the general did not cheat anybody "of one cent of money or property, or that he appropriated any money or property belonging to other persons to his own use." He would not believe Paine was guilty "until I have evidence outside of the editors of the Journal." Lush also defended himself. "One thing, however; I know I did not either directly or indirectly share with him any property or money in any manner, shape, or form, whilst he was in command at Paducah or any where else. Any statement made in the Journal to the contrary I pronounce unqualifiedly false and untrue."[10]

Next, Anderson addressed the *Journal*'s claim that Paine had citizens shot. The congressman noted that among those the paper named was "one Kesterson" who Lush said he "happened to know." Anderson said James Kesterson, who lived in Graves County, was hardly an innocent civilian. For six months before he fell in front of a firing squad, Kesterson was a guerrilla leader who "aided" the murder of J.B. Happy, who was shot to death "in the dead of night … in presence of his wife and children." Kesterson was "one of the *citizens* shot by order of Gen. Paine, and for which he has incurred all the ill will, hatred and denunciation of the Journal." Lush added that local Confederate sympathizers were as outraged at Kesterson's execution "as the editors of the Journal are, and they made their threats that if he was shot, they would burn my house and kill me, by way of retaliation." The congressman added that he knew nothing of other alleged executions.[11]

Anderson also asserted that the real motive for the *Journal*'s "unprovoked and malignant attack on" him was his support for Colfax as house speaker. "Here I am charged with betraying my faith and pledges for my course in Congress…. Not only so, but the *epithet* scoundrel is applied to me for that course." Lush promised that "so far as the term scoundrel is concerned, I will at a proper time and in a proper way reply." Meanwhile, he declared that his "course in Congress is now a part of the history of the country. By my vote, voice, and in every other way I sustained the legal and constituted agents of the Government in the prosecution of the war for the suppression of the rebellion." Anderson said he was pledged to so act before he was elected. "For thus acting I am arraigned and denounced before the people of my district and State as an abolitionist by the editors of the Journal." In a little more than three months, Anderson would vote to constitutionally abolish slavery forever. Yet in the autumn of 1864, it seemed he was still trying to duck the abolitionist label.[12]

Lush maintained that the *Journal*'s abolitionist accusation came "with a bad grace." Again, he turned the charge against pro-Clay Prentice, citing an editorial from long before the war. "Mr. Clay views slavery in the abstract with unmingled abhorrence," Anderson quoted the editorial. "He justly considers it a *monster of evil; a deadly vampire draining away the lifeblood of the Republic.*" Clay "proclaimed in vivid colors the *sufferings*, the bodily degradation, of the slaves. He spoke of the dangers to be apprehended from the insurrection of the blacks; when *in every abiding place of slavery there were fierce hearts brooding over the accumulated wrongs of years, and dark hands ready to grasp the firebrand and the dagger.*"[13]

Anderson invited *Press* readers to note "what the Louisville Journal has to say about the right of all men to liberty: 'All men have a right to liberty, no matter what color.'" Lush also quoted from a *Journal* editorial on adding Texas to the Union. Texas statehood, which came in 1845, was controversial; opponents of slavery charged that pro-slavery Southerners wanted Texas because it would be another slave state. According to the editorial, supporters of Texas annexation were "above all others, the men upon whose heads rests the sin *of extending the area of slavery*, for they were warned and besought, through the public press and by their fellow-citizens, to frown down all connections with Texas and her 'peculiar institutions.'" The *Journal* "hoped for the day when 'in Kentucky *all* men would enjoy the right to liberty—*no matter what color*,'" and piled on more quotations from the paper: "Many of the best minds of the States are engaged with the subject, and they will express freely their opinions, and act freely upon them. We must make up our minds to meet that question, for no human power can stop it." Anderson cited more from the journal: "*We have ever looked forward to the day when Kentucky should contain within her bounds no bondsmen, and* WE HOPE TO LIVE TO SEE THE LIGHT OF SUCH A DAY." Finally, according to Lush, the paper declared it was ready to help abolish slavery: "We believe there is a settled conviction in the minds of a large majority of the people of Kentucky that their interests—social, moral and financial—would be promoted by disposing of the slaves, and we believe that one day they will themselves begin to move in the matter. WE AWAIT THE MOVEMENT, AND SHALL STAND READY TO SECOND IT WHENEVER OUR AID CAN BE OF ANY AVAIL."[14]

The *Journal*'s attack on Anderson was not signed, but Lush obviously believed Prentice wrote it, and he probably did. "This is the man who calls me an abolitionist because I voted to sustain the armies of the Government in order that the rebellion now against its authority might be crushed." Lush jabbed, "Does he suppose that the people of this State are so blinded by the present aspect of the slavery question, or so ignorant as to forget his history[?]" Anderson claimed Prentice "is now, and has been, all his life, an anti-slavery man" and "would to-day, if in his power, wipe it out from the soil of the United States, for he considers 'all men have a right to liberty, no matter what color.'" Nonetheless, the editor "for base and malignant purposes, charges me with being an abolitionist," Lush declared. "If the charge was true would it not be the *kettle calling the pot black*? When did the editors of the Journal become the defenders of slavery? There is not a well informed man in the State to-day who believes that they are the friends of slavery, but all know and believe they have assumed their present position for selfish purposes."[15]

Anderson demanded to know when Prentice and the other *Journal* editors became Democrats. "Was it in 1863, when they denounced every member of that party from Ex. Gov. Wickliffe down to the lowest private in the ranks of traitors?" Who had changed, Lush mockingly mused, the *Journal* or Wickliffe and the Democrats?

> We and them all together in 1864, drawing consolation from, and contending for, a platform which declares that the war on the part of the Government against the Rebellion is a failure, and demanding a cessation of hostilities, so that a white rag may be raised whenever a rebel or a guerrilla shall invade the *sacred soil of the State*.[16]

Anderson concluded that the *Journal*, not the Democrats, had changed. The paper's editors "have basely surrendered up the position of the Union men of the State and nation, into the hands of men who in 1863 they denounced as traitors." Lush demanded,

> Can anything *more corrupt* in the whole range of political turpitude be conceived of than the action of that paper? They have not only done this, but are now and have been for months, pursuing with fiendish malignity every Union man in the State, who will not basely desert his faith and flag, and follow their lead into the meshes of treason and rebellion.[17]

Anderson declared that despite the *Journal's* abuse, slander and denunciation of him, he would

> never desert my country; and if the vote of my native State in the coming elections, is to be cast on a *platform* which surrenders up the *sacred* cause of the nation to rebels in arms against it, by a base and infamous coalition which is known to exist in Kentucky, concocted and fixed up at Chicago by demagogues and political *jugglers*, I will not be instrumental in having it done.

Regardless of "malice, detraction and slander" toward him, Anderson swore that "as long as a I have a voice to raise or an arm to strike" he would "fight open rebels and disguised traitors."[18]

In concluding his lengthy letter, Anderson said there was "not one word of truth in" the *Journal's* charge that he dodged Fry and Brown when they came to Paducah. Lush vowed he did go before the commission and answered every question put to him. "Why should I skulk?" Lush challenged. "I have never, since the rebellion began, skulked from rebels and traitors," Anderson thundered. The skulking charge "was made by the editors to answer their purpose. I am not astonished. A press which is now the slanderer of Union men and Federal officers, the defender of traitors and apologist for guerrillas, will not hesitate to say or do anything."[19]

The *Journal* counterattacked the next day, describing him as "The dishonorable Hon. Lucien Anderson." The paper stood by its story, declaring "what we said of him we said upon authority." The *Journal* also defended Craddock as its source, adding

> if he reported incorrectly, let the facts be proved by those who feel themselves aggrieved. We presume that the decision of the Commission will soon be given officially to the public, and this will settle the matter, or, if it doesn't, a civil or military trial of Paine and Anderson upon the charges against them may.[20]

Paine had recently called at the *Journal* demanding to know the source of the September 27 article, the October 25 story said. When he approached Prentice's office, the general met an army officer he did not know; he asked him to witness his meeting with the editor. "I have come to ask who authorized this statement," Paine demanded. The officer interjected, "*General Paine, you need inquire no further; I authorized everything stated in that article; and everything in is true, as I am ready to prove.*" The paper did not name the officer but took him for a lieutenant colonel. "After a little while," Paine asked the officer for a written statement admitting that he made the charges in the article. The officer wrote out a statement and handed it to Paine, thus ending the interview "soon afterwards," according to the *Journal*.[21]

Switching back to Anderson, the story suggested that Lush, who "volunteers what he intends as a defense of Paine," might have a harder time defending himself. "He insinuates an intention to hold us personally responsible for applying to him the term 'scoundrel.' Well, we hear his 'bark'; we may feel the 'bite' if it ever comes." The *Journal* mused that "perhaps our Hon. hero, laboring under a grievous mistake, would a little rather focus on an *Editor* for personal responsibility rather than upon a *military officer*. Even your fire-eaters, your red and blazing salamanders, sometimes remember what they deem a little *discreet*."[22]

The paper figured Anderson felt "sick as death at being reminded of his proving false and treacherous to his constituents after his election to Congress." Nonetheless, he "can't relieve himself of the infamy. He can't erase or modify the black blot upon his name." The *Journal* repeated its accusation that Anderson

> got elected by making the strongest conservative, anti-abolition promises and pledges, then went right off to Washington and voted for every abolition man and abolition measure. Whether it was flattery or money or the promise of official favor or all three that induced him to incur the guilt of such monstrous perfidy, we of course know not, but we do know than any man of ordinary sensibility, standing before the community as he does, would desire, more than aught else, to hide his dishonored head six feet under ground.

But the paper maintained that if Lush "by holding persons to personal responsibility, can get himself killed, it will be great gain to him—as well as to the world."[23]

On October 26, Bolinger had his say in the *Press*, prompting the *Journal* to rebuke both "Paducah culprits" the next day. Lush and Bolinger were slow to reply to Fry and Brown's report "and neither would have lost anything by being a great deal slower," Prentice's organ sneered. "Bolinger tries to put a bold face upon the matter, but succeeds only in putting an impudent one." The *Journal* ridiculed Bolinger's rejoinder: "It is easy to see guilt peeping out from every sentence of his letter like a rat from a hole. He offers a reward of five thousand dollars for proof of the charges against him. He may find that the proof will cost him a good deal more than that." The issue "is or ought to be in the hands of the authorities, and we trust that justice, strict and exact justice, will take its course," the *Journal* declared. "If the persons accused want to defy anybody, let them defy the members of the Commission and the authors of the affidavits." Bolinger also accused Craddock of being the *Journal*'s informant about the proceedings in Paducah. "But we can tell him that Col. C. is not our *only* informant." A commission member who was at the *Journal* when its September 27 story was composed "said that the whole was true, and, that the Commission were ready to establish that Bolinger had been for a considerable time the agent of a guerrilla band!" Such a charge seems preposterous given that Confederates kidnapped him in 1861, that guerrillas tried to rob his store in 1862 and rebel cavalry tried to abduct him in 1863. The paper again insisted the story was true and identified the lieutenant colonel who rebuked Paine as a member of Burbridge's staff who was judge advocate for Fry and Brown in Paducah. The *Journal* said the officer told an editor, "You might have referred General Paine to me, 'for every statement in the article of the Journal article is perfectly true."[24]

The *Journal* predicted that

> the accused parties, before they get through this ugly business, will probably find, unless their abolitionism has the virtue to save them, that they have more persons to deal with than Col. Craddock and the Editors of the Louisville Journal. As Anderson proposes to hold us personally responsible for *calling* him a scoundrel, what in the world will he do to the members of the Commission if they *prove* him one! But will the Administration permit this matter to go any further than it has gone?[25]

A majority of Anderson's fellow Mayfield citizens—and most Purchase dwellers—doubtless rejoiced at the hasty departure of his friend, Paine. "His removal ... was hailed with delight by the citizens of the town and surrounding country, many of whom had been subjected to the greatest cruelty on account of their suspected friendship for the Southern cause," Battle, Perrin and Kniffen wrote.[26]

Despite Meredith's evidently gentler rule, most citizens clung to their rebel ways. Smugglers still plied their illicit trade with the South. Guerrillas still scourged the countryside. Though Paine was deposed in the Purchase, Judge Williams defended the general in an October 3 letter to the president that mainly centered on the election. The general "may have done some indefensible things," Williams admitted. Yet he said Copperheads had greatly exaggerated Paine's alleged wrongdoings. Perhaps to encourage Lincoln to look favorably on Paine and himself, the judge painted a rosy—and inaccurate—picture of the president's chances in the Bluegrass State. "Let me assure you that our prospects are daily brightening and we have a constant increase in Kentucky." Williams heaped on the soft soap, too, declaring, "This is a triumph solely attributable to your greatness and goodness, and in some measure a reward to your single devotedness to our nationality." He compared Lincoln to George Washington and Andrew Jackson, vowing, "If impartial history has written that Washington was the father of his country, this same history shall write Lincoln its preserver." He was correct that Lincoln would also go down in history as a great president. But he was wrong about the Lincoln vote in Kentucky in 1864. At any rate, the judge added, "Thousands like myself yield you unqualified support, and other thousands will yet do so in

Kentucky: that we have great reason to hope and believe Kentucky will go for you in November." He told the president that the McClellan partisans were short on enthusiasm and that "a very large portion of the conservative Union men" really sensed they were "not discharging their duty to the country by" getting behind Little Mac. Either Williams was merely telling Lincoln what he thought the president wanted to hear, or he profoundly misunderstoon political realities in Kentucky. The state was pro–Union, but not pro–Lincoln and anti-slavery.[27]

Not long after Paine departed, Meredith heard Forrest was on the way back to the Purchase. "Much excitement prevails ... respecting a raid that is being made into Western Kentucky," the *New York Times* reported. Forrest purportedly had politics on his mind. He told his Kentucky troops "he was coming to free their State from the hand of the oppressor, and to enable them to vote right at the coming election," the paper said. His Bluegrass State contingent—from the Purchase and elsewhere in the western part of the state—included the Third, Seventh and Eighth mounted infantry regiments and the Twelfth Kentucky Cavalry. Their commander, Brigadier General Abraham Buford, addressed them, echoing Forrest. They were indeed homeward bound, mainly on a political mission. "The people of the First District of Kentucky were being misled by the General in command (Gen. Meredith)— and that he (Buford) was going to see that it was stopped. He came to attend the elections and to allow Kentuckians to vote as they pleased." Of course, Forrest and Buford hoped the locals would back the Democratic ticket, though a Yankee general topped it. The *Times* said Meredith was so desperate for reinforcements that he called on civilians to help him defend the Paducah, which sustained considerable damage when Forrest came calling on March 25.[28]

The *Chicago Tribune* provided more details of Union military preparations to fight Forrest. Meredith ordered Mayfield abandoned on October 15 and pulled his troops back to Paducah. The move was supposed to bolster the city's defenses against Forrest and did not cause any "loss to the Government, inasmuch as every dollars' worth of public property was removed; but it was a severe blow to individuals many of whom lost considerable quantities of goods, etc., which were abandoned in the flight."[29]

Perhaps Uncle Sam did not lose any money when the Yankees abandoned Mayfield, but at least three civilians reportedly lost their lives when the town almost immediately became a guerrilla target again. On October 17, sixteen "rebel soldiers rode into the town," bought a few items and departed. Other Confederates were observed in Graves and Ballard County on the same day, prompting Meredith to send cavalry after the enemy. Two days later, "forty rebels" returned to Mayfield, burned the courthouse "and committed many depredations," according to the to the *Cleveland Daily*

*Leader.* On October 29, "a small squad of guerrilla cut-throats" attacked May-field and carried out "various depredations on civilians," the *Tribune* reported. They shot to death two men and hanged seventy-year-old Peter Wortham "who had been in the habit of taking information of the Rebel movements to Gen. Meredith in Paducah." The Chicago paper claimed "Rebel soldiers occupy Mayfield whenever they feel inclined without ... hindrance." About forty were in town on October 29 and 30 "purchasing goods which they paid for in Confederate money. They molested no private citizens and destroyed no property."[30]

The *Tribune* also said that Forrest's invasion was designed to disrupt voting for president on November 8. Apparently, the general heard that Meredith, with Lush "and several others of our most influential citizens," were out campaigning for Lincoln "with the most flattering prospects of success." Union Clubs were organized everywhere the dignitaries visited "and a large majority of the citizens pledged themselves to vote for Lincoln and Johnson." Thus, Forrest headed for western Kentucky, according to the Chicago paper.[31]

The *Tribune,* too, reported that Forrest told his Kentucky soldiers, nearly all of them from the Purchase, "that he intended to redeem their State from Abolition rule and to enable them to 'vote right.'" Buford, from Woodford County, in the Bluegrass region, vowed "that he was determined to 'drive the damned Yankees from Kentucky soil, and to have the polls in my own hands on the 8th of November.'" He promised to "prevent Abe Lincoln from getting a vote outside of a military post." Nonetheless, the Chicago paper predicted that "if force sufficient to drive the scoundrels from the country be furnished, this district will give a large Union majority, notwithstanding the former political status of the people."[32]

Forrest reputedly aimed to attack Paducah as well. The threat prompted Meredith called on civilians to help his soldiers defend the city. On October 18, he "issued a stirring appeal to the citizens to organize for home defense." Lush and others backed up the general with speeches. As a result, four hundred men were organized into a home guard battalion which the *Tribune* was sure would "form an important auxiliary to our defenses." That night, the Union Club put on "a grand demonstration. The torchlight procession was a great success, and excited much attention. Hundreds of ladies were on the streets to witness the proceedings, which were of the most gratifying character."[33]

The *New York Times,* quoting the *Chicago Evening Journal,* also said politics spurred Forrest and Buford to return to the Purchase. Forrest "told Kentuckians that he was coming to free their State from the hand of the oppressor, and to enable them to vote right at the coming election." The paper added that Buford told his men "that the people of the First District of Kentucky were being misled by the General in command (Gen. Meredith) and that he (Buford) was going to see that it was stopped. He came to attend the elections and to allow Kentuckians to vote as they pleased."[34]

In his October 17 missive to Lincoln, Anderson also tried to ingratiate himself with the president. Lush said he had delivered a trio of pro–Lincoln speeches in three Purchase counties in line with Meredith's policy, which he called "wise & conciliatory." He said the people listened attentively "and they *profess to be all right* in many places," including Mayfield where he believed voters "intend to do right," meaning vote for the president. But the congressman could not resist a dig at Meredith, telling Lincoln that Union troops had given up Mayfield, thus leaving much of the Purchase wide open to rebel and guerrilla control. Subsequent events proved Lush right, at least where his hometown was concerned. Anderson advised that "unless these Counties are held of course no votes will be polled." Lush promised the president that Meredith had said he would reoccupy Mayfield "in a few days." But, according to the congressman, Meredith believed he had insufficient forces "to hold beyond a doubt the whole of these Counties therefore he desires more troops immediately." Anderson trusted Meredith would get reinforcements, and declared, "the whole district shall be canvassed if tis possible to do so," assuring Lincoln "nothing on my part shall be wanting." He also hoped Kentucky would "do her duty in this contest," but he admitted, "I am not however sanguine." Should Kentucky go for McClellan, Lush said, "it will not be the fault of the *true men* of the state," meaning men like him.[35]

As it turned out, Forrest's foray was more military than political. He left Paducah and Columbus alone and instead sneaked into abandoned Fort Heiman on the Tennessee River in southeastern Calloway County and on October 29 and 30 used his artillery to shoot up steamboats and disrupt military traffic on the Tennessee River. Afterwards, Forrest headed south, slipping along the river's western bank and emplacing his guns opposite the big Union supply base at Johnsonville, Tennessee. On November 4, his gunners shelled the post, smashing and setting ablaze large, well-stocked warehouses and supply vessels. After reducing the base to an inferno, Forrest and his troops got away.[36]

On the day Forrest's gunners blasted Johnsonville, Lush again wrote the president, this time endorsing Treasury Secretary Salmon P. Chase of Ohio for chief justice of the Supreme Court. Anderson understood Lincoln was well acquainted with the longtime abolitionist's "antecedents, his qualifications etc for the place," adding that anything he might say in Chase's "favor would amount to but little." Nonetheless, Anderson assured the president that the secretary's elevation to the high court "would be received with satisfaction by all truly loyal men in this part of the State and they would regard his appointment as another indication that the true principles of the Gov were intended to be carried out." Shortly after his reelection, Lincoln named Chase, a former Buckeye State governor and senator, chief justice. Chase served from 1864 to 1873 and presided over the impeachment trial of President Andrew Johnson in the Senate in 1868.[37]

Lincoln easily won a second term on November 8, but without his home state's electoral vote. McClellan carried Kentucky by a wide margin, 64,301 to 27,787. To be sure, Lincoln fared considerably better in his native state than he had in 1860. But his total amounted to just 30.2 percent of the votes cast. Percentage-wise, Kentucky was Lincoln's worst state. Still, he considerably improved on his 1860 total of a scant 1,364 votes. Lincoln carried no counties in his home state the first time he ran; in 1864, he pocketed twenty-five.[38]

Union authorities had desperately wanted Kentucky in the Lincoln column. Burbidge considered "it of the utmost importance for Kentucky's future that the State should be carried for Mr. Lincoln." The general tried his best to win votes for Lincoln, employing old-fashioned patronage and "honorably" granting favors. He sent claims commissioners to Unionist slave owners whose bondsmen were in the federal forces. Burbridge's emissaries strongly implied that a vote for Lincoln meant compensation for lost slaves, a McClellan vote did not. But taking no chances, the general ordered "a judicious disposition of the troops." As a result, 54,000 fewer ballots were cast in 1864 than in 1860. The depressed vote also reflected "the great demoralization which prevailed in the state." Military heavy-handedness was not as widespread as it had been in previous elections, but some of the falling off was the result of intimidation by soldiers.[39]

Indeed, in the Purchase, only 4,097 of 13,721 eligible voters—less than thirty percent—went to the polls; Calloway County reported no returns. The statewide turnout was 40.5 percent. McClellan managed to edge Lincoln in the Purchase, 2,064 to 2,033. Lincoln carried Fulton, Hickman, Marshall and McCracken counties—and Livingston and Crittenden counties elsewhere in the First District, but just as statewide, the turnout was tiny. Lush's home county went for McClellan 769 to 643.[40]

Predictably, the *Louisville Journal* lamented Lincoln's victory. "The future of the Republic is gloomy," the paper editorialized. "It is dark. Yet we do not despair. And we exhort Constitutional Unionists everywhere to be of good cheer." The *Journal* urged,

> The Union MUST BE PRESERVED AT ALL HAZARDS. And among the commonest of these hazards is the temporary prostration of the Union's most rational and most devoted friends. We are vanquished; but our principles are not. They are unvanquishable; though the present success of their false friends, and consequently of their worst enemies, renders their final triumph more costly in all that is dear to citizens and men.[41]

The outcome of the presidential election in Kentucky did not settle the struggle for political supremacy in the state or the controversy among the citizenry over slavery's future. The fused Union and Peace Democrats, now calling themselves the Conservative Democrats or just Conservatives, clearly had the upper hand in Frankfort over Lush and the Unconditional Unionists. But the Unconditional Unionists were on good terms with the Republicans who controlled the White House and both houses of Congress.[42]

The Lincoln vote was so small in Kentucky because the president made the Civil War a conflict to save the Union and destroy slavery. Most Conservatives—indeed most white Kentuckians—were still for the Union and slavery. But time was fast running out on the South's peculiar institution when Lush and his fellow congressmen returned to Washington for the second session of the Thirty-eighth Congress. The main issue was the future of slavery, whose demise began on January 1, 1863, when the Emancipation Proclamation took effect. But it only freed slaves in Confederate-held territory on and after that date. Almost all Kentuckians fiercely opposed the proclamation, though it did not apply to Kentucky.[43]

The second step toward slavery's eradication came on April 8, 1864, when the Republican Senate by a vote of thirty-eight to six, ratified the Thirteenth Amendment to the constitution, which in its final form declared "Neither slavery nor involuntary servitude, except as a punishment for crime whereof the party shall have been duly convicted, shall exist within the United States, or any place subject to their jurisdiction." Kentucky's Union Democratic senators, Garrett Davis and Lazarus W. Powell, voted against the amendment.[44]

Anderson and Randall did not speak on the amendment in Congress but Smith did, and forcefully. Smith, born in 1826, represented the strongly pro–Union Sixth Congressional District in northern Kentucky. A Mexican-American War veteran, he began practicing law in Covington in 1858. Voters sent Smith to the state house of representatives on the Union ticket in 1861, but he soon opted for military service. His army record is unclear, but he evidently volunteered as a private in 1861. He was promoted to major of the Third Kentucky Cavalry Regiment and was put in charge of recruiting. In March, 1862, he became colonel and commander of the Fourth Kentucky Cavalry and played a key role in the Union defeat of Morgan's cavalry at the battle of Lebanon, Tennessee, on May 5, 1862. The next month, Smith earned brigadier general's stars. He resigned his commission on December 1, 1863, four months after he was elected to Congress, and headed for Washington. Nonetheless, on March 13, 1865, he was promoted to brevet major general of volunteers.[45]

"We all know that slavery will resist the government until it is destroyed," Smith said. He added that slavery caused the war and that peace required its

From *Harper's Weekly* "Scene in the of the Passage of the Proposition to Amend the Constitution, January 31, 1865 (Library of Congress).

abolition. With slavery gone, the reunited country would be stronger than before. Kentuckians should welcome an end to slavery because the peculiar institution had held Kentucky back. Slavery, he argued, stifled individual initiative and prevented the growth of industry. At the same time, Smith maintained that the rancorous political battles in Kentucky were mainly "over Negroes. And if every Negro were taken from the Commonwealth of Kentucky there would not be in thirty days a man in the state to raise his voice against the Government." The congressman hoped his country was beginning a new era of growth in industry and agriculture and he urged his fellow Kentuckians to be part of it. "Shall we not look forward one hundred and fifty years and see millions of freedmen who know no masters, and one free country stretching from the Atlantic to the Pacific under one Constitution, with the one motto Union and liberty forever?" he asked.[46]

Meanwhile, the Kentucky legislature reconvened on January 4. In his opening message, Bramlette told lawmakers he was sending them a copy of Fry and Brown's report and a copy of his letter to Lincoln about Paine and his alleged misrule in Paducah. Representative H.C. McLoed of Woodford County was so angry over the report that on January 30 he urged the House to call on Lush to quit Congress. He charged that Anderson "used his influence over, and was in complicity with, the notorious General Paine and others, in their acts of tyranny, insult, oppression, bribery, and plunder." Thus McLeod proposed a resolution declaring Anderson unfit to represent the people of Kentucky "and unworthy to hold any office of honor, trust, or profit within the gift of the people of Kentucky ... and he is hereby requested, to resign his position as a member of the Federal Congress." Nothing came of the resolution.[47]

Though Conservatives like McLoed controlled the House and Senate, Lush was not without friends in Frankfort. Senator Landrum, who had been kidnapped with Anderson, defended his fellow townsman against the governor, Fry and Brown. On February 1, the Unconditional Unionist called on the Senate to appoint a committee to investigate the "grave charges" against Paine and Anderson contained in Bramlette's message. Landrum said that "persons thus implicated charge that said commission was *ex parte* and done them injustice, and did not make a full and fair investigation; and as this report is appended to a State paper, it is but right and just that a full and fair investigation should be made." Landrum's proposed panel was to be composed of one senator and two representatives with the authority

> to investigate those matters and charges; that said committee have a sitting at Paducah, with power to send for persons and papers..., and that they give notice of their sittings by one publication in the Louisville daily newspapers and by letters respectively addressed through the mails to Brigadier General Paine and Hon. L. Anderson."

Landrum got nowhere; the senate voted 17–11 to table his proposal.[48]

The next day, Landrum tried again, this time offering a briefer resolution: "...That so much of the Governor's message, and documents appended thereto, as relates to Hon. L. Anderson and other citizens of Western Kentucky, be referred to a select committee, and that they report at as early a day as possible." The result was the same; the Senate voted it down.[49]

Anderson fared better at the Union State Convention, which met in Frankfort on January 4. The Unconditional Union men, including Judge Williams, approved a resolution declaring "That the thanks of all loyal men in Kentucky are justly due, and are hereby rendered to the Hon. Green Clay Smith, Hon. Lucien Anderson and Hon. W.H. Randall, for their truly patriotic efforts in the Union cause, and that their past official conduct as members of Congress is hereby fully approved." Though, percentage-wise, Kentucky gave the president the smallest vote he polled in any state in 1864, the Unionists also "resolved, that the sagacity of President Lincoln in conceiving, and his heroic firmness in sustaining, wise measures for the maintenance and perpetuity of our Republican institutions entitle him to the gratitude and support of all loyal men of Kentucky and the nation." The delegates asked the state's senators and representatives to vote for "submitting a proposed amendment of the National Constitution abolishing and prohibiting slavery throughout the domain of the United States, and that we invite the co-operation of the legislature of Kentucky in carrying forward this request."[50]

The sagacious Lincoln interpreted his election to a second term as a mandate for passing the Thirteenth Amendment, James M. McPherson wrote in *Battle Cry of Freedom: The Civil War Era*. While Lincoln won another term, several Democrats who opposed the amendment lost their seats. However, they would remain in office until March 5, 1865, when the Thirty-Eighth Congress was to adjourn. The amendment required a two-thirds majority to pass; the Republicans would enjoy a three-fourths majority in the Thirty-Ninth Congress, making passage a certainty. If the amendment failed in the Thirty-Eighth Congress, Lincoln was ready to call the next Congress into special session in March. But he wanted Congress to approve the amendment "sooner, by a bipartisan majority, as a gesture of wartime unity in favor of this measure that Lincoln considered essential to Union victory," McPherson explained, quoting the president's message to Congress on December 6, 1864: "In a great national crisis like ours, unanimity of action among those seeking a common end is very desirable—almost indispensable." Lincoln's words were stirring but "an expression of an ideal rather than reality, since most war measures, especially those concerning slavery, had been passed by a strictly Republican vote," the author cautioned. "For the historic achievement of terminating the institution, ... Lincoln appealed to the Democrats to recognize 'the will of the majority' as expressed by the election."[51]

Nonetheless, almost all Democratic house members stubbornly opposed the amendment. A few, however, could see the handwriting on the wall. One lawmaker said the party was drubbed at the polls in 1864 "because we [would] not venture to cut loose from the dead carcass of negro slavery." Such resignation encouraged the Lincoln administration to target "a dozen or so lame-duck Democratic congressmen" for "a barrage of blandishments," McPherson wrote. Secretary of State Seward, an ex-senator and thus wise in the ways of Capitol Hill, headed the lobbying campaign. "Some congressmen were promised government jobs for themselves or relatives; others received administration favors of one sort or another."[52]

Still, no one could predict if the "arm-twisting and log-rolling" would pay off until the House voted, McPherson wrote. The House chamber was packed for the vote on January 31. "The nation, realizing the transcendent magnitude of the issue, awaited the result with profound anxiety," wrote Henry Wilson in *History of the Antislavery Measures of the Thirty-Seventh and Thirty-Eighth United States Congresses*. "The galleries, and the avenues leading to them, were early thronged by a dense mass intensely anxious to witness the scene." Members of the senate, Lincoln's cabinet, supreme court justices "and even strangers, crowding onto the floor of the House, watched its proceedings with absorbing interest." The roll was called alphabetically; Lush was seventh in order. His "aye" vote broke a three-to-three tie. The amendment passed one hundred nineteen to fifty-six with eight abstentions.[53]

The Republican *New York Times* hailed the vote as "the great feature of the existing rebellion" and "an epoch in the history of the country," that would "be remembered by the members of the House and spectators present as an event in their lives." The roll call started at 3 p.m. and when "when prominent Democrats voted aye, there was suppressed evidence of applause and gratification exhibited in the galleries, but it was evident that the great interest centered entirely upon the final result." When the total was announced

the enthusiasm of all present, save a few disappointed politicians, knew no bounds, and for several moments the scene was grand and impressive beyond description. No attempt was made to suppress the applause which came from all sides, every one feeling that the occasion justified the fullest expression of approbation and joy.[54]

Besides Unconditional Unionists Anderson, Smith and Randall, Union Democrat George H. Yeaman of Owensboro voted "aye." The remaining five Kentucky representatives, all Conservatives, voted "nay": Clay, Mallory, Grider, Harding and Wadsworth. In a last-ditch attempt to derail the amendment, Mallory tried to postpone the vote, to no avail.[55]

The thirty-five-year-old Yeaman represented the Second District which sprawled across the Pennyrile Region of western Kentucky. He had seniority over Anderson, Randall and Smith, but barely. He made it to Washington in 1862, via a special election to fill out the unexpired term of James S. Jackson of Hopkinsville. Elected in August, 1861, Jackson resigned, joined the Union army, made brigadier general and was killed at the battle of Perryville on October 8, 1862. Yeaman's district leaned toward the Union, but included a significant Confederate minority. A Hardin County native, Yeaman was the nephew of John L. Helm, who was governor of Kentucky from 1850 to 1851. Elected lieutenant governor in 1848, Helm became governor when John J. Crittenden resigned to become President Millard Fillmore's attorney general. Yeaman became a lawyer in Elizabethtown, the Hardin County seat, in 1852 but

George H. Yeaman (National Archives and Records Administration).

moved to Owensboro, the seat of Daviess County. Voters elected him their county judge in 1854 and their state representative in 1861, the latter on the Union ticket. He won his own term in 1863, and though he came to support the Thirteenth Amendment, he had bitterly opposed the Emancipation Proclamation.[56]

The *Commonwealth* was pleased, though surprised, at the vote, maintaining that had it

been taken two weeks ago it would doubtless have been otherwise. The debate on the question up to the time at which it was postponed for a fortnight, shewed that the Democratic portion of the House was expected to hang together in opposition to the measure, and it was feared that the members would all act in accordance with the party requirements. Probably the interim has been improved by instructions from constituents to their representatives, which have taught them that lesson the Democracy has been so slow in learning—that country is more worth than party, and patriotism than demagoguery.[57]

While "ayes" from Anderson, Randall and Smith were expected, Yeaman's support for the amendment "surprised his friends in Congress," according to the Frankfort paper, which added, he spoke as he did because he saw slavery already destroyed by its friends, and that now the best interests of his country and his State demanded its removal. Others have taken the same view, and voted accordingly. They have acted as statesmen and patriots, and will win the esteem and respect of their countrymen, no matter how much they may now differ from them on this point.[58]

The *Commonwealth* claimed the amendment's constitutionality

was ably and fully debated, and those who are in the habit of sneering at and condemning all that is done by the supporters of the Administration as unconstitutional, will do well to remember, that the question had this full discussion, and after hearing the arguments *pro* and *con*, men have voted, who, at least, are as capable of a just and impartial judgment as those who condemn the act.

The paper conceded that the issue was not yet decided because the amendment was only approved by Congress.

It is to go before the States for the ratification of the people, and if they can be convinced of its unconstitutionality the measure will yet fail. It will require a vote of three-fourths of the States before it can be adopted, and surely if, after a fair and thorough canvassing of the country on this question, this requisite vote is gained, the amendment must be regarded as constitutional, necessary and just.[59]

The *Commonwealth* predicted a storm of criticism from die hard Kentucky secessionists and conservative, pro-slavery Unionists.

The denunciation of true Union men by rebeldom and its well-wishers in our midst will now be severer than ever, but whatever in the late action of the House is unjust, or dishonest, or despotic, the rebellion is alone responsible for it—the rebellion has left us no choice between the destruction of slavery and the salvation of the country.[60]

The *Daily Union Press* of February 1 welcomed the amendment, telling its readers that when it passed, "thereupon arose a general shout of applause. The members on the floor huzawed in chorus with the galleries. The ladies in the House assemblage waved their handkerchiefs again and again, and the applause was repeated. The audience was wildly excited, and the friends of the measure were jubilant." The next day, the Press told how Kentucky's congressmen voted. Anderson, Randall, Smith and Yeaman helped plant "another great land-mark in the process of human history." The paper "dared not hope that this Congress would make itself illustrious by enacting the anti-slavery amendment ... but we are none the less gratified that it has done so." The *Press* pointed out that Clay, Grider, Harding, Mallory and Wadsworth opposed the amendment. "Mark them," the paper advised its readers. "To every one of them it will prove the unluckiest vote he ever cast." The *Press* published the names of every congressman who voted "aye" and "nay," italicizing the Democrats, including Yeaman, and observing that every lawmaker who opposed the amendment was a Democrat. But the paper said Yeaman was only "technically" a Democrat.[61]

Passage of the Thirteenth Amendment wrought yet another shift in political alignments in Kentucky. Some Conservatives accepted, however reluctantly, that slavery was doomed. So they called on all Democrats to support ratification of the amendment. They feared a resurgence of the old secessionists who bitterly opposed ratification and who were rising fast in the party. The concerns of pro-ratification Conservatives presaged a postwar split in Democratic ranks between the Bourbons, conservatives who clung to the state's slavery and agricultural past, and the New Departure faction, which accepted the end of slavery and called on Kentucky to industrialize like its northern neighbors.[62]

Some Kentuckians had resigned themselves to slavery's inevitable demise. Even the *Louisville Journal* urged the people to accept the Thirteenth Amendment. On the other hand, Bramlette still hoped slavery might be ended gradually and that freed slaves could be colonized in Africa. He proposed to the legislature that masters be allowed to keep their slaves for two years and pay them so they could earn enough money to pay their way to Africa. But when the amendment was presented to lawmakers for ratification, Bramlette favored it. Surprisingly, Magoffin did, too.[63]

Realizing the legislature was disinclined to ratify the amendment as it was written, Bramlette proposed that it be approved conditionally. He suggested that approval be contingent upon the federal government compensating slaveholders more than thirty-four million dollars, the assessed value of the state's slaves in 1864. The legislature rejected the governor's plan and voted outright not to ratify the Thirteenth Amendment. On February 23, the House voted for a resolution rejecting the amendment, fifty-six to twenty-eight. Unconditional Unionist Representatives E.W. Smith of Graves County and T.J. Birchett of McCracken voted against the measure. Conservative Thomas P. Hayes of Ballard County favored the resolution, and the Purchase's three other Conservative representatives did not vote. The next day, the senate approved a similar resolution, twenty-three to eleven. Landrum opposed the anti-ratification legislation. Conservative Senator T.W. Hammond of Cadiz, whose district included Calloway County, voted for it, and the other senator from the Purchase did not vote.[64]

Bramlette was disgusted with the House and Senate for refusing to ratify the Thirteenth Amendment, but he dutifully notified Washington. Unconditional Unionist lawmakers subsequently tried to reverse the vote but to no avail. Kentucky clung to slavery while the number of states approving the amendment moved steadily toward the requisite constitutional majority. At the same time, slavery, though legal in Kentucky, continued to disintegrate.[65]

Also in February, Lush's name innocently surfaced in connection with an alleged White House bribery scandal. A young man from Gibson County, Tennessee, came to Washington seeking the release of five Confederate prisoners of war held at Camp Morton in Indianapolis and Camp Douglas near Chicago. He asked Anderson for help, and Lush agreed to write Lincoln on the captives' behalf. In his letter of support, Anderson confessed that he did not know any of the soldiers but assured the president that they were "recommended by ten true men (with whom I am personally acquainted) as proper persons to be permitted to take the oath and return home." Thus, based on "recommendations and information received," Lush requested Lincoln to free them if they swore allegiance to the Union.[66]

Anderson gave his letter to the Tennessean who took it to the White House. The doorkeeper to Lincoln's office demanded a bribe, but Emerson Etheridge, the recently ousted clerk of the House of Representatives, claimed he foiled the extortionist. The ex-Tennessee congressman told his self-serving story to the *Washington Constitutional Unionist,* and other papers published his account.[67]

Etheridge evidently knew the young man; Gibson County was part of his old congressional district. Doorkeeper C. O'Leary denied the young man entrance, Etheridge said. But when the visitor told O'Leary what he wanted, he pulled the man aside and said for fifty dollars "he (O'Leary) would take charge of the papers and procure the President's order for the release of these prisoners; that otherwise he would have to remain for many days without any probability of having an interview with the President." Etheridge wrote that his fellow Tennessean saw two other people "on a similar errand pay money to O'Leary, and saw the desired papers, a few minutes afterward, given by O'Leary to such persons."[68]

The young man "had but little money at the

Emerson Etheridge (National Archives and Records Administration).

hotel; nothing like that amount with him." Even so, he left the papers with O'Leary and informed Etheridge. At any rate, Etheridge said he immediately accompanied the man back to the White House "intending to play a simple and rustic part." Etheridge claimed that "with some difficulty" he managed to win O'Leary's confidence "and arranged with him to pay the fifty dollars so soon as the President's order for the discharge of these prisoners should be handed to the gentleman."[69]

O'Leary agreed to meet the young man at his room in the National Hotel. He showed up at the appointed time with the president's order freeing the prisoners, which he wrote on the back of Anderson's letter. Etheridge hid and watched as the cash and the release order changed hands. Etheridge swore,

> Just as O'Leary was bowing himself out, I intercepted him, forced him back into the room, denounced him as a swindler, and caused him to surrender the money (thirty dollars), that being the amount which he had agreed to take finally, because of the assurance that nothing would be advanced for two of the prisoners, and the inability of the gentleman to pay more for the others.[70]

Etheridge was all too happy to embarrass Lush and Lincoln. He turned against the president over the Emancipation Proclamation, which he considered a betrayal of pro-slavery Southern Unionists like himself. In December, 1863, he joined a harebrained plot to hand control of the House to a coalition of northern Democrats and border state Unionists. Etheridge was supposed to use his position as clerk to invalidate the credentials of several Republican lawmakers. The scheme failed, and he was voted out as clerk. He remained in the capital city as a bitter critic of Lincoln and the Republicans.[71] He claimed,

> I make this matter public from motives of humanity. During the last year I have made many applications for the discharge of prisoners of war upon the terms mentioned in the above order of the President, but in no instance have I been successful. I have often written to the friends and kindred of prisoners that there was no end to their captivity but peace. I rejoice, however, to be able at last to inform those who feel an interest in the matter that a cheap and expeditious remedy is within their power.[72]

Meanwhile, Paine, who heartily supported the Thirteenth Amendment, returned to Paducah in February, 1865, for court martial proceedings that lasted into March. Paine faced twenty-five charges which ranged from abuse of power and corruption to extortion, oppression and profanely denouncing Halleck. The *Journal* closely followed the trial, hoping for a guilty verdict but pretending to be objective. "If General Paine shall be acquitted after an evidently fair and full trial, no one will be readier than ourselves to do him ample justice," the paper proclaimed. "We shall in that case be prompt to unsay what we have said of him upon the strength of very strong testimony." Then came the inevitable qualification: The *Journal* had received a damning communication "from a very gallant officer at Paducah" that claimed the trial was rigged in Paine's favor. The unnamed officer said that among the charges Fry and Brown sent to Washington "was one to the effect that he ordered two men, a citizen and a soldier, summarily shot, upon his own responsibility without trial." Another charge had Paine personally levying "various sums, from $1,000 to $10,000, upon men and women in Paducah and its vicinity." But when Judge Advocate General Joseph Holt, a Kentuckian and an Unconditional Unionist, forwarded to Paducah the list of charges against Paine, he left out "those two very ugly ones as well as others that could easily be proved, setting down only such as might probably got over with ease." Further, the officer alleged, Major General David Hunter, who was heading the court martial, said he had no right to add charges that Holt omitted.[73]

The *Journal* was in high dudgeon.

> The author of the letter further says that important witnesses for the prosecution are away—*why* he knows not; and, that a very strong outside pressure is brought to bear, the friends of Paine proclaiming that he will be reinstated in thirty days, and that his enemies will have need to look to themselves.

Thus, the paper concluded, "If these things are true, the trial, so called, is a cheat, an imposition, a humbug."[74]

The *Journal* and his other detractors aside, Paine steadfastly maintained his innocence, claiming he was the victim of the relentless hostility of Confederate sympathizers throughout his time in western Kentucky. He said stern measures were needed because he had to deal with hypocrites, perjurers and traitors, adding that if anywhere deserved martial law, it was the Jackson Purchase. An attorney before the war, Paine skillfully defended himself and in the end, he was acquitted of all charges except cursing Halleck. His punishment was a reprimand in general orders.[75]

Meanwhile, die-hard secessionists and Conservatives remained suspicious. The *Journal* on March 10 rehashed its early denunciation of Holt. The story began with a sop to the judge advocate.

> For a number of years, we have thought exceedingly well of the Hon Joseph Holt.... He has seemed to us to be eminently patriotic. He has, notwithstanding a pretty strong tendency to radicalism, given his energy and eloquence to the cause of the Union. We have thought that the country owed him much.[76]

Yet the paper failed to "see the propriety of Mr. Holt's action in the case of General Paine." The *Journal* cited Fry and Brown's enquiry, adding that the two officers, after hearing the sworn testimony of witnesses, sent Holt a list of charges against Paine based on what the witnesses said under oath. The paper again claimed that Holt left out

> one that Gen. Paine, upon his own responsibility, had ordered and enforced the execution of two men, a citizen and a soldier, without trial or examination, and another that he had, without even the shadow of authority, levied heavy pecuniary contributions upon such

men and women in Paducah as he chose to select for his purpose, and compelled them to pay as the only means of escaping a far severer punishment—probably death.

The *Journal* insisted that the proof of both charges was "said to have been unquestionable." The paper asked, "Why was all this? What is the explanation of the part acted by the distinguished Advocate-General?" The *Journal* was unwilling to concede that based on the evidence that wound up on his desk, Holt dismissed the charges as groundless. Instead, the paper kept insinuating the judge advocate had his thumb on the scale of military justice. "For what reason or semblance of reason did he refuse to let Paine be tried upon the two most important of all the charges that the Examining Court [Fry and Brown] had represented as established?" The paper professed it "shall sincerely and heartily rejoice if satisfactory answers can be made to these questions." Meanwhile, the *Journal* mocked, "The friends of the Advocate-General need not think we would willingly do him wrong. Certainly we would not. We expect General Paine's dishonorable dismission from the service but not upon the worst charges proved on him."[77]

Stanton did not make public the detailed findings of the court martial until October 19. Paine was sentenced "to be reprimanded by the President of the United States in General Orders." Yet Secretary Stanton, based on the recommendation of the members of the court martial, did not enforce the sentence. "Even this shamefully inadequate sentence was remitted," groused Collins' *History of Kentucky*. At any rate, Paine's military career was over. Listed as "awaiting orders" after he lost his Paducah command, Paine finally resigned his commission, effective April 5, 1865. He returned to his law practice in Monmouth, Illinois, but in their later years, he and his wife alternated their homes between those of their two daughters. He died at the home of their Jersey City, New Jersey, daughter in 1882. Paine, who was sixty-seven, was buried in Oakland Cemetery in St. Paul, Minnesota.[78]

A decade before Paine's death, *History of Kentucky* started the anti–Paine ball rolling among historians by accusing the general of oppressing the Purchase with a "a fifty-one days' reign of violence, terror, rapine, extortion, oppression, bribery and military murders." Besides alleged "military murders" Paine was best known for exiling a group of known or suspected Southern sympathizers to Canada and apparently elsewhere. A "closer analysis of the general shows that many of his actions were well within the bounds of accepted wartime measures," Hoskins wrote. "Indeed, many of his 'crimes' were practiced by other Union generals, in particular Sherman, Grant, and Sheridan." Hoskins noted that Sherman advocated the practice of banishment "long before Paine implemented it." Too, "Sherman and Grant ... advocated the arrest of citizens and destruction of crops in areas where guerrilla depredations were strongest, and Paine certainly operated in a 'strong' guerrilla area."[79]

Hoskins added that "while Paine was accused of committing over forty murders, no records exist to corroborate the claim." The historian acknowledged that "an argument could be made that the names of the victims were conveniently lost during Paine's escape from Paducah," but she wrote that "no private letters or diaries, local histories, or newspapers contain a list of the supposed victim's names. Court martial and provost marshal records, which include testimony from dozens of citizens and accusers, detail only four executions ordered by Paine and seven by McChesney." Paine, McChesney and local Unionists said all of the men shot by firing squads were guerrillas. Kesterson confessed to murdering Happy and harassing pickets at Mayfield and Paducah. Another guerrilla admitted that he shot pilots steering navy transports on the Ohio River, according to Hoskins.[80]

"Under General Orders 100, or Lieber's code, moreover, Paine and McChesney were following official Union policy," Hoskins wrote.

> In 1862 legal scholar Francis Lieber created regulations designed to address the guerrilla warfare that plagued his friend General Henry Halleck, who then dealt with groups of lawless Missouri guerrillas who operated in civilian dress and ignored the rules of war. According to Lieber, partisans such as John Mosby and Forrest were soldiers since they were authorized by the government and wore the uniform of the Confederacy. Guerrillas, such as the ones facing Halleck in Missouri were defined as 'small parties of armed country people ... who resort to occasional fighting and occasional assuming of peaceful habits, and to brigandage ... devastation, rapine, or destruction.[81]

When Paine stressed that Kesterson "attacked 'defenseless old men'" while he was wearing "both Confederate and Union uniforms or civilian clothes, he was making the distinction that the guerrilla was a noncombatant, or a 'country' person." At the same time, Lieber's Code permitted severe punishment for populations that aided guerrillas. "Viewed through this lens, Paine's other crimes—banishment, assessments, and confiscation of property—existed within the bounds of wartime measures."[82]

In the last analysis, evidence is strong that the local animus toward Paine, perpetuated by nineteenth and twentieth century historians, was rooted in his strongly abolitionist views, in his support for the enlistment of African Americans into the Union forces and in his belief in black equality with whites. At the same time, he equated all but unconditional Unionism with treason, an opinion that courted the wrath of the *Louisville Journal*, Bramlette and the conservative, pro-slavery Union Democrats, and later Conservatives, who controlled the state. He was anathema to almost all Purchase whites. He was to them the worst sort of Yankee—he was an anti-slavery, pro–Lincoln "Black Republican."

Doubtless, Paine's detractors were equally angered when Anderson was neither expelled nor dragged into court for his alleged misdeeds in league with Paine. Indeed, Representative Green Clay Smith successfully defended

Lush on the House floor. On January 18, 1865, he argued for a congressional enquiry because "charges ... of a serious and damaging character," namely "corruption, bribery, and malfeasance in office," had been leveled at his colleague. Smith asked Speaker Colfax to appoint a committee of three "to investigate said charges, with power to send for persons and papers, and report thereon."[83]

Republican Congressman Elihu Washburne of Illinois—whose constituents included General Grant—suggested the "select committee to investigate the charges against Hon. Lucian Anderson" be expanded to five members. Colfax agreed and named Unconditional Unionist Smith chair. Two Republicans were apparently happy to serve, but the Democrats tried to thwart the investigation by declining to be part of the panel. Colfax kept naming Democrats who kept begging off. Finally, he found Democrats willing to serve and the committee started interviewing witnesses on February 6.[84]

Paine was first up, and the general testified under oath that neither he nor Anderson committed any criminal acts. Paine said he met Anderson in Paducah in 1861. And next saw Lush in 1864. Paine said Anderson was a lodger in the hotel where he briefly stayed. Anderson was in Paducah "because he could not go to his home," according to the general. Paine said that on the day he arrived, guerrillas attacked the Union picket line and that they struck again two days later. "I found that Union men could not go beyond the lines, for the reason that the whole country was held and controlled by guerrillas," the general said. Paine also testified that in early August, he led sixteen hundred soldiers to Mayfield, accompanied by Anderson and several other Unionist refugees. Like Lush, they had fled to Paducah "and ... had not been to their homes for several months." The general recollected that Anderson did not come back to Paducah until late August. "He then left for Cairo, and from there to Washington city, as I was informed." Lush came back about September 5, stayed in Paducah a day or two and went home to Mayfield, the general recalled.[85]

Paine addressed charges of corruption against Anderson, Bolinger and himself. Allegedly, Lush persuaded the general to reopen two Paducah stores he closed for trading in contraband. The implication was that Anderson bribed Paine. "Mr. Anderson knew nothing of this action until it was done," the general testified. "If he had, it would have made no difference in my orders." Paine said he knew of no money "paid to Mr. Anderson for his services for any party before me; he never offered me a dollar, or any amount of money or property, to induce me to issue or countermand any order or do any official act, or for any other purpose." The general also defended himself, declaring "I never received any money, property, or valuables of any kind whatever for any official or non-official act."[86]

Paine said he did not remember seeing the congressman again in Paducah until the army sacked him. The general also disputed other accusations: that he lavished lucrative trade allowances on Anderson and that he, Anderson and possibly Bolinger pocketed cash from a special tax levied on rebel sympathizers. "Mr. Anderson made no application to me at any time for permits to trade in merchandise, produce, mules, horses, or anything else," the general said. "He could not have traded in any such articles without my knowing it; I had a carefully prepared list of all persons engaged in every kind of trade." Paine said he "never seized, or ordered to be seized, any money or property of any kind for my own benefit or for the use of Mr. Anderson, Mr. Bolinger, or any other person." He maintained that the tax on pro–Confederate citizens was authorized "by order of the President of the United States, for the purpose of raising a fund called the relief fund, to be used in paying Union men their losses sustained by the raids of Forrest and Berford [sic], and guerrillas." Paine swore "he never took any property except such as was duly accounted for in the relief fund, or turned into the quartermaster's or other departments of the army." He concluded his testimony by declaring, "I never knew of an illegal, unlawful, or dishonorable act committed by Mr. Anderson." The next day, Paine left the capital for his court martial in Paducah, via Cairo.[87]

Another witness, a government official who worked under Paine, testified about the store closings, but nothing he said implicated the general, Anderson or Bolinger in any crime. Bolinger followed him and protested that he, Anderson and Paine were innocent. "General Paine did not, to my knowledge, while at Paducah, take money or property from any one and divide the same with myself and L. Anderson, or either of us, in any way, directly or indirectly." Bolinger added, "Neither do I know of any kind of speculation in which General Paine or L. Anderson was engaged in in any way whatsoever." Bolinger said he knew "that L. Anderson at all times refused to engage in any kind of speculation since the war began. I further know that he was and has been engaged, ever since the war began, doing all he could for the Union people of his district free of charge." Bolinger also swore that Anderson "had nothing to do with the assessment question." He admitted that he and others helped with assessing the tax, taking the tax books to Lush's hotel room "as it was the most convenient place we could get." But Bolinger insisted that he never "saw Mr. Anderson pay any attention to the books, or interfere, or make any suggestions about them or the tax in any way." Bolinger said he knew nothing about the stores Paine shut and allowed to reopen. He, too, was unaware "of ... collusion of any kind with anybody in any way about it."[88]

The witness parade continued. None of them, including two of the storeowners, produced the proverbial smoking gun to prove Paine, Anderson or Bolinger were crooks. Last to testify was Colonel Brown, who said he was "the recorder of the proceedings" at Paducah "to ... examine the conduct of General Paine." He said Anderson did not evade the commission, as the

*Journal* charged. Rather, he came before Brown and Fry "and made his statement in writing." Brown knew nothing more. "Mr. Anderson was sworn by me," he said. "The evidence was dictated by him and reduced to writing by me, read over to him, and then signed by him. The paper was forwarded through General Burbridge to the Secretary of War."[89]

The next day, Smith cleared Anderson. He announced that the committee had "examined all witnesses, pro and con, who were supposed to know anything about said charges, and in none of the testimony is there anything which would in the slightest degree sustain said charges." Furthermore, the chairman reported, "the evidence entirely exonerates said Anderson from all wrong, or any charge or charges made against him." Thus, Smith, on behalf of the committee, asked the house to approve a resolution "that the charges of bribery, corruption, and malfeasance in office against the Hon. L. Anderson, a member of this house, are not sustained by the proof in the case.[90]

Smith said every committee member supported the resolution except one of the Democrats. Even he did not think Anderson was guilty, according to Smith; he missed all of the committee meetings and "did not sign the report because he did not know anything about it. Having reported to the house, Smith called on lawmakers to endorse the committee's resolution exonerating Anderson.[91]

The Democrats were not about to rubber stamp the committee. Mallory, perhaps still angry over Anderson's refusal to support him for speaker, tried to stall the proceedings. He asked Smith to postpone the vote until he could "ask him a question in relation to the action of this committee." Smith agreed. "I want to have read at the Clerk's desk a paper which I now hold in my hand, being the statement of Colonel Brown, of the State of Kentucky, in the service of the United States; and to enquire of the gentleman," Mallory began. Seeing where Mallory was headed, Smith cut him off. "I did not withdraw to have any paper read." Mallory refused to budge. "I want to base my question on that paper, and to ask why that paper was not received by the committee."[92]

Smith shot back, "My colleague [Mr. Mallory] asked me to allow him to propound a question, and I withdrew the call for the previous question for that purpose only; instead of asking a question he sends a paper to the Clerk's desk to be read. I must resume the floor, and insist upon the previous question." Mallory challenged, "Does the gentleman intend to suppress any evidence?" Smith replied, "No, sir, I do not. The deposition of Colonel Brown has been taken, and is among the evidence reported from the committee."[93]

After Smith's rejoinder, the resolution received the requisite second. A division of the house followed, and congress proceeded to decide on whether to move to approve the resolution; sixty-five lawmakers were for a vote and nine were opposed. But the outcome was invalid because several Democrats refused to vote, deliberately denying Smith the needed quorum. Colfax asked

Smith and Mallory to be tellers; the latter requested to be excused. "As my colleague [Mr. Mallory] has declined to act as teller, I would also decline acting," Smith declared. Colfax named two new tellers, Republican John M. Broomall, a Pennsylvanian, and John O'Neill, an Ohioan and a Democrat.[94]

Following a second division of the house and vote, the resolution passed sixty-eight to two. But again, non-voting Democrats prevented a quorum. Colfax asked the clerk to read the house's thirty-first rule, which said that every House member present "when the question is put shall give his vote unless the House shall excuse him." The rule also stipulated that "all motions to excuse a member from voting shall be made before the House divides, or before the call of the yeas and nays is commenced." The speaker asked "gentlemen who have not voted to conform to the rules which they themselves have made and required the Chair to enforce." Dutifully, Broomall and O'Neill kept on with the count, reporting eighteen "noes"—still no quorum.[95]

Colfax again appealed to the Democrats to abide by the rule. He also reminded the recalcitrant lawmakers that "if members do not obey the rules they bring them[selves] into contempt." Representative James Brooks of New York, a Democrat, claimed many members of his party were not voting because "we do not know how to vote; we have no knowledge of the evidence." Congressman James M. Ashley, a Buckeye State Republican, saw through the ruse and shot back, "Does that excuse the gentleman from New York for violating the rules?" Brooks retorted, "Well, enforce the rules. It is nothing new for members to decline to vote. I have known it to happen a hundred times."[96]

Charles Eldridge, a Wisconsin Democrat, declared "If there is not a quorum, I move a call of the House." The tellers who kept on counting, reported a new tally and finally a quorum: sixty-seven "aye" and twenty-six "no" votes. So the resolution was put to the House. Even so, the Democrats would not relent. "If it is in order now, I desire to be ask to be excused from voting, and on that question, I wish to say a word," New York Democratic Representative John V.L. Pruyn besought the speaker. The "question is not debatable," Colfax snapped. Up popped Mallory again: "I demand the reading of the evidence on which the report is based. How can I vote upon the report of a committee without knowing what is the evidence?" The speaker agreed that Pruyn "has a right to ask to be excused from voting." But the House voted not to excuse him.[97]

One wonders what Anderson thought of the Democrats, led by Mallory, pulling out all the stops to keep the House from absolving him. Did he suspect it was payback time for Mallory, who could not forgive his fellow Kentuckian for favoring Colfax over him and for supporting the Thirteenth Amendment? In any event, the freeze continued. Wisconsin Democrat Charles Eldridge wanted to question Smith; Colfax said he could by unanimous consent. Smith said no to any queries. "Does the gentleman refuse to answer a question?"

Eldridge mocked. "Then he dodges." Representative Francis Le Blond, an Ohio Democrat, wanted the resolution tabled. Another Ohio Democrat, C.A. White, demanded a vote on Le Blond's offering. The tellers tallied five "ayes," eighty-three "nos" and ninety-four abstentions. "No quorum has voted," Colfax announced. Finally, Washburne moved that the clerk call the roll. After the names were checked off, the speaker said a quorum had been reached.[98]

Representative James F. Wilson, Republican of Iowa, moved "that all further proceedings under the call be dispensed with." The House agreed; the logjam was broken, and Le Blonde, via unanimous consent, withdrew his motion to table. The House vindicated Lush Anderson by a vote of seventy-nine to twenty-nine, with seventy-five still refusing to vote. Smith and Randall, who had stood with Anderson on the Thirteenth Amendment voted "aye." Yeaman parted company with them and did not vote. Anderson did not vote either, but obviously because he was the subject of the resolution. Grider and Mallory voted "no." Clay, Harding and Wadsworth also refused to vote. Defiant to the end, Mallory asked to be excused from voting when he name was called, then voted no when his request was denied.[99]

The Democratic *Cincinnati Enquirer* published an account of the proceedings that, not surprisingly, was less than flattering to Lush. "It will be recollected that charges of corruption and malfeasance in office were preferred against Hon. Lucian Anderson ... and that the House, some weeks ago, appointed a committee to investigate these charges." The *Enquirer*'s capital correspondent said it was close to midnight on March 3 when Smith issued the committee's report acquitting "Mr. Anderson of the charges preferred against him, and say that there was no grounds whatever for the accusation," the paper's capital correspondent wrote.[100]

The correspondent claimed that Smith was filled "with evident excitement and feeling" over Mallory's challenge and that "some of the more just and fair minded of the Republicans demanded the reading of Colonel Brown's statement" to no avail. "It is proper to say here that the affidavit of Hon. Lucian Anderson, upon which dependence was had to show his corruption, was in the possession of the Provost Marshal General in Washington, during the session of the Committee," the scribe added. "The Committee (or the chairman—Mr. Smith) was requested to call for the affidavit; and informed that, if not called for, it would be sent to the Court now acting on charges against General Paine." He said the committee failed to request the report and it was dispatched to the court martial. The *Enquirer*'s man claimed that when Brown heard the panel did not have Anderson's affidavit, he went to Washington, demanded to testify and was refused.

The paper included Brown's "statement" that Anderson testified to him in Paducah that he acted as the attorney for Ashbrook, Ryan & Co., one of the stores, and that one of the firm's officers gave him $1,500, which he halved with Major Henry Bartling, the Paducah provost marshal. Anderson also said that when he came back from Washington, he and Bartling equally split a $400 check from Prince & Dodds, the other store, "as a fee for permission to carry on their business," according to the colonel. Brown added that Anderson "deposed that he had not been retained as attorney by Prince & Dodds." Thus, the *Enquirer* concluded, "is proof that Mr. Anderson received a fee for representing a claim against the Government, contrary to the act of Congress, which makes such conduct punishable."[101]

Though a court martial cleared Paine, and congress absolved Anderson, their detractors claimed the former literally got away with murder and the latter got away with lining his pockets with ill-gotten gains. Perhaps Purchase secesh were at least somewhat mollified by the violent slaying of Thomas J. Gregory, the third member of their unholy trinity.

Like much of his life, Gregory's death is marked by mystery and misinformation. Gregory's Home Guard outfit mustered out of Federal service on February 12, 1865, yet he was still a captain commanding soldiers. According to Collins' *History of Kentucky*, his life ended on March 29 in a "desperate fight," with guerrillas "30 miles from Paducah."[102]

The April 4, 1865, *Frankfort Commonwealth* claimed Gregory died on March 22. The paper identified him as "Capt. Gregory … formerly of the 3d Battalion, Capital Guards." The *Commonwealth* responded he and his twenty-two-man company went off chasing guerrillas at the behest of Meredith and Paducah citizens. Gregory cornered a guerilla group led by a man named McDougal at Thomas Hayden's Hickman County home, about "thirty

**Grave of Thomas J. Gregory (Berry Craig).**

five miles south of Paducah." After ordering five men to guard the horses, Gregory and the rest surrounded the house. The captain beat down the door with the butt of his Spencer carbine, charged inside and shot McDougal dead.[103]

Gregory "was himself fired upon and instantly killed." His men avenged his death by "wrenching the pistols from the hands of the guerrillas and firing upon them with their own weapons." They shot dead six of the foe and wounded another twenty more, "most of them mortally." The balance of the marauders escaped, but forsook "forty horses and sixty guns and pistols, together with a number of blankets, hats caps &c." On the Union side, nobody was wounded, but one more soldier was killed. "The loss of Capt. Gregory is much lamented," the paper said. "He has proved himself an officer of great ability, both for his fighting and administrative qualities."[104]

The *Commonwealth* said Gregory "was also a conscientious and accomplished gentleman, and stood firmly by his state and country while most of his friends were seduced into the rebellion." Too, "he has suffered greatly from guerrillas by reason of his patriotism, almost all of his property having been destroyed, and a brother and sister murdered by the miscreants." The paper vowed that "he was never actuated by feelings of revenge in his treatment of them" but that "his death was well and terribly avenged by his men." The *Commonwealth* said Gregory was a Graves countian and maintained that McDougal was "a great scoundrel, having served four years in the Penitentiary." He had been "the terror of South Western Kentucky and Western Tennessee." Gregory's body was brought back to Paducah and buried in Oak Grove Cemetery alongside the body of his brother, John Franklin Gregory, a Union cavalry lieutenant shot by his commanding officer in an 1864 dispute.[105]

By the time Captain Gregory fell, the war was all but over. The only question was how long could the rebels last. General Robert E. Lee had begun the process of capitulation. On April 9, Palm Sunday, he surrendered his beleaguered army to Grant at Appomattox Courthouse, Virginia, effectively ending the Civil War. Other rebel commanders gave up in the weeks that followed, and the victorious Yanks and vanquished rebs began wending their way home.

By the end of the war, most of the rest of the state had moved toward the Purchase perspective following the Emancipation Proclamation and the enlistment of African American soldiers, both of which almost every white Kentuckian rabidly opposed. The shift became even more pronounced following the Confederate surrender. Coulter famously wrote that Kentucky "waited until after the war to secede." Historian Anne E. Marshall wrote, "this outward incongruity between the way white Kentuckians entered and participated in the Civil War and the way that they remembered it has become one of the great paradoxes of Civil War history." She added, "Though the commonwealth had not officially been a part of the Confederate defeat, white Kentuckians appeared to take up the Lost Cause as their own. As an ideology, the Lost Cause combined ideas about an idyllic agrarian past and the Confederacy's righteousness and valor in defending it." The paradox was not lost on never-say-die Unionists. "The 'Lost Cause' is found again in Kentucky," the *Commonwealth* complained. A Republican lamented, "Kentucky is today as effectually in the hands of rebels as if they had every town and city garrisoned by their troops.... What is to become of the poor blacks and loyal white men God only knows." African Americans would suffer as second-class citizens for a century; most white Republicans would be marginalized for many years. Kentucky would become the northern border of the white supremacist Democratic, Jim Crow "Solid South."[106]

Many of the former rebels became important political and social leaders and successful business owners and farmers, especially in Lush Anderson's hometown and elsewhere in the Purchase. Graves County-born U.S. Vice President Alben Barkley of Paducah wrote in his folksy 1954 autobiography *That Reminds Me*, "For years after the Civil War, a candidate for political office in our part of Kentucky who had not had at least one limb shot off while fighting for the Confederacy might as well have whistled down a rain barrel."[107]

# 10

# Back Home

The first post-war election in Kentucky came on August 7, 1865. The canvass pitted the Conservatives, or Democrats, against the Republicans, whom the Democrats called "Radicals." The Republicans counted on Bramlette and Kentucky-born Brigadier General John M. Palmer of Illinois, the new Union commander in the state, to keep ex-Confederate soldiers and rebel sympathizers from voting. The main issues were the Thirteenth Amendment and restoring the franchise to the returning Confederates. The Conservatives vehemently opposed ratification, and they enthusiastically embraced giving the vote back to the ex-rebels, knowing they would rally to the white supremacist standard. The Republicans favored ratification and keeping the ballot away from men they considered traitors.[1]

No sooner did the House pass the Thirteenth Amendment than it went to the states for ratification. On December 18, it was it declared approved by the requisite three-fourths of the states, Kentucky and Delaware not among them. In February, the legislatures of both states rejected the amendment, thus slavery remained legal in Kentucky and Delaware longer than anywhere else in the United States. Meanwhile, in Kentucky, the Republicans strove to win a majority in both chambers of the General Assembly in the August elections. But the tide was with the Conservatives statewide. It was a rip current in the Purchase, and Lush knew it.[2]

Undoubtedly aware that he had no chance to hold his seat, he chose not to run. Anderson's decision to bow out disappointed leaders of the First District's fledgling Republican Party, who met in Paducah on May 8. "Owing to the disturbed condition of the country," delegates represented only five of the district's fourteen counties: Ballard, Calloway, Graves, Lyon and McCracken. Even so, the Republicans, including Lush's old friend Bolinger, unanimously passed a resolution heartily approving Anderson's congressional tenure, however brief. They also were sorry "that he will not allow the use of his name for a renomination." Other resolutions—all approved with no dissent—urged the state legislature to ratify the Thirteenth Amendment and called the assassination "of the late most excellent President Abraham Lincoln ... a national calamity." John Wilkes Booth, a fanatically pro-slavery and pro–Confederate actor and spy, fatally wounded the president at Ford's Theatre in Washington on April 14. Lincoln died the next day. In addition, the First District Republicans resolved their "full confidence in the integrity, loyalty, and capacity of his successor, Andrew Johnson, and pledge to him our cordial and hearty support in his efforts to suppress the rebellion, punish treason, and restore peace to the country."[3]

Other resolutions reflected the party's strongly federalist and anti-slavery stand. The delegates declared "that we as a party are in favor of the supremacy of the national constitution and laws, the suppression of the rebellion, the restoration of the laws, and the punishment of traitors." They also outlined three principles they said the war established—"that these United States are one and indivisible ... that the States are not absolutely sovereign, and have no right to dismember the republic" and "that universal liberty is indispensable to republican government." The institution of slavery, the delegates resolved, should "be utterly and forever destroyed."[4]

The Republicans argued that slavery had become "not only effete but burdensome." Thus, they concluded, "it becomes us as wise men to provide for the removal of the remains of the institution from our midst, so that its place may be filled by compensated labor." Before adjourning they named district and country central committees and agreed to meet again on June 16 to nominate a congressional candidate.[5]

The Conservatives tried to portray the Republicans as extremists. Besides declaiming them as Radicals, they denounced them as Red Republicans, Radical Abolitionists and Jacobins—the latter the name of the French revolutionaries who ushered in the guillotine and the "Reign of Terror." The Conservatives charged that the Republicans favored racial equality as well as black suffrage and were for elevating African American rights over the rights of whites.[6]

The Conservatives also called themselves Southern Rights Party, the name of the secession party in 1861. The Republicans branded the Conservatives "the secession Democracy." Besides ex-Confederate soldiers and sympathizers, Conservative ranks included several former conservative Unionists, Trimble among them, who turned against the Lincoln administration mainly over the Emancipation Proclamation, the enlistment of black troops and the Thirteenth Amendment. The Conservatives were the party of reaction and white supremacy. Simply put, the Republicans looked to the victorious North for their inspiration, the Conservatives to the vanquished South.[7]

A third party emerged to challenge the Conservatives and the Republicans. Called the Conservative Union or Constitutional Union Democratic Party, it tried to build a base among old-line Whigs who found the Republicans too radical and the Democrats too reactionary. The party also attempted to attract Unionists who rejected making common cause with the increasingly Confederate-dominated Conservatives or the pro-black rights Republicans. Ultimately, the party faded away.[8]

In the First District, the Republicans settled on C.D. Bradley of Cadiz. The Conservatives chose Trimble, who hoped the third time would prove the charm for him. He ran as a Unionist and lost to Burnett in 1861; in 1863, Peace Democrat Trimble came up short against Lush. Though Confederate soldiers and known or suspected guerrillas and rebel sympathizers were not yet allowed to vote, Trimble won handily, defeating Bradley, 5,749 to 3,542. While Randall and Smith won again, Yeaman lost, and the Conservatives captured five of the state's nine House seats. At the same time, Conservatives won a close majority over the Republicans in the state House and Senate.[9]

Meanwhile, in Washington, Johnson and the Republicans were battling over how to reconstruct the Confederate states and return them to the Union. Like Lincoln, Johnson believed in a speedy process controlled by the president. Their terms were remarkably lenient given the fact that the Confederate states had engaged in bloody armed rebellion against the lawfully-constituted United States government. Congressional Republicans believed that reconstruction should be directed from Capitol Hill. The Radical Republicans, most of whom had been abolitionists, argued that the Confederates were traitors and should be punished.

Most House and Senate Republicans were moderates and inclined to restore the Union as quickly and easily as possible. But at the very least, they wanted to see some proof that the South had repudiated its slavery and secessionist past. Evidence pointed decisively the other way.

Many members of Congress and numerous state officials elected under Johnson's plan were ex-Confederate military and civilian leaders. At the same time, Southern state governments passed laws known as black codes. The measures were designed to create a labor system as close to slavery as possible under the Thirteenth Amendment. Further dismaying Northern opinion was a wave of murderous racial violence against the newly freed slaves. The Ku Klux Klan arose as a white supremacist terrorist organization whose first leader or imperial wizard was Nathan Bedford Forrest. In 1867, over Johnson's veto, Congress passed its own tougher version of reconstruction. The clash between Johnson and Congress over reconstruction resulted in his impeachment by the House in 1868. But his presidency survived in the Senate by one vote.

Meanwhile, the conservative, white supremacist Johnson, under sharp criticism from moderate and Radical Republicans, was desperate to rally support in advance of the 1866 mid-term Congressional elections. To boost presidential reconstruction, his backers organized a gathering in Philadelphia and called it the National Union Convention, the same name the Republicans gave their presidential nominating convention in 1864. Lush supported the conclave, according to a Louisville *Courier* correspondent. In a report from the Purchase, the scribe said "everybody down this way is a Johnson Democrat, not excepting Lucien Anderson." He claimed that Anderson "was insulted at the *honor* the Rads attempted to confer on him by placing his name among the delegates to the black-and-tan convention," apparently meaning the state Republican convention. "Black-and-tan" was a derisive term white supremacist Democrats applied to the growing bi-racial Republican Party in the old slave states. If the *Courier* story was true, Lush seemed to be drifting back toward his pre-war conservatism. At any rate, the GOP won big in the congressional elections held in twenty-one states, Kentucky not among them.[10]

Trimble was reelected on May 4, 1867, easily outdistancing Republican G.G. Symes, also of Paducah, by a hefty margin of 9,787 to 1,780 votes. But Symes challenged the vote and appealed to the Republican-majority House to seat him. He claimed that Trimble was a traitor and that the election was a fraud. To buttress his case, he took depositions from several citizens, including Anderson, whose deposition suggested he might not have gone over to the Democrats.[11]

Symes charged that during the war, Trimble smuggled supplies, food, medicine, military equipment and ammunition to the Confederates. He also charged that the congressman made disloyal speeches. Too, Symes protested that ex-Confederates ran the election and rigged it so Trimble would win. He said election officials frightened some Union men from the polls and denied the vote to others while extending the ballot to former rebel soldiers who had not been granted amnesty or who had not sworn the loyalty oath. Trimble claimed he was neither a smuggler nor a traitor and that the election was fair and was honest.[12]

Trimble was a "Johnson Democrat." If Lush were, too, he was not a Trimble Democrat. In his deposition, he recalled his dustup with Trimble when they crossed paths on the 1863 congressional campaign trail in Mayfield. Anderson testified that after pressing his opponent on whether he would vote men and money to support Union military forces, Trimble said he would not. "His entire speech was in denunciation of the authorities of the government for alleged violations of the Constitution in the prosecution of the war against the rebels," Anderson remembered. "His speeches aroused the old prejudices of rebels, infused new life into them; and the same men who two years before had denounced Trimble as an abolitionist were his warm supporters in 1863." Anderson said that after their Mayfield confrontation, they met again in Benton, the Marshall County seat. He said he promised to quit the race if Trimble would pledge to "vote men and money" to fight the Confederates. Trimble demurred and "reiterated his denunciations against the policy of the government in the prosecution of the war," according to Lush.[13]

On cross examination by Trimble's lawyer, Anderson confessed that in all the speeches he heard Trimble deliver, his opponent always said he was a Union man who wanted the Union restored. Further, Anderson admitted that he never heard Trimble say he wanted the Confederates to win. Lush also testified that Trimble argued that the Constitution "furnished ample powers to carry on war to suppress rebellion, but denied that federal authorities were then engaged constitutionally in putting down the rebellion."[14]

Trimble's attorney also brought up the "Loyal War Governors' Conference" in which anti-slavery governors of thirteen Union states met in Altoona, Pennsylvania, on September 24 and 25, 1862, and endorsed the Emancipation Proclamation. "Did not Trimble say that he had as much right to be opposed to the unconstitutional measures of the Lincoln administration as the governors of the different states, who met at Altoona to advise the administration to violate the Constitution?" the lawyer demanded. Anderson coolly responded to the loaded question. "He did contend that he had the right to judge of the constitutionality of the measures adopted by the authorities in putting down the rebellion, and said if he thought them unconstitutional he would not support them." Lush added, "I don't recollect whether he spoke of the governors of the different States meeting at Altoona or not; he may have and likely did so." In the end, Congress seated Trimble.[15]

The *Louisville Courier*, which preceded the *Journal* as an Anderson enemy, naturally impugned Lush over the election controversy. "The legally elected and qualified Representatives from Kentucky are excluded from their seats in Congress on the alleged ground of disloyalty," the paper editorialized.

> This charge is based in part upon the statements of Radical members who like [southern Illinois Representative and former Union Major General John A.] Logan, in becoming swift witnesses evinced a gross ignorance of Kentucky politics, and in part upon the statements, sworn and otherwise, of parties in Kentucky.

The paper scoffed at the notion that Lush and his friend Bolinger could enable non–Kentuckians "to arrive at a proper understanding of the meaning of disloyalty as applied to the case of the Kentucky members." The *Courier* quoted the *Frankfort Yeoman*, its secessionist ally in 1861. The capital city paper dredged up Fry and Brown's charges against Anderson, Bolinger and Paine. The *Courier* concluded,

> Thus do Lucien Anderson and John T. Bolinger stand condemned as unmitigated scoundrels by the report of two distinguished Federal officers, one of whom [Brown] is the present candidate of the Radical party in the State for Attorney General; and yet it is upon the testimony of Anderson and Bolinger that Mr. Trimble is treated as disloyal.

They testify that his speeches—made, let it be remembered, during the Paine administration—were calculated to deter men from enlisting. Doubtless, that is true as far as their sort of service was concerned. Further comment is unnecessary.[16]

Congressional Reconstruction began the year Trimble was elected to Congress. Because Kentucky did not secede, it was exempt from the process of restoring states to the Union. Under congress's plan, requirements for readmission included endorsement of the Fourteenth Amendment to the constitution. Ratified in 1867, it made African Americans citizens and extended them the right of due process of law and equal protection before the law. The Conservative-dominated Kentucky legislature rejected the amendment. Meanwhile, Kentucky took it upon itself to defend the old Confederate states, which it had helped defeat. The traitors became heroes to most white Kentuckians. The Democrats who came to rule state politics, relegated African Americans to second class citizenship status, passing laws that kept blacks separate and unequal from whites. Kentucky became the northern boundary of the Jim Crow South. Though the Fifteenth Amendment, ratified in 1870, extended the franchise to African Americans, the Kentucky legislature refused to adopt it.[17]

The late nineteenth century years were lean times for the Kentucky Republicans. The Democrats, though sometimes divided into squabbling factions, controlled the legislature. Not until 1895 were the Republicans able to elect a governor. Nonetheless, citizen Lush soldiered on for his party. He remained active in local Republican circles, narrow in diameter as they were. But he was not above helping a Democratic foe, even one who was an ex-secessionist aiming to be governor. In 1871, candidate John Quincy Adams King of Paducah appealed to Lush. Some Trigg County Democrats, in advance of the state Democratic nominating convention, claimed that during the war, King wrote a letter to Congressman Anderson betraying the rebel cause. King and Lush may have been old friends. He was a Whig and a Unionist before turning Confederate. In August, 1861, King was elected to the state house of representatives on the Southern Rights or secessionist ticket. Because he helped organize Kentucky's rump Confederate government in November, 1861, the Unionist-majority house expelled him as a traitor in December. At any rate, on April 22, 1871, the erstwhile pro–Confederate *Hickman Courier* reprinted a letter from the pro–Democratic *Paducah Kentuckian* in which King admitted that he wrote Anderson, but only to seek relief for himself and his beleaguered family. He pleaded,

I was expelled from the House of Representatives, driven from my home; my wife and children expelled from my own domicile; all my personal and real estate taken possession of by others, including my law office, library, accounts, notes, etc., deprived of all my slaves, an excellent residence worth $3,000 totally burned and destroyed.

King continued his long lament, claiming he was "twice drafted, and altogether suffered a heavy pecuniary loss, to say nothing of the mental anxiety, of myself, my wife and children, nor of the humiliating arrest, and transportation, under strong guard, as a criminal."[18]

King said he could have become a Unionist, "but with my *then* convictions of duty, it would have been dishonorable, because insincere." So he said he wrote Anderson in desperation. After all, Lush "was then in power in this district, and had and exercised great influence with his party, not only in this district, but at Washington." King stressed that "there was nothing in the letter against democracy, nor in favor of the republican party, but was alone for personal relief.... I did like hundreds and thousands of good Southern democrats, humble myself, for the time being, for the preservation and comfort of my family." King claimed "hundreds and thousands of sound, reliable democrats, who are trusted by the party this day, some of whom are now holding office, also humbled themselves in many ways, passed themselves off for Union men, induced Union friends to vouch for them, and many actually voted for Mr. Lincoln as the poll books show." King promised that had he been single, he "could have, and doubtless would have, avoided the trouble and humiliation that befell me." Yet as he was a family man he "was compelled to humble my pride, and to adapt myself to the circumstances surrounding me."[19]

Anderson confirmed King's version of what was in the letter, according to an article in the *Mayfield Democrat* the *Courier* reprinted. Lush was even willing to give King the missive "for its publication and his vindication," but regretted that the communication "with hundreds of others received by him during the war was destroyed." The *Courier* did not say how the letters were destroyed, and no copies of the *Democrat* are known to exist. It seems possible, if not probable, that the guerrillas who burned the Graves County courthouse in 1864 also torched Anderson's office. After all, it doubled as the local Home Guard headquarters. (The *Courier* article also may explain why so few of Anderson's personal papers survive.) Nonetheless, the article claimed Anderson's statement in support of King's claim "is a complete quietus of the whole thing. The object of Gov. King's enemies in bringing this electioneering ruse before the public, just on the eve of the nominating convention, is too plain to deceive anyone." Nonetheless, the Democrats tapped Preston H. Leslie as their candidate for governor.[20]

Lush's willingness to help King did not extend to Leslie. On July 29, the *Courier* reprinted a *Kentuckian* article with a less than flattering account of Lush's performance in an impromptu debate with Leslie in Mayfield. When the Democratic hopeful showed up, ex-Confederate soldier Ed K. Warren, the Graves Democratic chair—and brother and former partner of *Courier* publisher George Warren—handed Leslie a note from the local Republican chairman; Lush wanted to answer the Democrat's remarks. Leslie was amenable, as long as he could speak for ninety minutes and Lush for an hour. The candidate also wanted "to close the debate without restriction to time."

The Graves "radical [Republican] committee" rejected the terms, demanding that Anderson be allowed equal time with Leslie. Thus rebuffed, Leslie planned to go ahead "with his usual speech." But at the last minute, Anderson agreed to Leslie's terms. The less-than-objective scribe for the *Kentuckian* wrote that he had heard Leslie make four speeches, but claimed at Mayfield, "he was not only able but eloquent, and made radicalism, as it has exhibited itself in the management of both the State and Federal Governments, stink in the nostrils of honest men." Predictably, he panned Lush's rejoinder. "His time was principally up by attacking the last Legislature. He made mountains out of mole hills; the little appropriation of $16,000 made to refurnish the Governor's mansion, was expatiated upon at great length." According to the reporter, Lush carried on for ninety minutes "and then complained at the conclusion that the Governor had placed handcuffs on him and was forced to close." But Leslie got the last word. He suggested that "as Col. Anderson had accepted his proposition and made a speech in accordance with it he had precluded him from any complaint as to the conditions; but said he 'if I had the time I would be willing to let him speak for five hours if he could make no better speech than he had already made." In replying to Anderson, "the Governor was eloquent and forcible, and demolished every position the Col. had taken. The large audience was held for five long hours and were perfectly delighted…. In a word, he made a powerful speech." On August 7, Leslie won the governorship, defeated Republican John Marshall Harlan by a vote of 126,455 to 89,299. Six years later, President Rutherford B. Hayes nominated Harlan to the Supreme Court, where he served as an associate justice until his death in 1911.[21]

In the 1872 presidential race, the *Hickman Courier* endorsed Horace Greeley, candidate of the Liberal Republicans and of the Democrats. Greeley was the famous editor of the *New-York Tribune* and an old-time abolitionist. He helped organize the Liberal Republicans, a reformist group that split from the GOP over the scandal-plagued administration of President Ulysses S. Grant, who succeeded Johnson in 1868. On October 5, Lush and Greeley's names came up at a political gathering in Hickman that attracted Henry H. Houston of Paducah, the Republican candidate for Anderson's old congressional seat. Houston, according to the *Courier*, had been "a fire-eating Bourbon Democrat." After the Civil War, the Kentucky Democrats divided into Bourbon and New Departure factions. The Bourbons were conservatives who favored low taxes and limited government and an economy wedded to agriculture. Unyielding white supremacists, they mourned the end of slavery, rejected the Thirteenth, Fourteenth and Fifteenth amendments and "seemed to worship at the shrine of a dead past." They were named for France's royal family, which was bloodily deposed in the French Revolution. It was said that the Kentucky Bourbons, like the French Bourbons, "forgot nothing and learned nothing." The New Departure Democrats looked to the future and accepted the end of slavery and the Reconstruction amendments. They favored a state and federal role in the economy and wanted Kentucky to industrialize like the North. They also called for more spending on public education and at least some rights for African Americans. The Bourbons denounced the New Departure Democrats, whose leaders included Henry Watterson, editor of the new *Louisville Courier-Journal*, started in 1868, as quasi-Republicans.[22]

The *Hickman Courier* said Houston's

> line of argument was precisely the same laid down by St. Lucian Anderson, at this place, some weeks ago, with this exception, that St. Lucian contended that Mr. Greeley was to all intents and purposes a *Democratic* candidate—that the Liberal Republicans had sold themselves to and absorbed by the *Democracy*; whereas Houston argues exactly the opposite, that the Democracy has been absorbed—wiped out of existence, by the *Liberal* Republicans,—and that his party now having no existence, he elects to go for Grant."

On November 5, Grant was elected to a second term, though he lost Kentucky. Houston also came up short against the incumbent Democrat, and Confederate veteran Edward Crossland of Clinton, who also turned back Isaac H. Trabue, another Republican, and John Martin, another Democrat. Crossland was yet another Confederate veteran elected to office after the war.[23]

Though he had been out of office for seven years, Anderson was still providing what members of congress call constituent services. In November, 1876, he traveled to Washington to free a Mr. Colley from a jail cell in Mayfield. Colley had been behind bars "some time, charged with some violation of the revenue law," according to the *Mayfield Democrat*. Anderson saw Grant "and obtained a full pardon of all fines." The paper tendered "the thanks of the whole community" for Lush's "generous act," and added, "his heart and purse are always open to the calls of those in distress and need."[24]

Colley may have been related to the Union man the Confederates killed on the 1863 Mayfield raid in which Lush was kidnapped and taken to Tennessee. But ten years later, Anderson proved willing to join with ex-rebels in his hometown on a project to run a railroad from St. Louis through Cairo and Mayfield all the way to Savannah, Georgia, on the Atlantic coast. He, his brother, Ervin, John Eaker and others got behind the plan. Lush, Ervin and B.A. Neale, another ex-Union man from the war, addressed a mass meeting at the courthouse which resolved, with only one dissenting vote, for "the town of Mayfield, as a corporation ... take $50,000 stock in the line" and calling on Graves County's senator and state representative to back legislation permitting the citizens to vote on whether the town should invest up to $75,000, in the narrow-gauge line. "When accomplished, the paper predicted, the rail line "would be one of the greatest achievements of the nineteenth century." Nothing came of the railroad.[25]

In 1879, Lush joined a trio of ex-rebels from Mayfield—Congressman A. R. Boone of Mayfield, who succeeded Crossland and former Confederate Major Henry S. Hale in touting the Mayfield Elevator and Purifier, invented by Isaac Mayfield of Mayfield eight years before. The quartet signed an advertising letter swearing that they had used the contraption since 1871, heartily recommended it and claimed "that it will purify the foulest well or cistern ... will not freeze in the coldest weather" and "will last ten years." In addition, the machine was so handy "that a child ten years old can draw water out of fifty-foot well sufficient for the largest family use." Too, "wiggles, worms and water lice can not live in cisterns and wells where the Elevator is used."[26]

Three years before, Lush, who had tried to give a Union speech to his Confederate captors in 1863, proved he was still willing to address an enemy. He showed up at a Democratic rally in Murray, promising that though he was not a candidate for congress, the Republicans would soon have one. "He spoke at some length in behalf of his party and the corruption of the Democratic party, but failed to make any of his arguments substantial enough to withstand criticism," the Democratic *Murray Gazette* claimed. After Lush finished, the Democrats clamored for two of their own: Oscar Turner and former Representative Crossland, who succeeded Trimble in 1871 and won two terms. Turner, from Blandville, then the Ballard County seat, was challenging Congressman Andrew R. Boone, who followed Crossland to Washington. Boone was expelled from the Kentucky House of Representatives in 1861 for helping organize the state's bogus Confederate government at Russellville. Also a rabid secessionist, Turner, running as an Independent Democrat, helped lead the push for a military alliance between the Purchase and West Tennessee in 1861.[27]

The *Gazette* reported, "Turner again took the stand and defended the position of national politics he had been advocating. The debate between him and Anderson became of a personal character, they giving each other the lie." Crossland followed Turner, speaking "for several minutes in reply to Col. Anderson" and "showing conclusively that the Republican doctrine that Anderson was preaching wouldn't do to tie to." The ex-rebel promised "that if Anderson stumped the district in the coming campaign he would be with him when no one else better qualified was."[28]

On September 15, 1876, the *Hickman Courier* flayed Anderson in a long article headlined "Lucian Anderson He Don't Want the Bitterness of War Forgotten." The Republicans, especially in the North, never missed a chance to "wave the bloody shirt," or blame the Civil War on the Democrats. Before the war, the South was the party's base, and Democrats led the secession movement. Many northern Democrats, dubbed "Copperheads," opposed the war to one degree or another; some were Confederate sympathizers who smuggled goods South, joined secret pro–Confederate groups such as the Knights of the Golden Circle, engaged in sabotage and spied against the Union. Apparently, Anderson tried the tactic in western Kentucky. The paper claimed he evidently "has been engaged in making a series of inflammatory speeches, it is said, with the deliberate purpose of trying to arouse these long latent and dormant old war feelings." The *Courier* added that

> the Mayfield *Monitor* in order to show that this violent, extreme way of doing politics is peculiar to Mr. Anderson's nature, and that his extreme ideas are not shared by all the Republicans, prints some extracts from some old documents. These extremists in hitting back merely show they themselves are vulnerable, and allowing that the good conservative men of both parties, do not approve opening these old sores.[29]

The *Monitor's* snippets naturally were the old charges from the Paine era. The *Courier* quoted the *Monitor's* preface to the "extracts": "What can he (Anderson) say about his own character during the ... war—is it such that he would like to have it published to the world?" The paper reprinted from the 1864 *Senate Journal* Bramlette's September 2, 1864, letter to Lincoln accusing Paine and Anderson of extortion. Though a court martial cleared Paine on all but one minor charge and a congressional committee completely exonerated Anderson, the *Monitor* asked, "Would Gov. Bramlette have made such charges without foundation?" The paper answered its question, "Of course not," and added, "and those persons who were citizens of this county at the time know how near right he was." Interestingly, in quoting from the *Senate Journal*, the *Monitor* deliberately omitted Bolinger's name, drawing a line through places where his name appeared in the record.[30]

The *Monitor* also dusted off a pair of specific charges—one that Paine illegally arrested owners and clerks of stores, shut the businesses and commandeered the goods. "All that was required to explain such seizures and restore the goods to their rightful owners, was a liberal fee placed in the hands of the accommodating Lucien." The paper also accused Anderson of controlling the poll books used to tax Southern sympathizers to compensate Unionists harmed by rebel raiders and guerrillas. Supposedly, Paine cut Anderson in on the money. "And you seized the poll books, did you Lucien?" the *Monitor* sneered. "Another one of the blessings enjoyed by the people under Radical rule." The paper hammered away: "And how long after this was it, Lucien, when you were elected to Congress at the point of the bayonet? The people knew you too well to vote for you willingly, and you had to force yourself on them. Another evidence of your popularity." In its ardor to discredit Anderson, the *Monitor* got the timeline wrong. Lush was elected to Congress in August, 1863. Paine did not take command in Paducah until July,

1864. In any event, it is interesting that the *Monitor* did not blast Bolinger, who was also linked to Paine's purported perfidy.[31]

Undaunted, Anderson hit the campaign trail for Houston, who was making his second bid for Congress on the Republican ticket. Lush, of course, received less than rave reviews in the district's Democratic papers. The *Courier* scorned him as "the great Republican fugleman of this District" and quoted the *Princeton Banner's* account of his "little game." The Caldwell County seat organ hoped "the Democrats who heard Mr. Lucien Anderson on Monday will be able to see his game. He is in the field to rally the Republicans to the standard of Henry Houston, and believes that by a 'long pull, a strong pull, and a pull together,' he can get into Congress through a divided Democracy." The paper urged, "Democrats of Caldwell County and of the First District, will you not rally with enthusiasm under the banner of Boone and defeat them all?"[32]

In the same issue, the *Courier* published a less biased report of Anderson's Princeton speech. "Lush Anderson has mounted the stump, and says he thinks he sees a glimmer of light through the Democratic row going on in this District," the paper prefaced its story. "Mr. Anderson enjoys the reputation of being the leader of the Republican party in Western Kentucky and is justly entitled to the distinction," the account said. "His speech on Monday was a very good one, considering the burden the Republican ticket has to carry, though it was not so 'blood thirsty' as we had a right to expect judging from what we had heard of him and his speeches."[33]

Anderson appealed to white and African American Republicans to vote Republican, especially for Houston. In the post–Civil War period, blacks overwhelmingly supported the party of "Lincoln and Liberty." Poor, pro–Union whites also made up a big part of the party's base. Lush claimed Houston could win "if the Republicans would only give him their solid strength. The Republicans, he said, *could give him about* 8,000 *votes* and neither Boone nor Turner, in the divided present condition of the Democrats, could get so many—the strongest vote any Democrat got in this district since the war not running over 14,000." Lush missed the mark. On November 7, Boone won another term with 10,994 votes to 7,540 for Turner. Houston brought up the rear with 5,835 votes.[34]

Doubtless, another Democratic triumph distressed Lush, but in 1881, he got crosswise with his party over what Republican should be postmaster at Mayfield, according to a front page story in the *New York Times*. The dustup was part of "a general commotion among the 'outs' and the 'ins' in Kentucky" apparently stemming President James A. Garfield's assassination. Elected in 1880, he was murdered on September 19, 1881, and Vice President Chester A. Arthur was sworn in to succeed him. Walter Evans of Louisville, one of the Bluegrass State's top Republicans, tapped John T. Happy to replace the current Mayfield postmaster, also a Republican. John T. was a son of J.B. Happy, Lush's fellow Unionist, friend and neighbor whom guerrillas murdered during the war. A letter recommending Happy pointed out "with considerable flourish," that the Mayfield man's brother went to the 1880 Republican national convention and was in "the immortal band of 306," the nickname for the delegates who voted to re-nominate Grant, who nonetheless lost to Garfield. Lush sided with the "incumbent" postmaster and chided Evans. Lush sneered "that as he had a rebel in the Post Office at Louisville, where he was now living, and another in Hopkinsville, where he hailed from, it would look better if he would first direct his efforts to removing them, before he began on good Republicans." Happy got the job.[35]

Lawyer Lush became banker Lush in 1882 when he founded the Bank of Mayfield. His chief cashier was J.N. Beadles, his brother-in-law and old Unionist comrade. In 1866, Beadles had married Mary Elizabeth Anderson Thompson, the Confederate colonel's widow.

Also in 1882, the *Courier-Journal* reported that Lush was mounting a political comeback. The paper named him "among three pronounced candidates" for Congress among the Republicans.[36]

Apparently, Lush chose not to run and the nod again went to Houston, whose nomination was not a surprise, according to the *Paducah News*.

> It was well known that the erratic annihilator of classic English and unrelenting enemy of English grammar, Lucien Anderson, of Mayfield, would not accept the nomination; and it was equally well known that Mr. Bagby, of Paducah, who is much better posted in the science of language than Anderson, did not want it—he being already Attorney for the city of Paducah."

The *News* predicted that if Houston, evidently a Confederate veteran, "will refrain from Anderson's vituperation and confine himself to fact and logic instead of reveling in the vagaries of a too fervid imagination he may make a very respectable speaker." Even so, incumbent Oscar Turner, running as an independent Democrat, beat Houston and Democrat John R. Grace.[37]

Meanwhile, Arthur had a reputation as a party hack; GOP reformers spurned him. Lush, who favored James G. Blaine for the party's presidential nod in 1880, was among Arthur's detractors. Anderson pounded the president at the 1883 Kentucky Republican convention. "He called the convention an office-holders' and office-seekers' convention, and went into the history of Arthur's Administration, personal and political, with a power that was appalling," the *Courier-Journal* reported. "He told the Republicans they would regret their indorsement of Arthur, whereat the yells were so deafening he was compelled to desist." He refused to sit and the delegates refused to hear him. Nonetheless, "they couldn't wear the old man out and he told them he would stay with them all night." At that point, Lush's old enemy, John Mason Brown, stood up "and poured oil on troubled waters with no visible effect. He spoke his mind and sat down."[38]

Lush went home even more dismayed. The party nominated Brown's fellow investigator, Speed S. Fry, for lieutenant governor. "Lush Anderson, the old original boss Republican of this District, is furiously mad with the doings of his party," the *Hickman Courier* chortled. "He says their late state convention 'was a conclave of office-holders, post-masters, collectors, deputy marshals, gougers, etc. who met to burn incense under the nose of President [Chester A.] Arthur.'"[39]

Anderson was evidently fine with the Republican gubernatorial nominee, Thomas Z. Morrow, an ex-Yankee colonel. He was otherwise mortified. Lush denounced the Arthur administration for removing E. Case from the Hickman post office and flayed the convention as "no better than a lot of d——d rebels." The *Courier* invited Case and Anderson "to quit 'em and come over to the only *loyal* party—the Democrats." The Republicans might have been glad to see Anderson defect. Convention-goers "set down roughly on Lush Anderson and Jno. D. White, hissing them down when they tried to speak," according to the paper. "This is hard on old veteran Republicans. Democrats believe in free speech, but Republicans hiss down old members of their own party who dare to oppose the machine. And this party expects to grow in Kentucky!"[40]

In the presidential election of 1884, reformers called "Mugwumps" refused to support Lush's man Blaine. They either stayed home on Election Day or defected to Democrat Grover Cleveland, who won Graves County, Kentucky and the presidency. Cleveland, the first Democrat elected since the Civil War, polled better than seventy percent of the Graves vote. Some locals who lived a few miles north of where the Andersons first settled named their community Folsomdale in honor of Frances Folsom, who the bachelor Cleveland married in the White House in 1886.[41]

By the time the Clevelands were wed, Lush seemed to be more interested in banning booze than in Republican politics. In 1888, he attended the state Prohibition Party convention in Louisville which endorsed his old friend Congressman Green Clay Smith for president. Lush was named a delegate to the national convention in Indianapolis, which nominated Clinton B. Fisk of New Jersey, the Kentucky party's second choice.[42]

The next year, Lush the Republican-turned-Prohibitionist found himself at odds with Republican President Benjamin Harrison over who was getting the government jobs in western Kentucky. (Harrison beat Cleveland in 1888, but Cleveland topped Harrison in 1892 and reclaimed the White House.) "There has not been an appointment by President Harrison in this end of the state where there has not been a great deal of kicking by the disappointed ones," the *Paducah Standard* reported. "Col. Lush Anderson went all the way to Washington to try to get the Happy crowd kicked out at Mayfield." He evidently failed, but was "one of the leading lights" at the 1892 First District Prohibition convention in Paducah. The same year, he joined the board of directors of the Ocala and Silver Springs land company in Florida, whose president was Colonel Joshua Chamberlain of Maine, a Union hero of the Battle of Gettysburg, where he won a Medal of Honor for bravery.[43]

Lush was just shy of his seventy-fourth birthday when his health began to fail. "Col. Lucien Anderson, of Mayfield, has been seriously ill for several days, and his recovery is considered doubtful," the *Louisville Courier-Journal* reported on May 6, 1898. On September 3, the paper said Anderson had been "adjudged of unsound mind" the day before. "He is a wreck in mind and body, caused by old age, being seventy-four years old." The paper explained that the court would appoint a trustee to see to "his property and business," adding, "He is one of the oldest practitioners at the Mayfield bar and served two [sic] terms in Congress from" the First District. The *Courier-Journal* noted that Anderson "was formerly a Republican leader in the First district, but in later years affiliated with the Prohibition [party]." The paper said Anderson "had been bedridden since April."[44]

Death claimed Lucian Anderson on October 18, 1898. The Republican *Paducah Sun* put his obituary on page one, but misspelled his name, "Lucien." He perished at home where he had suffered "a lengthy illness from paralysis," the paper said. On October 11, "he was stricken again, and one entire side was involved, the patient being unable to take food, or medicine. He began gradually to sink and the end came yesterday."[45]

The death notice described him as "one of the best known men in this end of the state, and ... one of the pioneers of the state." The *Sun* also advised its readers that Lush's father, John Anderson, "laid out the city of Mayfield." The paper said Lush was a lawyer, county attorney, congressman and banker. The *Sun*, published in deeply Democratic Paducah, was silent about his Republican affiliation and his vote for the Thirteenth Amendment. Lush's survivors included three sons and two daughters. His beloved Anne Rebecca died on July 24, 1890 at age 59; the couple's first child, Henry Clay, died in 1863 at age thirteen. Anderson left "a large and valuable estate," according to the paper. The *Mayfield Monitor* remembered him as one of the town's "most noted citizens." The paper was confident that Anderson's "many friends will mourn his death, even though it comes after he lived more than the allotted three score and ten." The *Nashville Tennessean* also reported the news of Anderson's death, describing him as "one of the most extensively known citizens in Western Kentucky. He succumbed "after a long confinement from paralysis."[46]

Lush's friend Bolinger is buried in Mayfield's old Maplewood Cemetery, a short distance from the Anderson family burial ground. Like Lush, he ultimately abandoned the Republicans but for the anti-monopoly, short-lived Greenback Party, which denounced the increasingly conservative and pro-business policies of the GOP. Bolinger helped start Greenback Clubs in the Purchase. Like many Greenbackers in the 1890s, he joined the pro-farmer, pro-worker and pro-union Populist Party. "If the Republicans triumph and pass the Force bill, how would it do to put Bolinger in command in Western Kentucky with the rank of Major General!" the *Hickman Courier* mocked. "The old men of the District remember that Bolinger had experience with bayonet rule." Bolinger's life ended in Mayfield on January 19, 1895 at age seventy.[47]

Grave of John T. Bolinger (Berry Craig).

His old friend Williams chose not to run for another term on the Court of Appeals in 1870 and came home to Mayfield. Though not a Mormon, he moved to Utah Territory in 1878 and practiced law until his death on July 22, 1889, at age seventy-two in Logan. The Ogden bar praised him as a lawyer "industrious and true to his client's interests." The attorneys were sure there were "scores of young and middle-aged men in Utah, Kentucky and elsewhere who will shed silent tears as they hear of Judge Williams death." Perhaps so, but when Williams turned Yankee in 1861, the Columbus *Daily Confederate News* predicted that "whatever may be the issue of our unhappy difficulties, he is doomed. Nothing but curses and execrations will ever greet his ear from his old friends and constituents."[48]

# Chapter Notes

## Chapter 1

1. John F. Kennedy, *Profiles in Courage*, 50th Anniversary Edition (New York: HarperCollins, 2006), 1.

2. *The Constitution of the United States Of America As Amended, Unratified Amendments Analytical Index, Unum E Pluribus Presented By Mr. Brady Of Pennsylvania* July 25, 2007 Ordered to be printed (Washington: United States Government Printing Office, 2007), 16. https://www.gpo.gov/fdsys/pkg/CDOC-110hdoc50/pdf/CDOC-110hdoc 50.pdf (Accessed online Feb. 18, 2016).

3. *Evansville* (IN) *Journal*, Dec. 1, 1863, quoted in the *Chicago Tribune*, Dec. 9, 1863.

4. Interview with Lon Carter Barton of Mayfield, Jan. 18, 2001.

5. J.H. Battle, W.H. Perrin and G.C. Kniffen, *Kentucky: A History of the State* (1st ed.; Louisville and Chicago: F.A. Battey and Co., 1885), 7. Paducah, the region's principal town, was the "Charleston of Kentucky," according to Battle, Perrin and Kniffen. During the Civil War, the Jackson Purchase consisted of seven counties: Ballard, Calloway, Fulton, Graves, Hickman and Marshall. Today, the region has eight; the legislature carved Carlisle County from southern Ballard County in 1886.

6. *Biographical Directory of the United States Congress, 1774-Present*, Anderson, Lucien (1824–1898) http://bioguide.congress.gov/scripts/biodisplay.pl?index=A000201. (Accessed online Feb. 24, 2016).

7. John C. Rives, *The Congressional Globe, the Official Proceedings of Congress, Thirty-Eighth Congress, 1st Session.* Appendix (Washington: Globe Printing Office, 1864), 102; Republican Party Platforms: "Republican Party Platform of 1864," June 7, 1864. Online by Gerhard Peters and John T. Woolley, *The American Presidency Project.* http://www.presidency.ucsb.edu/ws/?pid=29621 (Accessed March 7, 2016).

8. See William Birney, *James G. Birney and His Times* (New York: G. Appleton and Co., 1889; H. Edward Richardson, *Cassius Marcellus Clay: Firebrand of Freedom* (Lexington: The University Press of Kentucky, 1976.

9. James Larry Hood, "For the Union: Kentucky's Unconditional Unionist Congressmen and the Development of the Republican Party in Kentucky, 1863–1863," *Register of the Kentucky Historical Society*, 76 (July, 1978), 197–198, 209–210.

10. J.B. Shannon, and Ruth Mcquown, *Presidential Politics in Kentucky 1824–1948: A Compilation of Election Statistics and an Analysis of Political Behavior* (Lexington: Bureau of Government Research, College of Arts and Sciences, University of Kentucky, 1950), 32–36.

11. Berry Craig, *Kentucky Confederates: Secession, Civil War, and the Jackson Purchase* (Lexington: The University Press of Kentucky, 2014), 292–293; "Legislative Document, No. 26. Response of the Adjutant General of Kentucky to a Resolution of Inquiry in Regard to Federal Enrollments in the State, Made to the House of Representatives Wednesday, March 1, 1865," (Frankfort: George D. Prentice, State Printer, 1865); D.W. Lindsey, *Report of the Adjutant General of the State of Kentucky* (Frankfort: John H. Harney, Public Printer, 1866) Vol. I and II; J. Tandy Ellis, *Report of the Adjutant General of the State of Kentucky Confederate Volunteers War 1861–1865* (Frankfort: The State

Journal Company, 1915) Vols. I and II. Union totals are expressed in enlistments, which means that if a man joined up to fight for a specified period and reenlisted, he would be counted twice.

12. Craig, *Kentucky Confederates*, 71–92.

13. *Ibid.*, 99–101, 156–159; Missouri did not secede, but it became the 12th Confederate "State" via a similar extralegal convention.

14. *Ibid.*, 165–167; 213.

15. Battle, Perrin and Kniffen, *Kentucky*, 220.

16. *Louisville Courier*, Aug. 11, 1855.

17. *Frankfort Commonwealth*, June 29, 1863; *Louisville Journal*, Dec. 9, 1863; *Louisville Democrat*, Dec. 10, 1863.

18. *New York Times*, Nov. 15, 24, 1863; *Chicago Tribune*, Nov. 11, 1863; *New Orleans True Delta*, Nov. 28, 1863; *Evansville Journal*, Dec. 1, 1863, quoted in the *Chicago Tribune*, Dec. 9, 1863.

19. William Lochridge Wells, *The Lochridge/Anderson Family of Graves County, Kentucky: From 1819 to the Present* (Mayfield: Mayfield Printing Co. 1990), 5.

20. Hood, "For the Union," 205–208.

21. Craig, *Kentucky Confederates*, 261–279.

22. Barton interview, Jan. 18, 2001.

23. Shannon and McQuown, *Presidential Politics*, 37–40.

24. Lewis Collins and Richard Collins, *History of Kentucky: By the Late Lewis Collins, Judge of the Mason County Court, Revised, Enlarged Four-Fold and Brought Down to the Year 1874, by His Son, Richard H. Collins, A.M., LL.B., Embracing Pre-Historic Annals for 331 Years, Outline, and by Counties, Statistics, Antiquities, and Natural Curiosities, Geographical and Geological Descriptions, Sketches of the Court of Appeals, the Churches, Freemasonry, Odd Fellowship, and Internal Improvements, Incidents of Pioneer Life, and Nearly Five Hundred Biographical Sketches of Distinguished Pioneers, Soldiers, Statesmen, Jurists, Lawyers, Surgeons, Divines, Merchants, Historians, Editors, Artists, Etc., Etc.* (1874; reprint, Berea, KY: Kentucke Imprints, 1976) I, 163; Lowell H. Harrison and James C. Klotter, *A New History of Kentucky* (Lexington: The University Press of Kentucky, 1997, 240.

25. Email, James C. Klotter to Berry Craig, Dec. 20, 2014.

26. Collins, *History of Kentucky*, 155.

27. Biographical Directory of the United States Congress, 1774-Present, Anderson, Lucien (1824–1898.) http://bioguide.congress.gov/scripts/biodisplay.pl?index=A000201; Hood, "For the Union," 197, 214.

28. Anne E. Marshall, *Creating a Confederate Kentucky: The Lost Cause and Confederate Memory in a Border State* (Chapel Hill: University of North Carolina Press, 2010.), 5; Harrison and Klotter, *A New History*, 241, 244.

29. Barton Interview; D. Trabue Davis, *Story of Mayfield Through a Century 1823–1923* (Paducah, KY: Billings Printing Co., 1923), 93–94; Battle, Perrin and Kniffen, *Kentucky*, 220.

30. *Mayfield Weekly Monitor*, October 19, 1898; William Lochridge Wells, letter to the editor published in the *Mayfield Messenger*, March 3, 2016.

31. Klotter email.

# Chapter 2

1. Davis, *Story of Mayfield*, 12–13; "Anderson, Lucien, 1824–1898," *Biographical Directory of the United States Congress 1774-Present* http://bioguide.congress.gov/scripts/biodisplay.pl?index=A000201 (accessed online March 7, 2016; Wells, *Lochridge/Anderson*, 4.

2. Jackson beat the Creek Indians at the Battle of Horseshoe Bend, Alabama, on March 27, 1814. Shelby fought Indians in Lord Dunmore's War of 1774, and battled the British and their Native American allies in the Revolutionary War and the War of 1812. He was dubbed "Old King's Mountain" for helping lead patriot militia to victory over loyalist militia in the Revolutionary War Battle of King's Mountain, South Carolina, on October 7, 1780. Battle Perrin and Kniffen, *Kentucky*, 7; John E.L. Robertson, "Western Kentucky and Paducah in Legend and Lore," *The Filson History Quarterly*, Vol. 76 (2002), 186.

3. Craig, *Kentucky Confederates*, 11–12.

4. Battle, Perrin and Kniffen, *Kentucky*, 7; Robertson, "Western Kentucky and Paducah in Legend and Lore," 187–188.

5. Craig, *Kentucky Confederates*, 12; interview with Mayfield educator, historian and author Lon Carter Barton, April 10, 1998.

6. Davis, *Story of Mayfield*, 6.

7. *Ohio History Central* online "Land

Ordinance of 1785," http://www.ohiohistory central.org/w/Land_Ordinance_of_1785? rec=1472 (accessed Feb. 24, 2016).

8. Lon Carter Barton, "The History of Graves County, Kentucky," MA thesis, University of Kentucky, 1960, 13.

9. Robert M. Rennick, *Kentucky Place Names* (Lexington: The University Press of Kentucky, 1984), 192.

10. Rennick, *Kentucky Place Names*, 192; Davis, *Story of Mayfield*, 6.

11. Wells, *Lochridge/Anderson*, 2–3.

12. Harrison and Klotter, *A New History*, 5–6; William Lochridge Wells, *The Lochridge/ Anderson Family of Graves County, Kentucky: From 1819 to the Present* (Mayfield, KY: Mayfield Printing Co., 1990), 4.

13. Wells, *Lochridge/Anderson Family*, 3–4; Davis, *Story of Mayfield*, 48–49, 65; John Anderson Journal, 1838, Forrest C. Pogue Special Collections Library, Murray State University, Murray, KY, Martha Nell Anderson, a descendant of Ervin and the last resident of Lucian's home, owned the journal for many years before donating it to Murray State in 2014.

14. Lon Carter Barton, "A History of Graves County, Kentucky," master's thesis, University of Kentucky, 1960, 13.

15. Davis, *Story of Mayfield*, 13, 25, 50; Battle, Perrin and Kniffen, *Kentucky*, 50; Barton 22.

16. Barton thesis, 38.

17. Anderson Journal. Typhus is a bacterial disease spread by lice and rats and is commonly treated with antibiotics, according to the National Institutes of Health.

18. Anderson Journal.

19. *Ibid.*

20. *Ibid.*

21. Battle, Perrin and Kniffen, *Kentucky*, 53, 220; Dictated letter, Lucian Anderson to Charles Lanman, Oct. 29, 1863, in the Charles Lanman Collection, Filson Historical Society, Louisville, KY Lanman was the U.S. House of Representatives librarian. He collected biographies of House members that ultimately became the *Biographical Directory of the United States Congress*. Thus, it seems likely that congressman-elect Anderson was replying to Lanman's request for information; Wells, *Lochridge/Anderson Family*, 4.

22. Battle, Perrin and Kniffen, *Kentucky*, 52; Lewis Collins, *Historical Sketches of Kentucky: Embracing Its History, Antiquities, and*

*Natural Curiosities, Geographical, Statistical, and Geological Descriptions; with Anecdotes of Pioneer Life, and More than One Hundred Biographical Sketches of Distinguished Pioneers, Soldiers, Statesmen, Jurists, Lawyers, Divines, Etc.* (Maysville, KY, Lewis Collins, and Cincinnati, U.P. James: 1848), 326; Wells, *Lochridge/Anderson*, 28.

23. Wells, *Lochridge/Anderson Family*, 4.

24. Harrison and Klotter, *A New History*, 112. South Carolina, led by John C. Calhoun, Jackson's vice president, vehemently opposed the Tariffs of 1828 and 1832 and threated to nullify the import taxes and even secede. Jackson vowed to use federal troops to collect the duties and privately threatened to hang Calhoun, who resigned and soon afterwards returned to Washington as a South Carolina senator. In 1833, Clay proposed a compromise tariff; South Carolina backed away from nullification making Jackson's use of force unnecessary.

25. Shannon and McQuown, *Presidential Politics*, 3. Jackson won the most popular votes, but not the requisite electoral college majority. As a result, the election went to the House of Representatives where Speaker Clay threw his support to Adams, who won and named Clay secretary of state. Jackson and his followers accused Clay and Adams of striking a "Corrupt Bargain." But Adams was a nationalist like Clay and supported the American System.

26. *Ibid.*, 5–6.

27. *Ibid.*, 7–31.

28. Louisville *Courier*, Aug. 11, 1851, July 10, 1852.

29. *Ibid.*, Oct. 16, 1852. The Locofocos were reformist Democrats in New York city who opposed Tammany Hall, the Democratic machine that controlled local politics. Many Locofocos belonged to labor unions. "Locofoco" was the name of a popular match; the reformers were dubbed "Locofocos" when Tammany turned off the gaslights at one of their meetings and they struck matches to relight the hall.

30. *Ibid.*

31. *Ibid.*

32. *Ibid.*

33. Shannon and McQuown, *Presidential Politics*, 23–27. John P. Hale and George W. Julian also ran on the ant-slavery Free Soil party ticket. But they were not on the ballot in Kentucky.

34. Harrison and Klotter, *A New History*,

123; Raleigh, NC, *Semi-Weekly Standard*, July 28, 1855.

35. Harrison and Klotter, *A New History*, 123; Collins, *History of Kentucky*, I, 75.

36. *Louisville Courier*, Aug. 11, 1855.

37. *Ibid.*, Oct. 4, 1855.

38. *Ibid.*, Oct. 17, 1855.

39. *Acts of the General Assembly of the Commonwealth of Kentucky: Passed at the Session Which Was Begun and Held in the City of Frankfort, on Saturday the 31st of December, 1853, and Ended Friday the 10th of March, 1854.* (Frankfort, KY: A.G. Hodges, state printer, 1854), II, 251; Wells, The Lochridge/Anderson Family, 28–29, 33.

40. Carlton J. Corliss, *Main-Line of Mid-America: The Story of the Illinois Central* (New York: Creative Age Press, 1950), 263–264.

41. *Louisville Courier*, Jan. 10, 1856.

42. *Nashville Union and American*, Sept. 5, 1856.

43. Shannon and McQuown, *Presidential Politics*, 28–31.

44. Patricia Ann Hoskins, "'The Old First Is with the South,' the Civil War, Reconstruction, and Memory in the Jackson Purchase Region of Kentucky," PhD diss., Auburn University, 2008, 48–49, 98–103; Craig, *Kentucky Confederates*, 24.

45. Harrison and Klotter, *A New History*, 168.

46. *Ibid.*

47. *Ibid.*, 169–170.

48. *Ibid.*, 179; Marion B. Lucas, *A History of Blacks in Kentucky: From Slavery to Segregation, 1760–1891* (Lexington: University Press of Kentucky, 1992), 326.

49. Harrison and Klotter, *A New History*, 171.

50. *Ibid.*, 170.

51. Lucas, *A History of Blacks*, 326.

52. Hoskins, "The Old First," 99; Craig, *Kentucky Confederates*, 24.

53. Barton, *History of Graves County*, 27; Collins, *History of Kentucky*, II, 260–261.

54. Aaron Astor, *Rebels on the Border: Civil War, Emancipation, and the Reconstruction of Kentucky and Missouri* (Baton Rouge: Louisiana State University Press, 2012), 29; Shannon and McQuown, *Presidential Politics*, 35–36; Craig, Kentucky Confederates, 24–25.

55. Craig, *Kentucky Confederates*, 24–25; Hoskins, *The First*, 99–100.

56. Craig, *Kentucky Confederates*, 25.

57. Alan Bearman, "'The South Carolina of Kentucky': Religion and Secession in the Jackson Purchase, *Filson Club History Quarterly* 76 (2002), 497, 502; Craig, *Kentucky Confederates*, 26.

58. Walter Brownlow Posey, *Frontier Mission: A History of Religion West of the Southern Appalachians to 1861* (Lexington: University of Kentucky Press, 1966), 341; Bearman, "The South Carolina," 503, 505–6, 513; Craig, *Kentucky Confederates*, 26–27.

59. Bearman, "The South Carolina," 514; Craig, Kentucky Confederates, Craig, *Kentucky Confederates*, 26.

60. Bearman, "The South Carolina," 509, Craig, *Kentucky Confederates*, 27.

61. Bearman, "The South Carolina," 516, Craig, *Kentucky Confederates*, 27.

62. *Frankfort Yeoman*, May 15, 1858.

63. *Ibid.*, May 27, 1858.

64. *Louisville Courier*, Jan. 10, 12, 1859.

65. *Ibid.*, Jan. 10, 1859.

66. Collins, *History of Kentucky*, I, 81.

67. *Louisville Courier*, Jan. 11, 1860.

68. "Judge R.K. Williams," *Tullidge's Quarterly Magazine*, April, 1882, 473–474.

69. *New-York Tribune*, Feb. 1, 1865.

## Chapter 3

1. *Graves County, KY, Census of 1860*, Transcribed by Pat Record (Melber, KY: Simmons Historical Publications, 1979), 202–203.

2. Collins, *History of Kentucky*, I, 84.

3. *Mayfield Southern Yeoman*, quoted in the *Louisville Courier*, July 17, 1860; Battle, Perrin and Kniffen, *Kentucky*, 53.

4. *Louisville Courier*, Sept. 11, 1860.

5. J.E. Anderson to A.R. Boone, July 22, 1860, typescript, Noble J. Gregory Papers, Pogue Special Collections Library; *Graves County, KY, Census of 1860*, 201.

6. Anderson to Boone.

7. *Ibid.*

8. *Ibid.*

9. *Louisville Democrat*, July 26, 1860.

10. *Louisville Democrat*, Sept. 9, 1860, Oct. 27, 1860.

11. Shannon and McQuown, *Presidential Politics*, 35–36.

12. William George Pirtle *Memoirs*, the Filson Historical Society, Louisville, KY.

13. Lowell H. Harrison, *The Civil War in*

*Kentucky* (Lexington: University Press of Kentucky, 1975), 5.

14. Eliza Gregory letter, Dec, 13, 1860, quoted in Barton, "A History of Graves County," 97; J. David Hacker, "A Census-Based Count of the Civil War Dead," *Civil War History*, no. 4 (Dec. 2011): 307–48. Hacker says 752,000 is the most likely number of fatalities, but he adds that the total could reach as high as 851,000.

15. Shannon and McQuown, *Presidential Politics*, 35–36.

16. *Journal of the Called Session of the House of Representatives of the Commonwealth of Kentucky, Begun and Held in the Town of Frankfort, on Thursday, the Seventeenth Day of January, in the Year of Our Lord 1861, and of the Commonwealth the Sixty-Ninth* (Frankfort: John B. Major, State Printer, 1861), 19.

17. Collins, *History of Kentucky*, I, 84–85; Harrison and Klotter, *A New History*, 185.

18. Harrison and Klotter, *A New History*, 185.

19. "The Address of the People of South Carolina, Assembled in Convention, to the People of the Slaveholding States of the United States" (Charleston, SC: Evans and Cogswell, Printers to the Convention, 1860), 25–26; E. Merton Coulter, *The Civil War and Readjustment in Kentucky* (Chapel Hill: University of North Carolina Press, 1926), 25–28. Charles B. Dew, *Apostles of Disunion: Southern Secession Commissioners and the Causes of the Civil War* (Charlottesville: University of Virginia Press, 2001), 93, 96, 97–98; Craig, *Kentucky Confederates*, 39–40.

20. Collins, *History of Kentucky*, I, 85–86.

21. *Hickman Courier*, quoted in the *Louisville Courier*, January 11, 1861; Craig, *Kentucky Confederates*, 41, 43–44.

22. *Louisville Journal*, Jan. 29, 1861.

23. Report by John Eaker and William N. Cargill to Senator John J. Crittenden, January 22, 1861, in *The Papers of John Jordan Crittenden, Library of Congress*, microfilm copy in the Pogue Library at Murray State University. Eaker also wrote Crittenden and Senator Lazarus W. Powell on January 23; Craig, *Kentucky Confederates*, 45–46.

24. John Eaker to Crittenden and Lazarus W. Powell, January 23, 1861; R.K. Williams to Crittenden, January 23, 1861, *Crittenden Papers*, microfilm, Pogue Library; Craig, *Kentucky Confederates*, 45–46.

25. *Louisville Journal*, Feb. 8, 1861.

26. Craig, *Kentucky Confederates*, 46–47.

27. *Ibid.*, 48; Collins, *History of Kentucky*, I, 86.

28. Collins, *History of Kentucky* 1, 86.

# Chapter 4

1. Collins, *History of Kentucky*, I, 87.

2. *Ibid.*

3. Richard Nelson Current, *Lincoln's Loyalists: Union Soldiers from the Confederacy* (New York and Oxford, England: Oxford University Press, 1992), 3.

4. Collins, *History of Kentucky*, I, 87; Craig, *Kentucky Confederates*, 56.

5. Robert Emmet McDowell, *City of Conflict: Louisville in the Civil War* (Louisville, KY: Louisville Civil War Roundtable, 1962), 26–28; Craig, *Kentucky Confederates*, 56–57.

6. *Paducah Herald*, quoted in the *Louisville Courier*, April 29, 1861; Craig, Kentucky Confederates, 57.

7. Battle, Perrin and Kniffen, *Kentucky*, 81–82.

8. Coulter, *Civil War and Readjustment*, 41, 46; Collins, *History of Kentucky*, 1, 89.

9. Craig, *Kentucky Confederates*, 71–92; Wells, Lochridge-Anderson, 5; the *Frankfort Yeoman* and *Lexington Statesman* also printed accounts of the meeting.

10. *Ibid.*, 88, 99.

11. *Ibid.*, 116–123.

12. *Louisville Journal*, July 15, 1861.

13. *Ibid.*

14. *Ibid.*

15. *Ibid.*

16. *Ibid.*

17. Collins, *History*, I, 92; Craig, *Kentucky Confederates*, 121–122.

18. Craig, *Kentucky Confederates*, 121–122.

19. *Louisville Journal*, Aug. 21, 1861; Craig, *Kentucky Confederates*, 104–106.

20. *Louisville Journal*, Aug. 21, 1861.

21. Coulter, *Civil War and Readjustment*, 114.

22. *Louisville Journal*, Sept. 16, 1861.

23. Allen H. Mesch, *Teacher of Civil War Generals: Major General Charles Ferguson Smith, Soldier and West Point Commandant* (Jefferson, N.C.: McFarland, 2015), 177.

24. Mesch, *Teacher of Civil War Generals*, 177; Craig, *Kentucky Confederates*, 163; *Louisville Journal*, Nov. 25, 1861.

25. *Louisville Journal*, Nov. 25, 1861.

26. *Ibid.* M.M. Conner survived the war and afterwards owned the American Hotel in Paducah. See Battle, Perrin and Kniffen, *Kentucky*, 81.

27. Mesch, *Teachers of Civil War Generals*, 177, Craig, *Kentucky Confederates*, 197.

28. Mesch, *Teacher of Civil War Generals*, 177.

29. *Ibid.*; Craig, Kentucky Confederates, 164.

30. Mesch, *Teacher of Civil War Generals*, 177–178; Craig, *Kentucky Confederates*, 164–165.

31. Mesch, *Teacher of Civil War Generals*, 178.

32. *Ibid.*, 182.

33. *Ibid.*

34. *Ibid.*,182–183.

35. *Ibid.*, 183.

36. *Ibid.*,181–182.

37. *Louisville Democrat*, Jan. 8, 1862.

38. *Ibid.*

39. *Ibid.*

40. Craig, *Kentucky Confederates*, 146.

41. The anchor and a short section of chain are among featured attractions at Columbus-Belmont State Park. The wooded preserve also includes trenches and a cannon lost when part of the bluffs caved off during World War II. The cannon was recovered, remounted on a reproduction carriage and placed a safe distance from the edge of the bluffs, which continue to crumble. One of the best accounts of the battle is Nathaniel Cheairs Hughes, Jr. *The Battle of Belmont: Grant Strikes South* (Chapel Hill: University of North Carolina Press, 1991).

42. Craig, *Kentucky Confederates*, 156–159.

43. *Louisville Democrat*, November 21, 1861.

44. *Ibid.*

45. *Ibid.*, Nov. 22, 1861.

46. *Ibid.*

47. For an excellent account of Grant's signal victories see Kendall D. Gott, *Where the South Lost the War: An Analysis of the Fort Henry—Fort Donelson Campaign, February 1862.* (Mechanicsburg, PA: Stackpole Books, 2003).

48. Craig, *Kentucky Confederates*, 165.

49. *Ibid.*, 165–166.

50. Craig, *Kentucky Confederates*,167; Rennick, *Kentucky Place Names*, 52.

51. Craig, Kentucky Confederates, 167.

52. *Louisville Journal*, April 7, 1862.

53. *Ibid.*, April 17, 1862.

54. *Louisville Democrat*, April 24, 1862.

55. *Ibid.*, May 10, 1862.

56. Craig, *Kentucky Confederates*, 166, 168.

57. *Louisville Journal*, June 10, 1862.

58. *Ibid.*, July 1, 1862.

59. *Kentucky Secretary of State Elections Register 1855–1872*, 261, 279; *Louisville Journal*, August 12, 1862; Collins, *History of Kentucky*, II, 39, 109, 292, 342, 542, 594; J.K. Roberts and Daniel Woosley Crockett, *Kentucky Opinions Containing the Unreported Opinions of the Court of Appeals* (Lexington: Central Law Book Co., 1906), 62.

60. *Louisville Journal*, Jan. 14, 1863; Battle, Perrin and Kniffen, *Kentucky*, 53; Craig, *Kentucky Confederates*, 196.

61. *Louisville Journal*, Jan. 14, 1863; Craig, *Kentucky Confederates*, 196.

62. *Louisville Journal*, Jan. 14, 1863; Craig, Kentucky Confederates, 197.

63. *Ibid.*, 197–198.

64. *Ibid.*, 198.

65. *Louisville Journal*, Jan. 14, 1863; Craig, Kentucky Confederates, 197–198.

66. *Ibid.*

67. Marshall, *Creating a Confederate Kentucky*, 24; *Louisville Journal*, May 7, 1861; Lowell H. Harrison, *The Antislavery Movement in Kentucky* (Lexington: The University Press of Kentucky, 1978), 102.

68. Harrison and Klotter, *A New History of Kentucky*, 201.

69. Coulter, *Civil War and Readjustment*, 170–175.

70. *Ibid.*, 171.

71. *Ibid.*,174.

72. *Ibid.*, 174–175.

73. *Louisville Journal*, March 7, 19, 1863; Craig, *Kentucky Confederates*, 199.

## Chapter 5

1. Coulter, *Civil War and Readjustment in Kentucky*, 161–164; *Louisville Journal*, January 1, 1863; Craig, *Kentucky Confederates*, 196. All three were abolitionist Republican congressmen—Lovejoy from Illinois, Julian from Indiana and Bingham from Ohio.

2. James Larry Hood, "For the Union: Kentucky's Unconditional Unionist Congressmen and the Development of the Republican Party in Kentucky" *The Register of*

*the Kentucky Historical Society* 76 (July, 1978) 198; *Frankfort Commonwealth*, June 29, 1863; Harrison, *Civil War in Kentucky*, 83.

3. George Quigley Langstaff, Jr., *The Life and Times of Quintus Quincy Quigley 1828–1910: His Personal Journey 1858–1908* (Paducah, KY: The Paducah Area Community Foundation, 1999), 78; *Frankfort Commonwealth*, June 29, 1863. "Vanlandigham" was Representative Clement L. Vallandingham of Ohio, a bitter foe of Lincoln, the war and abolitionism.

4. *Louisville Journal*, June 4, 1863; Craig, *Kentucky Confederates*, 204–205.

5. *Louisville Journal*, June 4, 1863; Craig, *Kentucky Confederates*, 205.

6. *Ibid.*

7. *Louisville Journal*, June 4, 1863; Craig, *Kentucky Confederates*, 204–206.

8. Harrison and Klotter, A New History, 206; Harrison, *Civil War in Kentucky*, 84; *The War of the Rebellion: A Compilation of the Official Records of the Union and Confederate Armies*. Washington, D.C.: War Department, 1880–1902, Ser. 1, Vol. 23, Pt. 2, 572.

9. Harrison, *Civil War in Kentucky*, 85.

10. *O.R.*, Ser. 1, Vol. 23, Part 2, 570; Craig, *Kentucky Confederates*, 210.

11. Duke to Lincoln, July 6, 1863, Lincoln Papers; Craig, *Kentucky Confederates*, 211. The other candidates were N.N. Cowgill, Thomas Owens and R.B.J. Twyman.

12. *O.R.*, Ser. 1, Vol. 23, Part 2, 570–571; Craig, *Kentucky Confederates*, 212.

13. *Ibid.*

14. *O.R.*, Ser. 1, Vol. 23, Part 2, 568–569; Craig, *Kentucky Confederates*, 212. In 1857, Waring, an engineer, supervised the drainage of wetlands that became New York's Central Park. After the war, he designed a sewer system for Memphis.

15. *O.R.*, Ser. 1, Vol. 23, Part 2, 589; Craig, Kentucky Confederates, 212.

16. *War Eagle*, Columbus, KY, August 3, 1863, quoted in John Kelly Ross," Columbus Scrapbook," bound typescript, Pogue Library, 175–176; Craig, *Kentucky Confederates*, 212.

17. See Dieter C. Ullrich, "Confederate Operations in the Jackson Purchase: A History of Camp Beauregard," *The Filson History Quarterly*, Vol. 76, No. 4, pp. 459–493; *Elections Register 1855–1872*, 311–314, 327; Collins, *History of Kentucky*, I, 127–128. Boone, Carroll and Trimble counties elected

"No-Men-Or-Money" representatives; Craig, *Kentucky Confederates*, 213.

## Chapter 6

1. *Evansville Daily Journal*, Aug. 6, 1863.
2. *Chicago Tribune*, Oct. 28, 1863.
3. *Ibid.*
4. *Ibid.*
5. *New York Times*, Oct. 31, 1863.
6. *New York Times*, Nov. 15, 1863.
7. *Ibid.*; Craig, *Kentucky Confederates*, 216.
8. *Ibid.*, 216–217.
9. *Ibid.*, 217.
10. *Ibid.*
11. *New York Times*, Nov. 15, 1863; Lindsey, *Report of the Adjutant General*, Vol. I, 395, Vol. II, 769; Craig, *Kentucky Confederates*, 217.
12. Craig, *Kentucky Confederates*, 217.
13. *Ibid.*, Nov. 24, 1863.
14. *Chicago Tribune*, Nov. 7, 1863.
15. *Ibid.*
16. *Ibid.*
17. *New Orleans Times-Picayune*, Nov. 29, 1863; *New Orleans True Delta*, Nov. 28, 1863.
18. *Evansville Journal*, Dec. 1, 1863, quoted in the *Chicago Daily Tribune*, Dec. 9, 1863.
19. *Ibid.*
20. *Ibid.*
21. *Ibid.*
22. *Cincinnati Gazette*, Nov. 19, 1863, quoted in the *Frankfort Commonwealth*, Nov. 27, 1863.
23. *Louisville Democrat*, Dec. 3, 1863.
24. *Ibid.*
25. *Ibid.*
26. *Ibid.*
27. *Ibid.*
28. *Ibid.*
29. *Ibid.*
30. *Ibid.*
31. *Ibid.*
32. *Ibid.*
33. *Washington Evening Star*, Dec. 7, 1863.
34. *The American Annual Cyclopedia and Register of Important Historical Events of the Year 1864. Embracing Civil, Military, and Social Affairs; Public Documents; Biography, Statistics, Commerce, Finance, Literature, Science, Agriculture, and Mechanical Industry.* Vol. 4 (New York: D. Appleton & Co., 1869), 219.

35. *Louisville Journal*, Dec. 9, 1863.
36. *Ibid.*
37. *Louisville Democrat*, Dec. 10, 1863.
38. *Ibid.*
39. *Ibid.*
40. *Ibid.*
41. *Ibid.*
42. *Louisville Democrat*, Dec. 10, 1863; Cincinnati Enquirer, Dec. 17, 1863.
43. *Cleveland Morning Leader*, Dec. 12, 1863.
44. *Chicago Tribune*, Dec. 18, 1863.
45. *Ibid.*
46. *Ibid.*
47. *Ibid.*
48. *Ibid.*
49. *Ibid.*
50. *War Eagle*, December 12, 1863, photocopy at Columbus-Belmont State Park.; *New York Times*, December 24, 1863.
51. (Washington, D.C.) *National Republican*, Dec. 30, 1863; James M. McPherson, *Battle Cry of Freedom: The Civil War Era* (New York: Ballantine Books, 1988), 599.
52. Irasburg, VT, *Orleans Independent Standard*, Jan. 8, 1864.
53. *Indiana Journal*, Jan. 14, 1864, quoted in the *Belmont Chronicle*, Jan. 21, 1864.
54. Hood, "For the Union," 209.
55. *Louisville Journal*, Jan. 14, 1864.
56. *Ibid.*
57. *Ibid.*
58. *Louisville Journal*, Jan. 15, 1864; Craig, *Kentucky Confederates*, 220. "The Mock Doctor: Or the Dumb Lady Cur'd" was an 18th century play written by Henry Fielding. It debuted in London in 1732.
59. *Frankfort Commonwealth*, Jan. 15, 1864.
60. *Ibid.*
61. *Louisville Journal*, Nov. 3, 1863; Craig, *Kentucky Confederates*, 220.
62. *Ibid.*
63. Craig, *Kentucky Confederates*, 220–221; Lucian Anderson to Salmon P. Chase, January 29, 1864, *The Abraham Lincoln Papers at the Library of Congress*, http://memory.loc.gov/cgi-bin/query/P?mal:2:./temp/~ammem_66z2, accessed online Nov. 14, 2015.
64. *Biographical Directory of the United States Congress, ALLEN, William Joshua (1829–1901)*, http://bioguide.congress.gov/scripts/biodisplay.pl?index=A000152 (Accessed March 15, 2016); Craig, *Kentucky Confederates*, 107.

65. John C. Rives, *The Congressional Globe, the Official Proceedings of Congress, Thirty-Eighth Congress, 1st Session* (Washington: Globe Printing Office, 1864), 456–457.
66. *Ibid.*, 457.
67. *Ibid.*
68. *Ibid.*, 457–458.
69. *Ibid.*, 458–459.

## Chapter 7

1. Hood, "For the Union," 207; *Congressional Globe, 38th Congress 1st Session, Part I*, 333–334.
2. *Louisville Journal*, Feb. 26, 1864.
3. *Nashville Daily Union*, Feb. 7, 1864.
4. Hood, "For the Union, 207; *Congressional Globe, 1st Session, Part I*, 598.
5. *Ibid.*
6. Hood, "For the Union," 207–208; *Congressional Globe, 38th Congress 1st Session, Pt. I*, 598, 768.
7. *New York Times*, June 15, 1864.
8. "Report No. 18. Report of the Committee on the Judiciary on the Case of William Yokum," *Reports of Committees of the House of Representatives Made During the First Session of the Thirty-Eighth Congress, 1863–'64 Printed by Order of the House of Representatives in Two Volumes.* (Washington: Government Printing Office, 1864). Vol. II, 1–2.
9. *Ibid.*
10. *Ibid.*, 3–4.
11. Lowell H. Harrison, *The Civil War in Kentucky* (Lexington: The University Press of Kentucky, 1975), 89–90.
12. Hood, *For the Union*, 208–209.
13. William H. Mulligan, Jr., "African American Troops in Far West Kentucky During the Civil War: Recruitment and Service of the Fourth U.S. Heavy Artillery (Colored), Typescript of Speech Given at Fort Donelson National Military Park, Dover, Tenn., February 25, 2012, 4–5; Coulter, *Civil War and Readjustment*, 197; John David Smith, "The Recruitment of Negro Soldiers in Kentucky," *The Register of the Kentucky Historical Society* 72 (1974), 374–375.
14. Aaron Astor, *Rebels on the Border: Civil War, Emancipation, and the Reconstruction of Kentucky and Missouri* (Baton Rouge: Louisiana State University Press, 2012), 128; Craig, Kentucky Confederates, 224.

15. Ira Berlin, *Freedom: A Documentary History of Emancipation 1861–1867: Series II (Book I) the Black Military Experience* (Cambridge and New York: 1982), 255; Craig, *Kentucky Confederates*, 224.

16. Astor, *Rebels*, 128; O.R., Series 3, Vol. 4, 429; Ezra J. Warner, *Generals in Blue: Lives of the Union Commanders* (Baton Rouge: Louisiana State University Press, 1964), 502; O.R., Ser. 1, Vol. 32, Part 3, 157, Part 1, 548; Janet B. Hewett, ed., *Supplement to the Official Records of the Union and Confederate Armies, Part II, Record of Events*, Vol. 77, Serial No. 89 (Wilmington, N.C.: Broadfoot Publishing Company, 1998), 212; Craig, *Kentucky Confederates*, 224.

17. Collins, *History of Kentucky*, I, 132; Craig, *Kentucky Confederates*. 226, 239–240

18. O.R., Ser. 1, Vol. 32, Part 1, 417.

19. *Louisville Journal*, February 29, 1864; Craig, *Kentucky Confederates*, 225–226.

20. *Globe, Thirty-Eighth Congress, First Session, Appendix*, 98–99.

21. *Ibid.*, 99.

22. *Ibid.*

23. *Ibid.*

24. *Ibid.*

25. *Ibid.*

26. *Ibid.*, 99–100; Davis, *Story of Mayfield*, 57.

27. *Congressional Globe, Thirty-Eighth Congress, First Session, Appendix*, 100.

28. *Ibid.*

29. *Ibid.*, 101.

30. *Ibid.*, 101–102.

31. *Ibid.*, 100, 102.

32. *Ibid.*, 103–104.

## Chapter 8

1. Henry George, *History of the 3rd, 7th, 8th and 12th Kentucky, C.S.A.* (Louisville: Dearing Press, 1911), 78–79; Collins, *History of Kentucky*, I, 136.

2. *Cairo News* quoted in the *Evansville Daily Journal*, Aug. 12, 1864, and the *Louisville Journal*, Aug. 16, 1864. The story said the younger Gregory brother died in a skirmish but furnished no other details. Also, the paper referred to the captain as "Jim Gregory."

3. *Ibid.*

4. *Ibid.*

5. *Louisville Journal*, September 18, 1862; D.W. Lindsey, *Report of the Adjutant General of the State of Kentucky* (Frankfort: John H. Harney, State Printer, 1866), 1, 54–55, 765, 825–826.

6. George, *History of the 3rd, 7th, 8th and 12th Kentucky*, 79–81.

7. Craig, *Kentucky Confederates*, 232–233.

8. Stephen Berry, *House of Abraham: Lincoln and the Todds, a Family Divided by War* (Boston and New York: Mariner Books Houghton Mifflin Harcourt, 2009), 147.

9. Coulter, *Civil War and Readjustment*, 180; McPherson, *Battle Cry of Freedom*, 716.

10. *Frankfort Commonwealth*, Feb. 13, 1864.

11. *Louisville Journal*, Feb. 25, 1864; Coulter, *Civil War and Readjustment*, 180–181. The Louisville delegates included James Speed, a friend of Lincoln; and L.N. Dembitz, uncle of Supreme Court Justice Louis Dembitz Brandeis of Louisville.

12. *Louisville Journal*, Feb. 25, 1864. Secessionists and anti-war Northern Democrats often denounced abolitionists as Jacobins. The Jacobins were the most radical of the French revolutionaries. "Jayhawkers" was the nickname of anti-slavery Kansans. The "Apple of Discord" is rooted in Greek mythology. The gods were feasting the wedding of Peleus and Thetis when Eris, the goddess of discord, showed up uninvited. She tossed down a golden apple inscribed "For the Fairest." The goddesses Hera, Athena, and Aphrodite vied for the apple, a contest that triggered a chain of events that supposedly led to the Trojan War.

13. *Louisville Democrat*, Feb. 25, 1864.

14. *Ibid.*

15. *Ibid.*

16. Victor B. Howard, *Black Liberation in Kentucky: Emancipation and Freedom, 1862–1884* (Lexington: The University Press of Kentucky, 1983), 61; Coulter, *Civil War and Readjustment*, 180–181.

17. *New York Times*, May 29, 1864; *Louisville Journal*, May 26, 1864.

18. D.F. Murphy, reporter, *Presidential Election, 1864 Proceedings of the National Union Convention Held in Baltimore, Md., June 7th and 8th, 1864* (New York: Barker & Godwin Printers, 1864), 5–6, 92–93.

19. *Ibid.*, 31, 65.

20. Coulter, *Civil War and Readjustment*, 182; New York Times, May 29, 1864.

21. *Ibid.*, 182–183.

22. Roy P. Basler, Marion Dolores Pratt,

and Lloyd A. Dunlap, eds., The Collected Works of Abraham Lincoln, Vol. 7 (New Brunswick, N.J.: Rutgers University Press, 1953), 400; Murphy, Presidential Election, 1864, 91; J.K. Roberts and Daniel Woosley Crockett, Kentucky Opinions Containing the Unreported Opinions of the Court of Appeals (Lexington: Central Law Book Co., 1906), 62; Craig, Kentucky Confederates, 257–258.

23. The (Raleigh, N.C.) Daily Conservative, July 16, 1864; "Henry Emerson Etheridge," The Tennessee Encyclopedia of History & Culture Version 2.0 online, https://tennesseeencyclopedia.net/entry.php?rec=4 41 accessed Dec. 17, 2015.

24. Collins, History of Kentucky, Vol. 1, 134–135.

25. Collins, History of Kentucky, I, 135; O.R., Ser. 1, Vol. 39, Part 2, 171.

26. Louisville Journal, July 23, 1864; Lindsey, Report of the Adjutant General, Vol. 1, 54–55, 765, 825–826; Craig, Kentucky Confedertes, 258–259.

27. O.R., Ser. 1, Vol. 39, Part 2, 171.

28. Lon C. Barton, "A History of Graves County, Kentucky, 1818–1865," unpublished master's thesis, University of Kentucky, 1960, 115–116. According to Battle, Perrin and Kniffen's Kentucky, Paine executed sixty-one people, "Many of Them Entirely Innocent." See page 56; Patricia Ann Hoskins, "'The Old First Is with the South,'" 218. Her dissertation is an excellent and balanced account of Paine's time in Paducah and his subsequent court martial.

29. Harrison and Klotter, A New History, 206; Battle, Perrin and Kniffen, Kentucky, 56; Barton, "History of Graves County," 117.

30. "Journal of Private Hawley V. Needham, 134th Illinois Volunteer Infantry Regiment, Company G," 18–19, typescript in Pogue Library.

31. Evansville Daily Journal, Aug. 1, 1864.

32. Hood, "For the Union," 210.

33. Journal of the Adjourned Session of the Senate of the Commonwealth of Kentucky Begun and Held in the Town of Frankfort, on Monday, the Seventh Day of December, in the Year of Our Lord 1863 and of the Commonwealth the Seventy-Second (Frankfort: George D. Prentice, State Printer, 1865), 23. The letter was also published in the House journal.

34. Ibid., Series I, Vol. 39, Part 2, 349.

35. O.R., Ser. I, vol. 39, pt. 2, 349; Lucian Anderson to Green Adams, Sept. 10, 1864, Lucian Anderson to Abraham Lincoln, September 10, 1864. Abraham Lincoln Papers, Manuscripts Division, Library of Congress.

36. Hoskins, "The Old First Is with the South," 214.

37. Dieter C. Ullrich, "General E. A. Paine and the Military District of Western Kentucky," unpublished book manuscript, 68; O.R., Series 3, Vol. 4, 688–689.

38. Ibid.

39. Ibid., 68–69.

40. UIlrich, General E.A. Paine," 68–73; Senate Journal, 24, 31–32. The report is also in the House journal.

41. Senate Journal, 24.

42. Ibid., 27.

43. Ibid., 32.

44. Ibid., 30, 32. Verres was a famously corrupt and cruel Roman governor of Sicily. Hastings was accused of similar machinations while he served as the first British governor-general of India.

45. Ibid., 32.

46. Portsmouth Daily Times (Portsmouth, Ohio), Oct. 1, 1884; The Daily Milwaukee News, Oct. 2, 1864.

## Chapter 9

1. Louisville Journal, Sept. 27. 1864.

2. Ibid.

3. Ibid.

4. Ibid.

5. Ibid.

6. Ibid.

7. Ibid.

8. Louisville Journal, Sept. 28, 1864.

9. Ibid.

10. Louisville Daily Union Press, Oct. 24, 1864.

11. Ibid.

12. Ibid.

13. Louisville Daily Union Press, Oct. 24, 1864; Kleber, Kentucky Encyclopedia, 736.

14. Louisville Daily Union Press, Oct. 24, 1864.

15. Ibid.

16. Ibid.

17. Ibid.

18. Ibid.

19. Ibid.

20. Louisville Journal, Oct. 25, 1864.

21. Ibid.

22. Ibid.

23. Ibid.

24. Ibid., Oct, 27, 1864.

25. *Ibid.*

26. Battle, Perrin and Kniffen, *Kentucky*, 56.

27. Williams to Lincoln, October 3, 1864, *Lincoln Papers*, http://memory.loc.gov/cgi-bin/query/r?ammem/mal:@field(DOCID+@lit(d3695000)), accessed August 26, 2013; Craig, *Kentucky Confederates*, 281–282.

28. *New York Times*, Oct. 23, 1864.

29. *Chicago Tribune*, Oct. 23, 1864.

30. *Chicago Tribune*, Oct. 23, Nov. 1–2, 1864; *Cleveland Daily Leader*, Oct. 24, 1864.

31. *Chicago Tribune* Oct. 23, 1864.

32. *Ibid.*

33. *Ibid.*

34. *Chicago Evening Journal*, n.d., quoted in the *New York Times*, Oct. 23, 1864.

35. Anderson to Lincoln, October 17, 1864, Lincoln Papers; Craig, *Kentucky Confederates*, 282.

36. *OR*, Ser. I, vol. 39, pt. 1, 870–871; John Allen Wyeth, *Life of General Nathan Bedford Forrest* (New York: Harper & Brothers, 1899), 520–529; Hall Allen, *Center of Conflict: A Factual Story of the War Between the States in Western Kentucky and Tennessee* (Paducah: The Paducah Sun-Democrat, 1961), 142–144.

37. Anderson to Lincoln, Nov. 4, 1864, Lincoln papers.

38. Shannon and McQuown, *Presidential Politics in Kentucky*, 37–40; Hood, "For the Union," 210.

39. Coulter, *Civil War and Readjustment*, 185–187.

40. Shannon and McQuown, *Presidential Politics in Kentucky*, 37–40.

41. *Louisville Journal*, Nov. 10, 1864.

42. Hood, "For the Union," 211.

43. *Ibid.*

44. *Globe*, Senate, 38th Congress, 1st Session, 1490.

45. John Kleber, ed. *The Kentucky Encyclopedia* (Lexington: The University Press of Kentucky, 1992), 829–830;

46. Hood, "For the Union," 211.

47. *House Journal, Adjourned Session*, 1863–1864, 18–19; 316–317.

48. *Journal of the Adjourned Session of the Senate of the Commonwealth of Kentucky Begun and Held in the Town of Frankfort, on Monday, the Seventh Day of December, in the Year of Our Lord 1863 and of the Commonwealth the Seventy-Second.* (Frankfort: George D. Prentice, State Printer, 1865), 231–232.

49. *Ibid.*, 239–240.

50. *Frankfort Commonwealth*, January 6, 1865; Shannon and McQuown, *Presidential Politics*, 37.

51. McPherson, *Battle Cry of Freedom*, 838–839.

52. *Ibid.*, 839.

53. Henry Wilson, *History of the Antislavery Measures of the Thirty-Seventh and Thirty-Eighth United-States Congresses, 1861–65* (Boston: Walker, Fuller and Co., 1865), 392–393.

54. *New York Times*, Feb. 1, 1865.

55. Globe, 38th Congress, Second Session, 531.

56. *Kentucky Encyclopedia*, 421–422, 971–972; *Biographical Directory, Yeaman, George Helm (1829–1908)* http://bioguide.congress.gov/scripts/biodisplay.pl?index=Y000015, (Accessed March 21, 2016); Collins, *History of Kentucky*, 1, 127.

57. *Frankfort Commonwealth*, Feb. 3, 1865.

58. *Ibid.*

59. *Ibid.*

60. *Ibid.*

61. *Louisville Daily Union Press*, Feb. 1–2, 1865.

62. Hood, "For the Union," 212.

63. Harrison, *Antislavery Movement*, 108.

64. *House Journal, Adjourned Session*, 1863–1864; 578–579; *Senate Journal, Adjourned Session*, 408–409.

65. Harrison, *Antislavery*, 109.

66. *Washington Constitutional Union*, Feb. 26, 1865, quoted in the Columbus *Daily Ohio Statesman*, March 3, 1865.

67. *Daily Ohio Statesman*, March 3, 1865; Etheridge, *Henry Emerson, Ncpedia* online, http://ncpedia.org/biography/etheridge-henry-emerson (Accessed Jan. 21, 2016).

68. *Ibid.*

69. *Ibid.*

70. *Ibid.*

71. *Etheridge, Ncpedia* online (Accessed Jan. 21, 2016), *Constitutional Union*, Feb. 26, 1865, quoted in the *Daily Ohio Statesman*, March 3, 1865.

72. *Daily Ohio Statesman*, March 3, 1865.

73. *Louisville Journal*, March 2, 1865.

74. *Ibid.*

75. Craig, *Kentucky Confederates*, 289.

76. *Louisville Journal*, March 10, 1865.

77. *Ibid.*

78. *New York Times*, Oct. 20, 1865; Collins, *History of Kentucky*, Vol. 1, 164; Ezra J. Warner, *Generals in Blue: Lives of the Union*

*Commanders* (Baton Rouge: Louisiana State University Press, 1964), 356.

79. Hoskins, "The Old First," 216–217; Collins, *History of Kentucky*, Vol. 1, 136.

80. *Ibid.*, 217–218.

81. *Ibid.*, 218.

82. *Ibid.*, 218–219.

83. *Congressional Globe*, 38th Congress, 2nd session, 316.

84. *Globe*, 38th Congress, 2nd session, 369, 414, 539.

85. *The Reports of the Committees of the House of Representatives Made During the Second Session Thirty-Eighth Congress, 1864–1865* (Washington, D.C.: Government Printing Office, 1864), "Report No. 29," 1–3. Report No. 29," 1–2.

86. *Ibid.*

87. *Ibid.*, 2–3.

88. *Ibid.*, 4–5.

89. *Ibid.*, 6–7.

90. *Ibid.*, 1.

91. *Globe*, 38th Congress, 2nd Session, 1411.

92. *Ibid.*

93. *Ibid.*

94. *Ibid.*

95. *Ibid.*

96. *Ibid.*

97. *Ibid.*

98. *Ibid.*

99. *Ibid.*, 1412.

100. *Cincinnati Enquirer*, March 14, 1865.

101. *Ibid.*

102. Collins, *History of Kentucky*, Vol. 1, 158; Lindsey, *Report of the Adjutant General*, II, 325–326, 765.

103. *Frankfort Commonwealth*, April 4, 1865; Craig, *Kentucky Confederates*, 287–288.

104. *Ibid.*

105. *Ibid.*

106. Coulter, *Civil War and Readjustment*, vii; Marshall, *Creating a Confederate Kentucky*, 2, 83–84. Harrison and Klotter, *A New History*, 241–242.

107. Alben Barkley, *That Reminds Me* (Garden City, NY, Doubleday & Co., 1954), 34.

## Chapter 10

1. Coulter, *Civil War and Readjustment*, 278.

2. Coulter, *Civil War and Readjustment*, 261; Harrison and Klotter, *A New History*, 235. Delaware ratified the Thirteenth Amendment in 1901, Kentucky in 1976.

3. *Paducah Herald*, May 15, 1865, quoted in the *Frankfort Commonwealth*, May 23, 1865.

4. *Ibid.*

5. *Ibid.*

6. Harrison and Klotter, *A New History of Kentucky*, 239.

7. *Ibid.*, 239–240.

8. *Ibid.*, 240.

9. Collins, *History*, Vol. I, 163; Coulter, *Civil War and Readjustment*, 282. Some sources say the Conservatives and Republicans were tied in the Senate.

10. *Weekly Louisville Courier*, Oct. 17, 1866.

11. "40th Congress, 2nd Session, House of Representatives, Mis. Doc. No. 14 Papers in the Case of G.G. Symes Against L.S. Trimble, First Congressional District of Kentucky," *Index to Miscellaneous Documents of the House of Representatives for the Second Session of the Fortieth Congress 1867-'68*. Vol. 1, from No. 1 to No. 84 (Washington: Government Printing Office, 1868), 1; Collins, *History*, Vol. I, 180.

12. *Ibid.*, 1–5.

13. *Ibid.*, 28–29.

14. *Ibid.*, 29–30.

15. *Ibid.*, 30.

16. *Louisville Daily Courier*, July 19, 1867.

17. Collins, *History of Kentucky*, 1, 175, 195.

18. *Hickman Courier*, April 22, 1871.

19. *Ibid.*

20. *Ibid.*, April 29, 1871. In the South and border states like Kentucky, "Governor" was a title of respect. Often, too, Southerners of standing in their communities were often addresses as "Colonel," though they were not in the military.

21. *Hickman Courier*, July 29, 1871; Collins, *History of Kentucky*, I, 216.

22. Harrison and Klotter, *A New History*, 242–243; *Hickman Courier*, Oct. 12, 1872; The *Louisville Courier, Journal* and *Democrat* merged in 1868.

23. *Ibid.*, Oct. 12, 1872; Collins, *History of Kentucky* I, 235; "Our Campaigns" Kentucky District 01 Online, http://www.our campaigns.com/racedetail.html?raceid= 627850 (Accessed Dec. 4, 2015).

24. *Mayfield Democrat*, ND, Quoted in the *Hickman Courier*, Nov. 16, 1872.

25. *Cairo Bulletin*, March 30, 1873.

26. *The Interior Journal* (Stanford, KY) Aug. 1, 1879.

27. *Murray Gazette*, ND, Quoted in the *Hickman Courier*, June 2, 1876.

28. *Ibid.*

29. *Hickman Courier*, Sept. 15, 1876.

30. *Ibid.*

31. *Ibid.*

32. *Princeton Banner*, ND, Quoted in the *Hickman Courier*, Nov. 3, 1876.

33. *Ibid.*

34. *Ibid., Hickman Courier*, Nov. 3, 1876; "Our Campaigns Kentucky District 01" (Accessed Dec. 4, 2015).

35. *New York Times*, Nov. 19, 1881; *Happy Family History*, http://www.angelfire.com/co3/jillymac/happy.html (accessed online Dec. 5, 2015).

36. *Paducah News* quoted in the *Louisville Courier-Journal*, Aug. 6, 1882.

37. *Louisville Courier-Journal*, Aug. 15, 1882; *Our Campaigns, KY-District 01, 1882* http://www.ourcampaigns.com/pages/RaceDetail.html?RaceID=628304 (Accessed March 25, 2016).

38. *Ibid.*, May 24, 1883.

39. *Hickman Courier*, June 1, 1883.

40. *Ibid.*

41. Shannon and McQuown, *Presidential Politics*, 58.

42. *Louisville Courier-Journal*, April 13, 1888; *Atlanta Constitution*, April 13, 1888.

43. *Paducah Standard*, n.d., quoted in the *Hickman Courier*, June 7, 1889; *Louisville Courier-Journal*, May 8, 1892; *Pittsburgh Dispatch*, March 23, 1892.

44. *Louisville Courier-Journal*, May 6, 1898, Sept. 3, 1898.

45. *Paducah Sun*, Oct. 19, 1898.

46. *Paducah Sun*, Oct. 19, 1898; *Mayfield Weekly Monitor*, October 19, 1898. Wells, Lochridge/Anderson Family, 28; *Nashville Tennessean*, Oct. 19, 1898.

47. Roberts and Crockett, *Kentucky Opinions*, 62–64; *Hickman Courier*, Aug. 1, 1879, June 10, 1887, Aug. 12, 1892.

48. *The Standard* (Ogden, Utah), Aug. 14, 1889; *Daily Confederate News*, n.d., quoted in the *Louisville Courier*, Oct. 29, 1861.

# Bibliography

## Archives

Abraham Lincoln Papers, Library of Congress.
Andrew Lucas Hunt Papers, University of North Carolina, Chapel Hill.
Charles Lanman Collection, Filson Historical Society, Louisville, KY.
John Anderson Journal, 1838. Forrest C. Pogue Special Collections Library, Murray State University. Murray, KY.
John Jordan Crittenden Papers, Library of Congress, Washington, D.C.
John Kelly Ross, "Columbus Scrapbook," Pogue Library.
"Journal of Private Hawley V. Needham, 134th Illinois Volunteer Infantry Regiment, Company G," Pogue Library.
National Archives Records Administration, Washington, D.C.
Noble J. Gregory Papers, Pogue Special Collections Library.
William George Pirtle Memoirs, Filson Historical Society.

## Newspapers

*Bardstown Gazette*
*Belmont Chronicle* (St. Clairesville, OH)
*Cairo Bulletin*
*Cairo Democrat*
*Chicago Evening Journal*
*Chicago Tribune*
*Cincinnati Gazette*
*Cleveland Morning Leader*
*Daily Conservative* (Raleigh, N.C.)
*Daily Milwaukee News*
*Daily Ohio Statesman* (Columbus)
*Evansville Journal*
*Frankfort Commonwealth*
*Hickman Courier*
*The Interior Journal* (Stanford, KY)
*Louisville Courier*
*Louisville Courier-Journal*
*Louisville Daily Union Press*
*Louisville Democrat*

*Louisville Journal*
*Mayfield Democrat*
*Mayfield Monitor*
*Mayfield Southern Yeoman*
*Murray Gazette*
*Nashville Tennessean*
*Nashville Union and American*
*National Republican* (Washington, D.C.)
*New Orleans Times-Picayune*
*New Orleans True Delta*
*New York Times*
*New-York Tribune*
*Orleans Independent Standard* (Irasburg, VT)
*Paducah Herald*
*Paducah Standard*
*Paducah Sun*
*Pittsburgh Dispatch*
*Portsmouth Daily Times* (Portsmouth, OH)
*Princeton Banner*
*Raleigh Semi-Weekly Standard*
*Sacramento Daily Union* (Sacramento, CA)
*Washington Constitutional Union*
*Washington Evening Star*
*Weekly Indiana State Sentinel* (Indianapolis)

## Primary Sources

*Adjourned Session of 1863–4, of the Senate of the Commonwealth of Kentucky, Begun and Held in the Town of Frankfort, on Monday, the Seventh Day of December, in the Year of Our Lord 1865, and of the Commonwealth the Seventy-Second*. Frankfort, KY: State Printer, 1865.

*The American Annual Cyclopedia and Register of Important Historical Events of the Year 1864. Embracing Civil, Military, and Social Affairs; Public Documents; Biography, Statistics, Commerce, Finance, Literature, Science, Agriculture, and Mechanical Industry*. Vol. 4. New York: D. Appleton & Co., 1869. Printing Office, George D. Prentice, State Printer, 1865.

*The Constitution of the United States of America as Amended, Unratified Amendments Analytical Index, Unum E Pluribus Presented By Mr. Brady Of Pennsylvania July 25, 2007*. Ordered to be printed (Washington: United States Government Printing Office, 2007), 16 https://www.gpo.gov/fdsys/pkg/CDOC-110hdoc50/pdf/CDOC-110hdoc50.pdf.

Ellis, J. Tandy Ellis, *Report of the Adjutant General of the State of Kentucky Confederate Volunteers War 1861–1865* (Frankfort: The State Journal Company, 1915) Vols. I and II.

"Excerpts from the Journal of Sergeant Eugene B. Read," Jackson Purchase Historical Society. Accessed December 31, 2012. http://www.jacksonpurchasehistory.org/jackson-purchase-during-the-civil-war/.

"40th Congress, 2nd Session, House of Representatives, Mis. Doc. No. 14 Papers in the Case of G.G. Symes Against L.S. Trimble, First Congressional District of Kentucky." *Index to Miscellaneous Documents of the House of Representatives for the Second*

*Session of the Fortieth Congress 1867–68.* Vol. 1, from No. 1 to No. 84. Washington: Government Printing Office, 1868.

Graves County, KY, Census of 1860. Transcribed by Pat Record. Melber, KY: Simmons Historical Publications, 1979.

"Legislative Document, No. 26. Response of the Adjutant General of Kentucky to a Resolution Of Inquiry in Regard to Federal Enrollments in the State, Made to the House of Representatives Wednesday, March 1, 1865." Frankfort: George D. Prentice, State Printer, 1865.

*Journal of the Adjourned Session of the House of Representatives of the Commonwealth of Kentucky Begun and Held in the Town of Frankfort, on Monday, the Seventh Day of December, in the Year of Our Lord 1863 and of the Commonwealth the Seventy-Second.* Frankfort: George D. Prentice, State Printer, 1865.

*Journal of the Adjourned Session of the Senate of the Commonwealth of Kentucky Begun and Held in the Town of Frankfort, on Monday, the Seventh Day of December, in the Year of Our Lord 1863 and of the Commonwealth the Seventy-Second.* Frankfort: George D. Prentice, State Printer, 1865.

*Journal of the Called Session of the House of Representatives of the Commonwealth of Kentucky, Begun and Held in the Town of Frankfort, on Thursday, the Seventeenth Day of January, in the Year of Our Lord 1861, and of the Commonwealth the Sixty-Ninth.* Frankfort: John B. Major, State Printer, 1861.

*Journal of the House of Representatives of the United States of America Being the Second Session of the Thirty-Eighth Congress.* Washington, D.C.: Government Printing Office, 1865.

Kentucky Secretary of State Elections Register, 1855–1872.

Lindsey, D.W. *Report of the Adjutant General of the State of Kentucky.* Frankfort: John H. Harney, Public Printer, 1866, Vol. I and II.

Murphy D.F., reporter. *Presidential Election, 1864 Proceedings of the National Union Convention Held In Baltimore, Md., June 7th and 8th, 1864.* New York: Barker & Godwin Printers, 1864.

"Report No. 18. Report of the Committee on the Judiciary on the Case of William Yokum." *Reports of Committees of the House of Representatives Made During the First Session of the Thirty-Eighth Congress, 1863–64 Printed by Order of the House of Representatives in Two Volumes.* Washington: Government Printing Office, 1864). Vol. II.

*The Reports of the Committees of the House of Representatives Made During the Second Session Thirty-Eighth Congress, 1864–1865.* Washington, D.C.: Government Printing Office, 1864. "Report No. 29."

Rives, John C. *The Congressional Globe, the Official Proceedings of Congress, Thirty-Eighth Congress, 1st Session.* Washington: Globe Printing Office, 1864.

*The War of the Rebellion: A Compilation of the Official Records of the Union and Confederate Armies.* Washington, D.C.: War Department, 1880–1902.

Wilson, Henry. *History of History of the Antislavery Measures of the Thirty-Seventh and Thirty-Eighth United-States Congresses, 1861–65.* Boston: Walker, Fuller & Co., 1865.

Wyeth, John Allen, *Life of General Nathan Bedford Forrest.* New York: Harper & Brothers, 1899.

## Secondary Sources

Allen, Hall. *Center of Conflict: A Factual Story of the War Between the States in Western Kentucky and Tennessee.* Paducah: The Paducah Sun-Democrat, 1961.

Astor, Aaron. *Rebels on the Border: Civil War, Emancipation, and the Reconstruction of Kentucky and Missouri.* Baton Rouge: Louisiana State University Press, 2012.

Barkley, Alben, *That Reminds Me.* Garden City, N.Y., Doubleday, 1954.

Barton, Lon Carter. "A History of Graves County, Kentucky." Master's thesis, University of Kentucky, 1960.

Basler, Roy P., and Marion Dolores Pratt, and Lloyd A. Dunlap, eds. *The Collected Works of Abraham Lincoln,* Vol. 7. New Brunswick, NJ: Rutgers University Press, 1953.

Battle, J.H., and W.H. Perrin, and G.C. Kniffen. *Kentucky: A History of the State.* 1st ed.; Louisville and Chicago: F.A. Battey & Co., 1885.

Bearman, Alan. "'The South Carolina of Kentucky': Religion and Secession in the Jackson Purchase," Filson Club History Quarterly 76, 2002.

Berlin, Ira. *Freedom: A Documentary History of Emancipation 1861–1867: Series II (Book I) The Black Military Experience.* Cambridge and New York: Cambridge University Press, 1982.

Berry, Stephen. *House of Abraham: Lincoln and the Todds, a Family Divided by War.* Boston; New York: Mariner Books Houghton Mifflin Harcourt, 2009.

*Biographical Directory of the United States Congress, 1774–Present.* Anderson, Lucien (1824–1898). http://bioguide.congress.gov/scripts/biodisplay.pl?index=A000201.

*Biographical Directory of the United States Congress, 1774–Present.* Smith, Green Clay (1826–1895). http://bioguide.congress.gov/scripts/biodisplay.pl?index=S000544.

*Biographical Directory of the United States Congress, 1774–Present.* Yeaman, George Helm (1829–1908). http://bioguide.congress.gov/scripts/biodisplay.pl?index=Y000015.

Birney, William. *James G. Birney and His Times.* New York: G. Appleton & Co., 1889.

Collins, Lewis. *Historical Sketches of Kentucky: Embracing Its History, Antiquities, and Natural Curiosities, Geographical, Statistical, and Geological Descriptions; with Anecdotes of Pioneer Life, and More than One Hundred Biographical Sketches of Distinguished Pioneers, Soldiers, Statesmen, Jurists, Lawyers, Divines, Etc.* Maysville, KY, Lewis Collins, and Cincinnati, U.P. James: 1848.

Collins, Lewis, and Richard Collins. *History of Kentucky: By the Late Lewis Collins, Judge of the Mason County Court, Revised, Enlarged Four-Fold and Brought Down to the Year 1874, by His Son, Richard H. Collins, A.M, LL.B. Embracing Pre-Historic Annals for 331 Years, Outline, and by Counties, Statistics, Antiquities, and Natural Curiosities, Geographical and Geological Descriptions, Sketches of the Court of Appeals, the Churches, Freemasonry, Odd Fellowship, and Internal Improvements, Incidents of Pioneer Life, and Nearly Five Hundred Biographical Sketches of Distinguished Pioneers, Soldiers, Statesmen, Jurists, Lawyers, Surgeons, Divines, Merchants, Historians, Editors, Artists, Etc., Etc.* 1874; reprint, Berea, KY: Kentucke Imprints, 1976. 2 Vols.

Corliss, Carlton J. *Main-Line of Mid-America: The Story of the Illinois Central.* New York: Creative Age Press, 1950.

Coulter, E. Merton. *The Civil War and Readjustment in Kentucky.* Chapel Hill: University of North Carolina Press, 1926.

Craig, Berry. *Kentucky Confederates: Secession, Civil War, and the Jackson Purchase.* Lexington: University Press of Kentucky, 2014.

Current, Richard Nelson. *Lincoln's Loyalists: Union Soldiers from the Confederacy* New York; Oxford, England: Oxford University Press, 1992, 3.

Davis, D. Trabue. *Story of Mayfield Through a Century 1823–1923.* Paducah, KY: Billings Printing Co., 1923.

Dew, Charles B. *Apostles of Disunion: Southern Secession Commissioners and the Causes of the Civil War.* Charlottesville: University of Virginia Press, 2001.

Etheridge, Henry Emerson. NCPedia online, http://ncpedia.org/biography/etheridge-henry-emerson.

George, Henry. *History of the 3d, 7th, 8th and 12th Kentucky, C.S.A.* Louisville: Dearing Press, 1911.

Gott, Kendall D., *Where the South Lost the War: An Analysis of the Fort Henry— Fort Donelson Campaign, February 1862.* Mechanicsburg, Pa: Stackpole Books, 2003.

Hacker, J. David. "A Census-Based Count of the Civil War Dead." *Civil War History* 4 (Dec. 2011).

*Happy Family History.* http://www.angelfire.com/co3/jillymac/happy.html.

Harrison, Lowell H. *The Antislavery Movement in Kentucky.* Lexington: The University Press of Kentucky, 1978.

Harrison, Lowell H. *The Civil War in Kentucky.* Lexington: The University Press of Kentucky, 1975.

Harrison, Lowell H., and James C. Klotter. *A New History of Kentucky.* Lexington: University Press of Kentucky, 1997.

"Henry Emerson Etheridge." The Tennessee Encyclopedia of History & Culture Version 2.0 online. https://tennesseeencyclopedia.net/entry.php?rec=441.

Hewett, Janet B. *Supplement to the Official Records of the Union and Confederate Armies, Part II, Record of Events,* Vol. 77, Serial No. 89. Wilmington, NC: Broadfoot, 1998.

Hood, James Larry, "For the Union: Kentucky's Unconditional Unionist Congressmen and the Development of the Republican Party in Kentucky, 1863–1863." *Register of the Kentucky Historical Society* 76 (July, 1978), 197–198, 209–210.

Hoskins, Patricia Ann. "'The Old First Is with the South,' the Civil War, Reconstruction, and Memory in the Jackson Purchase Region of Kentucky." PhD diss., Auburn University, 2008.

Howard, Victor B. *Black Liberation in Kentucky: Emancipation and Freedom, 1862–1884.* Lexington: University Press of Kentucky, 1983.

"Judge R.K. Williams." *Tullidge's Quarterly Magazine,* April, 1882.

Hughes, Nathaniel Cheairs, Jr. *The Battle of Belmont: Grant Strikes South.* Chapel Hill: University of North Carolina Press, 1991.

Kennedy, John F. *Profiles in Courage,* 50th Anniversary Edition. New York: Harper-Collins, 2006.

*Kentucky Opinions, Containing the Unreported Opinions of the Court of Appeals.* Lexington, KY: Central Law Book Co., 1906.

Langstaff, George Quigley. *The Life and Times of Quintus Quincy Quigley 1828–1910: His Personal Journey 1858–1908.* Paducah, KY: The Paducah Area Community Foundation, 1999.

Lucas, Marion B. *A History of Blacks in Kentucky: From Slavery to Segregation, 1760–1891.* Lexington: University Press of Kentucky, 1992.

McDowell, Robert Emmet. *City of Conflict: Louisville in the Civil War.* Louisville, KY: Louisville Civil War Roundtable, 1962.

Mesch, Allen H. *Teacher of Civil War Generals: Major General Charles Ferguson Smith, Soldier and West Point Commandant.* Jefferson, NC: McFarland, 2015.

Mulligan, William H. Mulligan, Jr. "African American Troops in Far West Kentucky During the Civil War: Recruitment and Service of the Fourth U.S. Heavy Artillery (Colored)." Typescript of Speech Given at Fort Donelson National Military Park, Dover, TN, February 25, 2012.

"Obituary." *The Hub.* March, 1895.

*Ohio History Central* online. "Land Ordinance of 1785." http://www.ohiohistorycentral. org/w/Land_Ordinance_of_1785?rec=1472.

"Our Campaigns" Kentucky District 01 Online. http://www.ourcampaigns.com/ racedetail.html?raceid=627850.

Posey, Walter Brownlow. *Frontier Mission: A History of Religion West of the Southern Appalachians to 1861.* Lexington: University of Kentucky Press, 1966.

Republican Party Platforms: "Republican Party Platform of 1864." June 7, 1864. Online by Gerhard Peters and John T. Woolley. *The American Presidency Project.* http://www.presidency.ucsb.edu/ws/?pid=29621.

Rennick, Robert M. *Kentucky Place Names.* Lexington: University Press of Kentucky, 1984.

Richardson, H. Edward. *Cassius Marcellus Clay: Firebrand of Freedom.* Lexington: University Press of Kentucky, 1976.

Robertson, John E.L. "Western Kentucky and Paducah in Legend and Lore." *The Filson History Quarterly*, Vol. 76 2002.

Shannon, J.B., and Ruth McQuown. *Presidential Politics in Kentucky 1824–1948: A Compilation of Election Statistics and an Analysis of Political Behavior.* Lexington: Bureau of Government Research, College of Arts and Sciences, University of Kentucky, 1950.

Smith, John David. "The Recruitment of Negro Soldiers in Kentucky." *The Register of the Kentucky Historical Society* 72, 1974.

Ullrich, Dieter C. "Confederate Operations in the Jackson Purchase: A History of Camp Beauregard." *The Filson History Quarterly*, Vol. 76, No. 4

Warner, Ezra J. *Generals in Blue: Lives of the Union Commanders.* Baton Rouge: Louisiana State University Press.

Wells, William Lochridge. Letter to the editor published in the *Mayfield Messenger*, March 3, 2016.

Wells, William Lochridge. *The Lochridge/Anderson Family of Graves County, Kentucky: From 1819 to the Present.* Mayfield, KY: Mayfield Printing Co., 1990.

## Interviews and Emails

Lon Carter Barton of Mayfield, interview, April 10, 1998; Jan. 18, 2001.

James C. Klotter, email to Berry Craig, Dec. 20, 2014.

# Index

Numbers in **bold** italics refer to pages with photographs

**209**